The Ernie Diaries

A motorcycle adventure
from London to Iran in 1973

Anne Betts & Des Molloy

Publishing Collective

The Ernie Diaries
A motorcycle adventure from London to Iran in 1973

©Anne Betts 2023
© Des Molloy 2023

Text design by The Design Dept.
Cover design by The Design Dept.
www.thedesigndept.com.au
Display font: Norton by K-Type
Body font: Cronos Pro

Photo Acknowledgement: Photos belong to Des Molloy and Anne Betts.
Illustrations by Des Molloy, excluding page 236 which was done by Jim Gordon.

Printed by Ingram Spark

Published in 2021 by
Kahuku Publishing
PO Box 149 Takaka
Tasman 7142, New Zealand
www.kahukupublishing.com

All rights reserved.
This book or any portion thereof may not be reproduced or used in any manner whatsoever without the express written permission of the author except for the use of brief quotations in a book review. All inquiries should be made to the author.

ISBN. PB: 978-0-473-67443-4
ePub: 978-0-473-67444-1
PDF: 978-0-473-67445-8

"Much travel is needed before a
raw man is ripened."

Arab proverb

The Ernie Diaries

IV

Contents

Preface	VII
Gestation	3
London, UK to Bergen, Norway	20
Norway	38
Sweden	64
Denmark, West Germany, East Germany	76
Poland and Czechoslovakia	96
Oktoberfest, Munich	110
Munich, West Germany to Dubrovnik, Yugoslavia	136
Dubrovnik, Yugoslavia to Istanbul, Turkey	150
Istanbul, Turkey	170
Istanbul to Anamur, Turkey	186
Anamur, Turkey to Tehran, Iran	206
Northern Iran	232
Tehran to the Persian Gulf, Iran	262
Persian Gulf to Tehran, Iran	284
The Home Straight	304
The Cast	317
Acknowledgements	327

The Ernie Diaries

VI

Preface

Anne Betts

In 2020, the COVID-19 pandemic required stepping back from my blog at *Packing Light Travel*. Finding the motivation to write about travel was a challenge because readers seemed to have little interest in something out of imminent reach. It was an ideal time to reflect on travel as it had been and ponder what it might look like in a post-pandemic world. As a result, I published a blog post on what it was like to travel in the 1970s. It was followed soon after by a call from Des.

Des and I had travelled together in the 1970s on 'Ernie,' a 1957 Norton ES2 motorcycle. He wasted no time in getting to the reason for the call.

"Anne, you must turn *The Ernie Diaries* into a book. People have an appetite for travel stories from bygone years. You have a rich repository of journal entries and photographs that point to a solid foundation for a book. It's time."

I initially rejected the proposal, but finally acquiesced in the face of dogged persistence. The one condition of accepting it was that Des and I would share the writing. We were living in separate countries; I was in Canada and Des in New Zealand. However, we forged ahead by loosely breaking The Ernie Diaries into geographical chunks resembling chapters and divided them accordingly.

The Ernie Diaries was a retirement project undertaken in the Canadian winter of 2009. It began by poring over handwritten journal entries and scanning slides chronicling travels with Ernie.

Until the materials were unpacked and dusted off, they remained virtually untouched for over 30 years. It was one of those get-to projects when time permitted. Perhaps the yet-to-be-defined project was fuelled by the innumerable times the boxes of diaries, slides, and related paraphernalia were relocated from one residence or one country to another and how I justified those endeavours with *I'll do something with them when I retire*. It might have amounted to merely reading them or, who knows, transforming them into something others might appreciate. The result was *The Ernie Diaries*, a digital account of the five-month trip.

The idea of doing something with them became indelibly imprinted on my psyche with little thought about why I would do so more than three decades later. It felt much like the choice to leave home back in the 1970s. It wasn't that my life at the time was lacklustre or lacking in purpose, or I was yearning for an altogether different existence. Simply put, it was something young Australians and New Zealanders did. It was our zeitgeist. We'd set off for the United Kingdom (UK), work and winter over in London, and travel within Europe during the warmer summer months. Then, after a year or two, we'd return to our homelands to pick up our antipodean lives somewhere near where we'd left off.

Somewhat analogous to that original decision to leave Australia for the UK on the SS *Australis* in January 1972, digitizing the journal and later converting it to a book brought unforeseen benefits.

As I delved into the depths of my memories to revisit the places mentioned in my notes, I thought about how my worldview had been reshaped by travel. It had been a journey of learning, unlearning, and relearning. While opportunities slipped from our grasp because of other priorities or limited financial means, I was grateful for the rich experiences we'd lived because we were young, frugal, and adventurous. As I read the musings of my twenty-something self (at times cringing), I relished those times when life had been less complicated, material possessions few, and money viewed as a short-term commodity to fund short-term needs. I savoured the fact we'd rarely thought about our safety or the need to safeguard our stuff. Our youthful naivety and mistaken optimistic belief in our invincibility had been fused with the reality that we'd been treated as honoured guests in the countries we'd passed through. I was awestruck by how we'd lived and travelled without a great deal of planning, guided by spontaneous and adventurous spirits, and how well we'd adapted to changing circumstances.

I cherished how easily we'd struck up conversations and formed friendships with total strangers. It was a social era when face-to-face interaction with others informed our travel plans. Our living arrangements invariably involved large groups of people with similar dreams crammed into flats or sharing overnight accommodation on the road. I reflected on the many wonderful relationships forged all those years ago and how several of them have withstood the test of time and geography to endure to this day. As I worked my way through the pages, I wondered about the whereabouts of people mentioned in my journals and I recorded in my address books. With the help of Facebook and Google, I was able to re-establish contact with several former travelling companions and, in some cases, make plans to meet up again for subsequent travel adventures.

Another epiphany concerned my journalling journey. I winced at the earlier entries — a few lines containing mundane summaries about what we ate, where we camped, and when we could find a hot shower. But, I was pleased to discover that as the journey unfolded, my account of the trip had evolved into more detailed descriptions of people and places and their history, and their influence on my learning and growth. I'd realised that reflecting on the day's events and being more detailed in describing them made me a more curious, observant, and grateful traveller.

As the book took shape, it became clear that it wasn't a travelogue. A travelogue is an insightful account of what a traveller sees, hears, and feels about the people and places encountered along the way. It incorporates what's learned about the history and culture of a place.

Instead, the book describes a youthful travel experience in the 1970s. It is based on a daily summary of how money-poor, time-rich young people travelled in an earlier era. It was one devoid of guidebooks for many places, and before smartphones, online research, email, and financial cards became the modern tools of savvy and connected travellers.

Another revelation concerned the gift of memories. By the time the digital journal was completed in 2010, I had tracked down Des. I'd last seen him on a trip to New Zealand in 1987, but as work and life got in the way, we'd failed to maintain contact. I sent him the journal, and his response along the lines of, "Were we on the same trip?" spoke volumes about how recollections could differ. From my perspective, there were references in my handwritten journal of which I had absolutely no memory. On the other hand, some encounters that hadn't been recorded were as vivid as if they'd occurred yesterday. As Des and I worked on the book, I was amazed at how our memories and perceptions of various events differed, converged, and expanded.

And finally, as I received the early drafts of Des's chapters, I loved seeing how he'd sprinkled his narrative with expressions that had long since left my vocabulary. After 45 years in Canada, my down-under idioms were mostly gone but not forgotten. As our writing unfolded, we decided to keep many of the terms we'd grown up with in Australia and New Zealand because they reflected how we described our adventures with Ernie at the time. For readers unfamiliar with Australian and New Zealand slang, we trust you can figure it out from the context.

Along the same lines, Des was working with British English, as was I, but my Canadian English had absorbed some influences from south of the border. We did our best to maintain consistency by relying on several references, most importantly, the Collins Online Dictionary. So, for readers who hesitate over the use of words such as skeptical and cosy (as opposed to sceptical and cozy), Collins was our arbitrator.

The writing of The Ernie Diaries: A motorcycle adventure from London to Iran, 1973 was a pleasant step back in time, and almost as enjoyable as the original journey of 1973.

Preface

Chapter 1:
Gestation

Des Molloy

"Much travel is needed before a raw man is ripened."
Arab proverb

I think that at some stage in every young person's life, they dream of riding off into the sunset on a noisy, anti-social motorbike. Sometimes it is merely a thirst for adventure; at other times, it is to throw off a yoke of convention threatening to define ... and constrict.

It is often said that youth is wasted on the young. I agree to the point that many don't realise there is only a small window between the time you leave the influencing umbrella of your upbringing and the embracing of grown-up responsibilities such as relationships, mortgages, children, career pathways, and planning for retirement. The Ernie adventures took place in that sweet spot.

Although Anne and I both travelled to the UK on the same sailing of the SS *Australis* in January 1972, our paths didn't cross (that we recall). With 2,000 young escapees on board, you can't know them all. A couple of my gang teamed up with a couple of her crew though, and whilst she went into an Aussie flat (including one pom) and I went into a Kiwi flat (including one Aussie), our paths would have crossed at Anzac parties.

In the spring of 1972, I moved into Anne's flat in Finsbury Park. This coincided with the departure of Bernie and Barry, two of her flatmates, and most of

the occupants of my Ealing flat. It was a common practice that flats would dissolve or merge as people departed, and those left behind would find a spare bed or piece of floor until they, too, were ready to move on. The departees were embarking on their respective European adventures, or in the case of the one Aussie, Cheryl, her sights were on the USA. Chris and Annette set off in their Austin Mini Van, and my mates Darcy, Graham, and Phil left in our Volkswagen (VW) Kombi. All of us had been passengers on the SS *Australis*.

In November 1972, after our summer travels, several of our mates remained in the UK and were keen to find suitable accommodation. Many of the remaining occupants of the Ealing and Finsbury Park flats consolidated into a happy bunch of 10 young 'colonials' in the Orthodox Jewish area of Stamford Hill. This was probably the zenith of communal living for me. The 'girls' were mainly teachers who had shorter working hours, enabling them to manage and expedite the shopping and the cooking. The 'boys' looked after the dishes and post-meal clean-up. These roles felt fair, and everyone seemed comfortable with the arrangement.

There were always enough people around to make life enjoyable. The group gelled well, and life was fun-filled. With any spare moment, we'd be in the park throwing a Frisbee, kicking a rugby ball, or playing tennis. Most of the girls were physical education teachers from Queensland. Nurtured by sun and exercise, they were splendid examples of the benefits of both. Real visions of vim and vitality, they could have been featured in an Aussie tourist promo video.

The world of young women was utterly alien to me at the time. I wasn't especially shy, but I'd grown up in a mostly male household, had all-male schooling, gone into an all-male cadetship, played all-male rugby, and none of my mates had sisters. My only romance had ended disappointingly after six months when the object of my desire decided she liked her older stepbrother more than her gauche would-be beau. I had awesome female country cousins but only saw them occasionally, and they *were* cousins. It didn't help that mum was pretty dismissive of the giggling, powdered-and-primped examples at church. Early skirmishes with my mates at dance halls also hadn't produced good results. I didn't have the chat; I didn't have the swagger. And I didn't know how to woo. I was also not totally easy with the hunting philosophy of some of my peers. Going out on a Saturday night with the sole aim of 'scoring' never felt quite right, and my half-hearted efforts reflected this.

Mixed flatting was still a concept that our parents (mums especially) would tut over and become a little pursed lipped when it was mentioned. It wasn't really an acceptable convention for *nice* young people. For us, 20,000 kilometres away from home and hearth, it was liberating; there was non-judgemental freedom. It was an adventure, and for me, it was an awakening. Our girls weren't preening, delicate little flowers sitting against the wall in the church hall, waiting to be asked to dance. They weren't desperately trying to look cool and attract attention in a tavern. Our girls didn't simper. They laughed, debated, and argued. They had opinions and dreams. There was robust banter, and there was fun. And none of them ran like penguins. (I had always wondered why city girls ran like penguins with their elbows pinned to their hips, arms flapping, and knees barely moving apart.)

In fact, our girls had way more adventures than the boys did, as they wasted very little of their spare time. Weekends and school holidays would see Devon and Cornwall visited, or France and Spain, or Ireland, or wherever took their fancy. Most of us boys played rugby, so we could only get away at the end of each season or on holiday weekends. However, we all enjoyed living vicariously through our flatmates' travels.

With any group like this, there were always embryonic plans being touted, dreams being dreamed. We were all away on our 'OE' — Overseas Experience — so there was little time to dally. Every possible spare moment was spent seeing the unseen, doing the previously not-yet-done.

My problem was that I seemed to lag behind most of the others regarding the funds I was able to assemble. I have never been profligate with money, yet I struggled to accumulate and retain it in any quantity. I'd arrived in the UK with the barest amount required. When Darcy, Graham, and Phil set off for Europe in our VW Kombi a couple of months before the 1972 Olympic Games in Munich, I hadn't saved enough to go with them. Steve and I remained in London as working Joes, desperately trying to top up the coffers so we could enjoy three months with the crew, post-Munich. That's when we moved into Anne's Finsbury Park flat until the summer.

Buying a Vincent Comet motorbike didn't help; then having it stolen. Twice. When it went the second time, I heaved a sigh of relief because the burden of ownership was lifted off my shoulders. It was one less end to tie off before hitching to Germany. The experience left me perilously impecunious and a little chastened.

I had a small stash of money to enable me to buy a brand-new Ducati 750cc motorbike and take it home after the required 12 months of ownership and

21 months of absence from New Zealand. Whilst waiting out the optimum nine months before purchasing, I succumbed to temptation again and bought an E-Type Jaguar sports car, a British racing green convertible. This was something way beyond the grasp of a young Kiwi lad at home. It was the sort of thing that would be the subject of a poster on a spotty-faced petrolhead's wall. I could now live the dream of the playboy rich. Sadly, it was never the chick-magnet that I hoped it would be, as I always seemed to have a mate with me riding shotgun. This was so there would be someone to help with petrol costs. I didn't have a plan for the car — I just had to own it — because I could. Back in New Zealand, it was worth about five times what I had paid for it. How I would get it there and realise this gain was never planned.

There had been a loose agreement that a colleague would store it whilst I adventured in Europe in 1972 and pay me a rental so he could use it. Disappointingly, the money never eventuated, and I recovered the car after returning to London. This, however, meant that I had little money for adventuring in the summer of 1973. I'd been in deficit at the end of the previous European adventure, and the coffers were taking a long time to fill. In the Stamford Hill flat, plans were falling into place for many of the crew. Darcy left to join a travel company as a tour leader and hopeful gigolo. Jo, Kerry, Kris, Rhyll, and Robyn were heading off to Europe in 'Fanny,' the girls' Kombi. Steve and Graham had decided to fly to the United States, buy an old Yank tank and explore the land of the free with Phil, Andy, and Donna from our Ealing flat. They managed many weeks doing just that in an enormous old Buick. Freddie Laker, the airline entrepreneur, had just revolutionized air travel with his budget-priced flights across the Atlantic, making this an achievable dream.

Meanwhile, Dessie-no-money (I don't believe I was ever Dessie-no-mates) couldn't really put his hand up for any adventures. I had a pretty good job in the Kentish Town area of London as a site contracts' manager, running the money side of a significant conversion of old council flats. The funds were coming in okay; I just needed time and a dream. My dream of all dreams, of course, was to ride off into the sunset on a noisy anti-social motorbike, a bit like *Easy Rider* but with fewer drugs and more interesting scenery.

When Anne entered the dream, I didn't know how to react. It was in early March of '73 when the suggestion of taking a motorbike to Europe at the end of her school term in July surfaced. This was like offering catnip to a feline. I'd been an avid motorcyclist since the age of 15 and was pining for another bike, having to make do with reading magazines and getting out to the motor racing circuits of Brands Hatch, Silverstone, and Mallory Park to get my fix. I'd even brought my racing leathers with me to the UK in the event a motorcycling adventure presented itself.

As a teenager, I'd toured the South Island of New Zealand with a mate on a couple of Triumphs, tenting along the way. It had been a mixture of euphoric fun and abject misery. Time had already banished the memories of the cold, wet hours in a sodden tent and the sheer hard work of the whole adventure.

The Ernie Diaries

Was Anne agreeing to come with me because I was the only cab left at the rank? I couldn't sense any Florence Nightingale in her, and she was already known for being resolute and staunch. I don't think I had ever been alone with Anne at this point. Surely she didn't have romantic intentions? If she did, I thought, that would be amazing. Of course, I fancied Anne, but then again, I fancied all six of 'our' girls; they were all most fanciable. The thought of sharing a small tent with Anne was pretty overwhelming. As an adult, I was still wearing an L plate. I felt like walking around chanting: I'm *not worthy, I'm not worthy!*

I didn't reflect on Anne's reasons for coming on board; I just grabbed hold of the idea and started the planning in case she'd change her mind. What would be would be! She had the Austin Mini Van that Chris and Annette (flatmates from the Ealing flat) had used to campaign through Europe — this would have been a far more sensible option for what she was suggesting. However, being sensible was never my forte, and I figured I should move quickly before she came to her senses.

Besides the plethora of monthly motorcycle magazines available at the newsagency, two weeklies were distributed on Wednesdays. They were *Motorcycle News* and the *Motorcycle*, and both were filled with classified advertisements. I don't recall how I settled on an old Norton single, as my experience was with BSAs and Triumphs, but a non-running 1957 500cc ES2 was found in Gloucester for £40, a price commensurate with its condition. We went up to settle the deal in my E-Type, and I can remember humming along the motorway home, hood down at 120 mph musing: *Fast car, pretty girl ... just bought a motorbike ... how good does life get!*

The Easy-two quickly assumed the moniker of Ernie after the cheesy Benny Hill parody song, 'Ernie (The Fastest Milkman In The West).' Soon Ernie was back at home base at Stamford Hill and in many pieces. Whilst the backyard was the main workshop, it should be admitted that big chunks did occasionally come inside, and the tolerance shown by the other flatmates should be recognised.

Gestation

Various bits were refurbed by suitable artisans. A new big end was fitted, Lucas reconditioned the magneto, a new exhaust system was added, and he was painted a patriotic McLaren Orange to honour the New Zealand race-car designer and driver, Bruce McLaren. I sourced a second-hand Craven fibreglass top box, and it was convenient that Ken and Mollie Craven were still making rear carriers to suit. I liked having a connection with the Cravens. They had opened up motorcycle touring of Europe just after World War II by organising and leading what they called 'PartiTours.' Year after year, they took reticent English riders off for a European adventure and a taste of riding on the 'wrong' side of the road.

None of their side panniers could be found, but our carpenter mate 'Pommie Jim' (from the SS *Australis* and the Finsbury Park flat) made a pair of plywood boxes. These had dovetail joints all around and a piano-hinged opening top.

Of course, time flew by and, by luck and serendipitous good fortune, things more or less fell into place. At some stage, the boys' Kombi shat itself on the way to Cardiff. We (the boys: Darcy, Graham, Phil, Steve, and I) had patriotically been going to watch our national rugby team, the All Blacks, play. It was decided to 'Walk Away Renee' and left it abandoned at the side of the motorway. So that was another thing resolved.

The last day of the Stamford Hill flat era saw many photos taken and hugs and farewells shared. We all hoped there'd be a coming together in a few months at the Munich Oktoberfest, an event that had been enjoyed by all the previous year. There is one anecdote I must share because it illustrates that I was not the only one wearing an adult's L plate. Fanny, the girls' van, was a replacement for 'Sebastian,' a Kombi that had seized a day or so after purchase because the oil level had fallen disastrously. To ensure that the five girls knew the importance of oil levels, a demonstration of checking the level on the dipstick was given. They all nodded sagely, indicating that this had been taken on board. A slight pause followed before Jo tentatively asked, "How do we get oil into the little hole?"

So, where would Anne and I live for the six weeks between the flat dissolution and our departure? This was causing us a slight concern, as was the fact that Ernie wasn't yet finished, and I still had the E-Type. The coffers had taken a hit when the E-Type needed a new clutch. Being an exotic car, it was a demanding job because the entire interior had to be removed to gain access. Of course, unlike our Kombis, it couldn't be accomplished by following a borrowed workshop manual from the library. It had to be done by a specialist. Things were not going well, as it also showed signs of having significant rust.

The project I was working on was an old four-storey block of about 100 flats, all of which were being refurbed and reconfigured. It sat near a council-owned tower block that was what these days we politely call 'social housing.' Our site, although fully fenced with six-foot corrugated iron, had suffered a

The Ernie Diaries

series of break-ins and thefts. Accordingly, we had employed an old duffer as an on-site night watchman. This worked for a while, but as he wasn't doing seven days and would occasionally call in sick, it didn't totally stem the tide of thefts. Somehow, the perpetrators knew when he wasn't on site. After being cleaned out of a delivery of toilet suites, the site manager had had enough and sacked him.

Faced with a much higher cost to employ a professional security company seven days a week, I quickly put forward a proposal that I would provide the overnight security at a cheaper rate than being offered. Fortunately, Anne agreed to come with me. We would lock up the site at the end of the day and sleep on the floor in a site shed on a couple of airbeds. I must admit that I wouldn't have had the courage to do this on my own. The flats had work being done on all levels in all zones, and there always seemed to be doors swinging and banging in the wind. It was very spooky.

Initially, we carried out a walk around with a torch and a baseball bat at 10.00 p.m. before bed, and once in the night, usually about 2.00 a.m. This scared me to death, and we soon found it better to lock ourselves in each night and trust that we'd been seen to be on site. One evening, in the dim light, a spotlight from the tower block shrouded us in light. On another occasion, the site phone rang in the middle of the night. We got the feeling that our presence was constantly being monitored.

One night stands out for the fear it engendered. In the early hours of the morning, we heard the unmistakable sounds of a big truck backing down the short driveway leading to the gate into the compound. Over the top of the corrugated iron, I could see it was a pantechnicon, a furniture removal truck. Scared witless, we rang the cops and snuck up to one of the mid-floors to peer over the balcony, hoping to get a bit more of a view of what was unfolding. I was pleased Anne was with me; valour has never been my strong point. Nothing could be ascertained from our vantage point as the fence was just too high. Unsure as to whether there was anyone on our side, we remained quiet and hidden, trembling with fear, hoping to hear the *nee-noor-nee-noor-nee-noor* wail of officialdom. We waited and waited, but saw and heard nothing. Finally, we made a dash for our site shed and locked the door, making sure the baseball bat was close to hand. We must have dozed off because dawn awoke us as the early carpentry crew were opening up and getting on a brew. The truck was still there, and I heard a guy say to the supervisor, "We'd only just settled down when the f**n 'Old Bill' roused us — reckoned we were up to no good — bastards!" It was a joinery delivery from the Midlands that no one had told me about. They'd had a good run down in the quiet of the night and were just going to kip in the driveway. I said nothing.

This was an auspicious interlude that not only saved us the cost of six weeks of rent, but it brought in much-needed money for the trip. Ernie and the E-Type were brought to the site and worked on in our spare time. Anne still had the Austin Mini Van, which provided her transportation out to her teaching job in Walthamstow.

The fenced-in compound became our realm. I found Anne to be an adept helper, both willing and quick on the uptake. I remember being surprised at the ease with which we fitted Ernie's piston into the barrel. With no ring compressor, the task necessitates the squeezing of the fragile rings into their grooves on the piston whilst gently and progressively feeding the relatively heavy cylinder down over the piston and holding the con rod stationary at the same time. It is a delicate manoeuvre best done with your tongue held just so, and without breathing. If you are a believer in an imaginary friend, it is always best to pay homage before doing this job or wait until you have the correct tool. Anne's fingers seemed to sense the bits that needed squeezing on her side, and the job was done smoothly and effortlessly, first time up, with no broken rings.

In the early 1970s, London still had a million homes without bathrooms; the British weren't known as big bathers. Each local borough had civic bathhouses where you could get all you needed for your ablutions. These became our first point of call each morning. Anne would make her way across to St Pancras whilst I would usually go to Camden Town or Swiss Cottage. Each borough would have one day closed, so we used a variety. It was from the bathhouses that most of the colonial flats sourced their towels. It was almost de rigueur to hire two towels on the way in, along with soap and shampoo, and when leaving the actual bathing area, ostensibly call out "Thanks" and throw a towel on the pile awaiting the laundry process. Of course, this left you with one nicely folded up in your bag under your change of clothes. In the camping grounds of Europe, we would see towels branded from all the haunts. London Borough of Islington, London Borough of Acton — Ealing, Greenwich, Camden, Chelsea — all well represented. Although it is hard to defend the indefensible, the young often have a poor moral compass, and I offer a pitiful defence against my less-than-pure activities of those years. Whilst training as a Quantity Surveyor, we were subjected to many papers on pricing and estimating. I passed all these exams and could pontificate about how pricing is done. "All pricing includes components of waste, breakage, and theft. So if you're not doing your share of wasting, breaking, and thieving, you're paying too much for everything!" If I average out my life's following of that philosophy, the provedores are winning. It is not an activity I am proud of or encourage. If my parents were still alive, I doubt my artful dodger, light-fingered practices would be revealed.

With several balls in the air at once, it was reasonably predictable that not everything would be done well, or on time. With the rust on the E-Type threatening to be an issue, I sourced a pair of fibreglass (what was I thinking??) replacement door cills and hacked off the originals with an angle grinder borrowed from the site. I then didn't have the time or ability to complete the repairs, thereby halving the value of the car. But soon, gone was gone, another example of how to make a small fortune — start with a bigger one — and we moved on.

In the nick of time, Ernie was finished, and we relocated for the last few weeks to another legendary Anzac flat in Leyton. It was notable that we left the Kentish Town site at about 5.30 p.m. on a Saturday, and the first scheduled visit by the security professionals was 7.00 p.m. In that brief window of opportunity, the site was done over. Clearly, our departure had been monitored.

The Leyton flat's address was 603 High Road, Leyton. The '603 girls,' as they came to be known, welcomed us and helped with the final decoration of Ernie's wooden panniers that had been painted white. An Aussie sticker had been stuck on the back of one side box and a matching NZ one on the other. On the Aussie box, Michele (a Kiwi and possibly the funniest woman on the planet) painted a smiley face and a dancing Snoopy dog. On the NZ box, she painted a frowning face and a laid-out-flat, unhappy Snoopy. Our time in Leyton saw much banter and fun, most of it at my expense as I was hopelessly outnumbered by gender.

The Ernie Diaries

We even managed a Saturday at Wimbledon for the lawn tennis. Life was pretty good!

The closing weeks saw me desperately outfitting the expedition. I bought a small gas-cartridge cooker for our stove. Pedlar and Anne Palmer from the rugby club gave us a little single-skin nylon tent. We purchased some waterproofing spray and did our best with it. I also popped in to Read Titan, the local Honda motorcycle shop. They were renowned for go-faster parts for the marque and were most dismissive when I asked for some Araldite, the well-known two-tube epoxy said to hold aeroplane wings on.

"We're a motorcycle shop!" the sniffy sales attendant postulated. "We don't sell glue!"

"Araldite and a coil of wire are the most important spares a rider can have," I countered with an exaggerated antipodean accent, and left in a huff.

So how was the possible romance going? Well, it had got no worse. The proximity of our young bodies squeezed down in the site shed had changed nothing. Progress was static, with no signs either way. This whole adventure was so exciting for me that I didn't want to ruin things with an ill-considered clumsy move. Of course, it should be remembered that I wasn't noted for moves of any sort. I was shortly to embark on the most ambitious ride of my young life. Already it was a bonus having an attractive blonde along for the ride. If things never changed, I'd still be a very happy and proud boy. Maybe Europe would see Anne lose control of her senses and be overwhelmed by my sheer presence. Already we were looking like being a good team. What will be will be!

Chapter 2:
London, UK to Bergen, Norway

Anne Betts

"It is not the destination where you end up but the mishaps and memories you create along the way!"
Penelope Riley, Travel Absurdities

True to his word, Des had Ernie ready to go in the summer of 1973. Well, kind of ... almost.

Several months earlier, I'd planned to leave for Europe in May with the girls in our Kombi van, Fanny. The previous year, the teachers in our group had worked until the end of the school year, but we discovered that late July wasn't the most propitious time to begin a summer adventure on the Continent. Unwelcome as it must have sounded to our prospective employers, we were resolute in our plans to work only until Whitsun, the bank holiday at the end of May

In the early 1970s, as citizens of British Commonwealth countries (at least as it pertained to Australia and New Zealand), we were fortunate to be able to live and work in Britain.

It was an era before the gap year was a thing. We'd travel to the linguistically and culturally familiar UK, where entry requirements weren't stringent, and jobs were plentiful. Because it was so far away, costs to get there were outside the reach of students unless magnanimous parents with deep pockets could bankroll such a trip. For the rest of us, it took time to amass the necessary funds. Besides, post-secondary credentials and work experience in our homelands offered access to well-paid jobs in the UK.

So, with my teaching certificate and work experience in Australia, I had the good fortune to land a fantastic job at the Stoneydown Park Junior School in the London Borough of Waltham Forest. I'd worked at the Henry Maynard Junior School in the same borough the previous school year, so it was a logical place to look for work on my return from Europe in November. Unfortunately, vacancies weren't available until January. My response along the lines of "I understand; I'll look elsewhere" attracted a proposal that I could sit in a classroom drawing full pay for the four weeks until the start of the January term.

The prospect of four weeks of sitting on my butt while earning a decent salary wasn't something to pass up.

I don't know how the departing teacher felt about my observing her every move, but I learned more about teaching in those four weeks than my post-secondary studies and three years of teaching in Australia. She was a brilliant example of an exemplary educator. Her calm demeanour and rhythmic Welsh accent made every day a gift. I couldn't come close to replicating that lilting, melodious accent, but I could embrace her methods and in no time fell in love with the 37-student Year 4 class entrusted to my care.

It didn't hurt that I adored the principal and staff and the learning environment they'd created. Respect was a core value that permeated teacher-student and staff relations, school assemblies, and extra-curricular activities. It was a dream job.

By March, ambivalence about leaving in May was taking root. I was enjoying the work, and less comfortable with the notion that such a fantastic group of nine-year-olds would have to break in a third teacher in the same school year. So when Des's dream of touring Europe on an old motorcycle drifted in my direction, it spawned alternative possibilities.

Travelling on two wheels wasn't new. At teachers' college and university in the late sixties, my vehicle of choice was a 50cc Honda. It was a step-through bike that was more scooter than motorcycle and putted along at a speed I could handle. Filling the tank for 13 cents was one of its greatest assets.

The thought of helping Des realise his dream was tempting, if not irresistible, on so many levels. His plan to rebuild an old motorcycle from scratch resonated with my 13-cent-fill-the-tank frugal approach to transportation. His passion for the idea of travelling around Europe on two wheels was out of the ordinary; it appealed to my indefatigable thirst for adventure. We'd both suffered from the bite of the travel bug, and this was a unique opportunity to scratch the itch.

I was thousands of kilometres away from parents whose job description contained the universal entries of 'worry about children' and 'discourage them from making reckless decisions.' Surrounded by other young adventurers, there were no naysayers or critics flinging a farrago of paranoia or a litany of fear in my direction. I had no niggling doubts, just a few questions rattling around in my mind. Had the idea of an adventure on two wheels been lying dormant since the days of zipping around Brisbane on my little Honda? Might it become a trip of a lifetime I'd be recalling or talking about in future decades? At the very least, I could question the sanity of it in more mature years to come.

Our timelines were compatible, resolving my indecision about quitting in May. Des was open to leaving at the end of July, allowing me to finish the school year. The extra seven or eight weeks of pay would fund many more months of travel.

Travelling with Des offered other advantages. He was the consummate dreamer, and I saw this as a positive characteristic. It translated into transforming what sounded unrealistic or seemed impossible into something worth pursuing.

Engines and other mechanical wonders were as alien to me as a bicycle is to a fish. To someone who didn't know the difference between a carburettor and a crankshaft, I was impressed with Des's mechanical prowess. After several years of dormancy, Ernie had been rescued from probable oblivion. As Des toyed and tinkered, Ernie rose like a phoenix from the ashes and assumed some of the splendour of his glory years. As a result, I felt confident that we wouldn't be stranded when encountering the inevitable breakdowns. While Des has indicated that "the tolerance shown by other flatmates should be recognised," it's but a snippet of the entire story. Because the backyard was lacking as a workshop, motorcycle chunks slowly made their way inside. Fortunately, for Des, in a flat of 10 residents, the dining room with its small dining table was useless for the purpose for which it was intended. The unused, well-lit warm space was just too tempting to a part-

time motorcycle mechanic, so Des tested the waters by gradually moving in Ernie bits and pieces and then more bits and pieces. Slowly, the dining room was transformed into a full-blown workshop. I believe he exercised sufficient restraint to stay within the confines of the dining room, but perhaps he squirrelled away a few mechanical bits into the small bedroom shared with other flatmates. On that point, I'm not sure, but it's not beyond the realm of possibilities given his zeal for getting Ernie in working order.

Now what Des failed to mention was that our flatmates' "tolerance" wasn't accompanied by silence. The dining room was strategically located between the small kitchen and the commodious living room where we ate with plates balanced in our laps. There was a steady stream of traffic back and forth between the kitchen and the living room. So, as the workshop took shape, Des was astute enough to leave enough space for an uncluttered path through the hijacked passageway. Amid the scattered chaos of various Ernie components littering the table and the floor, Des bore the brunt of the playful banter that permeated our environment. We were an opinionated bunch, and it was an unspoken rule that passing through the workshop required a sceptical reference to Des's unremitting toil. He let the comments wash over him, accepting the good-natured raillery for what it was. This was one of several endearing traits that added to his appeal as a travelling companion.

Des was a good person and trusted friend, as solid as the other flatmates I'd had the good fortune to develop a relationship with over the previous year. Our shared desire to succumb to the gravitational pull of travel suggested we'd learn and grow together from our experiences and discoveries. He was a voracious reader and virtuosic yarn spinner so conversation would never be lacking, yet we'd both have an interest in carving out personal space to retreat into our novels.

A cautious, considerate, and conservative rider, he wasn't a show-off or the least bit reckless. Along the same lines, he wasn't on himself, and the occasional glimpses into his self-deprecating nature indicated he didn't take himself seriously. And finally, in his racing leathers and with a face covered in hair, Des projected a scary edge, one not to be messed with. This could be helpful should the sheer presence of a perceived protector of our travelling trio be required. That he was as mellow as a marshmallow on the inside was our little secret.

Combined with similar hopes and convergent dreams, these characteristics pointed to a secure and enjoyable few months ahead.

Short on cash but flush with time without an expiry date, our rough plan was to travel to Israel and Palestine via the Arctic Circle. It wasn't the most direct route, but we figured it could be worked out as we went along, following the winds and tides of our choosing, stopping whenever and wherever we wanted.

After five months of scrounging and fettling, Des had customized and personalized an almost 20-year-old relic into a worthy chariot to take us to the ball. So here we were on August 12, 1973, under a mercifully sunny sky and with a healthy dose of carpe diem, ready to push off from London. It was three weeks after the end of the school term, but Des and Ernie had needed the extra time to fine-tune their relationship and develop confidence in each other's ability to hit the road humming.

And hum we did from the first kick, heading north on the A1, an impressively long road, by British standards. Our destination was Newcastle, a distance of 285 of Her Majesty's miles (or 460 kilometres on the metric chart). Back then, the Newcastle – Bergen ferry was a convenient option for crossing the North Sea from the UK to Norway with a vehicle. Unfortunately, the service ended in 2008 after 140 years of operation. But in 1973, it was a perfect launching pad for a European adventure from Norway.

As a pillion, I felt comfortable from the outset. Most of it stemmed from trust in Des as the rider. It helped that Ernie wasn't a powerful and intimidating beast capable of three-digit speeds. Des's instructions helped: look ahead and follow his cues to lean just the right amount with Ernie as he was manoeuvred through the urban sprawl of London to reach the motorway. I soon realised that being a pillion isn't passive, like being a passenger in a car. A pillion is an active participant in the ride.

I smile at a much later recollection of a trip to New Zealand in 2017, 44 years after our adventure with Ernie. Des had planned a motorcycle trip comprising an itinerary worthy of publication by *Lonely Planet*. And, of course, we were on an old bike, this time a 1965 BMW R69S.

The quick test run along the shores of Golden Bay on the South Island brought back the pillioning skills developed four decades earlier. Unfortunately, a couple of days into the 2017 ride, it became clear my Canadian antibodies couldn't handle the unfamiliar Southern Hemisphere bugs. The debilitating cold sucked the energy out of me. That, and trust in Des's riding abilities, resulted in my falling asleep on the back of the bike as we hummed through the hydro-lakes region of South Canterbury.

The promise of a quick, uneventful ride up to Newcastle was short-lived when the first of many Ernie-related mishaps presented an omen of things to come. It seemed that the catch on the right pannier wasn't up to the challenge of Ernie's motorway-cruising speeds. His 500cc engine was more powerful than that of my 50cc Honda, so perhaps that was a contributing factor. Or, it might have been the constant battering of passing lorries that loosened the closure. When the catch gave way, several carefully packed possessions spewed outwards, leaving a trail of damage in our wake. Most were retrievable. Unfortunately, my most cherished possession was unsalvageable.

Vegemite was smeared down the highway as a horrible yeast-extract skid mark. I'd been saving it and savouring the thought of it for many months. From its arrival in the Christmas box, it had been guarded against marauding gangs of Australians and New Zealanders with ravenous designs on this difficult-to-obtain treasure. Its readily available Marmite cousin itching to hold the wanna-be crown of the yeast-extract world didn't come close to holding a candle to Vegemite.

As an aside, it was a few years later in the Canadian North that one of my long-held assumptions regarding the desirability of Vegemite was put to the test. The arrival of mail once a week in the isolated fly-in community in Saskatchewan, where I lived and worked, was a major event. One or two teachers would head to the post office and return to the staff room with the collection of teachers' mail. Opening a care package from Australia and seeing the Vegemite, I excitedly invited everyone to be introduced to this down-under delicacy. Crackers were hastily coated with just the right amount and distributed among my colleagues.

I didn't expect the gagging, clutching of throats, and shouts of "I've been poisoned!"

Undaunted, I tried another approach. "Okay, it makes a great beverage. I'll put the kettle on and fix everyone a cup."

Two brave adventurers stepped up to the plate. Nope, that didn't make the grade either. The result was that my Canadian friends extracted a promise that I'd never again subject them to any exotic purporting-to-be food arriving in a cardboard box from Australia.

I guess a person has to be weaned on the stuff to appreciate its not-so-subtle taste. For me, it was the ultimate comfort food, and losing it on an English motorway not two hours into the trip was heartbreaking.

There was no time to waste lamenting the loss or wallowing in grief. The detritus scattered along the side of the motorway was collected as best we could while navigating the river of metal and dodging the thundering juggernauts that threatened to wipe out our existence. Mission accomplished, we were soon on our way, sans Vegemite. A short time later, we ran out of petrol. Shortly afterwards, Ernie's kickstand broke. Could our first day get any worse?

Indeed it could. Our first meal on the road was an excruciating ordeal. The one-pot special was an insipid stodge of boiled rice with chicken flavouring produced from a source that resembled nothing that could be classified as poultry. Our pantry wasn't large, and our cooking facilities and utensils comprised a one-burner gas-cartridge cooker and a few small pots and pans. Some people can work wonders with such a limited inventory, but Des and I weren't among them. We were philistines in the kitchen, capable of burning water and barely able to fry an egg without a recipe. Thankfully, we weren't fussy eaters. Hence, our meagre travel budget and hopeless cooking skills resulted in some less-than-stellar meals. Only this first meal was so bad that a combination of rice and chicken flavouring was struck from our repertoire, never to be experimented with again.

Des described his travel budget as the size of a gnat's nostril. My parsimonious habits didn't involve impulsive spending decisions such as buying an E-Type Jaguar "because I could." So my budget extended to both nostrils and most of the gnat's nose. To fund our travels on a day-to-day basis, Des and I established a kitty, contributing equal amounts when circumstances demanded doing so. We shared a similar approach to money matters: the cheaper we travelled translated into travelling further and longer.

We found an acceptable roadside spot for our first free-camping experience of the trip, partly shielded by a screen of vegetation from passing traffic. Why pay to camp when fields, parks, forests, caves, or beaches offer free alternatives? Spending money on accommodation wasn't in our DNA or our budget until it was necessary to do so.

Our first attempt at pitching the tent was a breeze. The poles, tent pegs, and guy ropes came together as they should, like a perfectly designed jigsaw puzzle for beginners. The borrowed two-person single-skin nylon tent was as basic as they came. It was bereft of posh features such as spring-loaded poles, a built-in groundsheet, insect screens, zippers, windows, ventilation skylight, porch, or storage room. It was rectangular with a sloping roof, and once in the tent, the access point was secured by attaching three flimsy sets of ties to each other.

With our peripatetic style of travel and the space constraints associated with touring on two wheels, minimalism guided our approach to packing. Every square inch of space was precious. What couldn't be carried in our clothing or strapped to external points needed to fit into Ernie's four storage areas: the pair of wooden panniers generously contributed by Pommie Jim, the rear second-hand Craven fibreglass top box, and the small vinyl tank-top bag with a see-through pocket for a map. These were capacious enough for our needs, with no room for packing unnecessary extravagances. Souvenirs collected along the way would be limited to visas and passport stamps.

Ernie's fix-it kit contained the bare essentials. A screwdriver, a few spanners, an inner tube patch kit, a can of Finilec Instant Puncture Repair, the indispensable Araldite, a roll of electrical tape, and a small coil of wire were all that was needed for Des to unleash his inner MacGyver. And as I was to learn later in Norway, if we needed to filter gasoline or plug the open mouth of the crankcase, Des would reach into his wardrobe for a sock and a T-shirt. We allowed ourselves the luxury of airbeds, referred to as LI-LOs in the UK. But that didn't extend to a pump. We were young, and our lungs could easily handle the huff-and-puff method of inflating them each evening.

The tent and our LI-LOs were a compatible combination. Without the flash accoutrements of a high-end tent, its simplicity meant it was easy to pack. The tent, LI-LOs, towels, spare jeans, and anything else that could be combined to form a compact roll were wrapped in the sturdy, black PVC bike cover dubbed 'The Ernie House.' The more robust the roll, the more effective it worked as a pillion's backrest enthroned across the top box.

Somewhere between the backrest and the fibreglass top box was a snug space for temporarily storing potatoes, corn, or similar provisions collected along the way for the next meal.

England is a beautiful country. The best way to appreciate it is to follow the shape of the land on winding secondary roads and green lanes through charming hamlets and quaint villages separated by farmlands, green belts, copses, hedgerows, heathlands, meandering streams, and rustic stone bridges. A motorway insulates travellers from the landscape, offering the fastest way to get from A to B and not much else. It's boring and as enjoyable as a skunk at a backyard barbecue. The traffic interferes with enjoying the scenery, which adds very little to a road trip. That was our choice for our mile-eating trip to Newcastle, but we made a pact to avoid these types of roads once we got down to business when we reached Norway.

On our second day, as the sun strengthened and burned off the early morning mist, Ernie gleamed and glinted in the sunlight. But what tricks did he have up his sleeve to keep us on our toes? It didn't take long to find out after we arrived at a bike shop in Newcastle. We were there to have the generator checked. It's a good thing we hadn't booked passage on the ferry because the unwelcome news was that the generator needed to be replaced.

Tracking down a wrecker brought fortuitous results; he had just what Ernie needed.

It wasn't surprising that the miscellaneous assortment of bits and pieces required to make Ernie whole could be scrounged from different sources. After all, we were in Ernie's homeland, where Norton had been manufacturing "fittings and parts for the two-wheel trade" since 1898.

A nearby field provided a suitable camping spot for our second night. The meal of fried eggs and potatoes was way more palatable than that of the night before. Things were looking up on the culinary front.

The dawning of the third day revealed more mechanical gremlins. 'The Fastest Milkman In the West' was displaying an aspect of his personality that wasn't conducive to his being an appreciated member of the team. He seemed to be developing into a hypochondriac. Or maybe he needed assurance he was an integral member of our trio by gauging our reaction to his attention-seeking antics. Did he have a sinister streak and derive a perverse joy from throwing a spanner in the works to disrupt our departure from England? Whatever the source of his motives, insecurities, or ailments, they weren't the least bit engaging, and it was all wearing a little thin.

'Des and the Art of Motorcycle Maintenance' was being called upon with a recurrent frequency we could have done without.

We spent the morning at Gateshead trying to get Ernie's lights going. The afternoon was consumed with hunting for a stand. We were successful on both counts. Both came with a welcome treat; the wrecker's spouse made us a cup of tea, and the vintage bike collector who sourced the stand made us coffee.

One reason people travel is to connect with others. As our journey unfolded, coffee and tea would become delightful excuses for mixing conversation with residents and other travellers. We'd chatter like birds heralding the arrival of spring. It facilitated learning about the customs of a country from fascinating people who shared their stories. We were to discover that mixing commerce and conversation over coffee or tea looked a little different in England compared to, for example, Turkey. But, at their heart, they were similar. The need to forge connections involved the hospitable act of supplying tea or coffee.

An affable chap, the vintage bike collector in his grease-stained overalls and with the wizened face of a septuagenarian, was older than his oldest motorcycle. He fitted Ernie's new stand with wrinkled hands etched in lines marked by years surrounded by grease. His impressive harem of old motorcycles was too much for Des, who drooled over the discovery. Our new friend sensed a kindred spirit in the young Kiwi. After coffee, he led us past two-wheeled carcasses and scavenged motorcycle parts to his most prized possession. It was a rarity, a coveted 1930 Overhead Cam Vee-four Matchless Silver Hawk. Several decades later, Des recalled it was the only one he had ever seen 'in the flesh.' It added an unexpected highlight to the experience for Des. I was underwhelmed; it was just another old motorcycle. But I enjoyed Des's reaction and the shared enthusiasm of these two motorcycle aficionados with so much in common. Even though roughly five decades of life and several continents in distance had separated them, they were kin.

For the 10-mile ride from Boldon Colliery to Newcastle, a mist settled over us like a cold blanket of cobwebs, pooling like soup in low-lying areas. I was rediscovering that a key aspect of motorcycling is being exposed to the vagaries of the weather, be it hot, cold, sunny, wet, windy, glorious, or miserable. This was our first brush with cold and miserable. In response to our observations and with a quizzical glance in our direction, our crystal ball mused, You ain't see nothin' yet!

Warming up required the extraordinary measure of shouting ourselves a hot meal in a toasty café, followed by a movie in a warm theatre: the 1968 epic, Where Eagles Dare. A cinephile might have chosen another offering, but for a couple of cold travellers, it fit the bill. Camping beside the road near Gateshead brought our first experience putting up the tent in the dark. It was the first of many more to come.

We were hoping to make the afternoon departure of the ferry on the fourth day after collecting the battery charging at the motorcycle shop. Bugger, the shop was closed. This resulted in buying another. Attending to Ernie's every need was seriously eating into our travel budget and travel time.

So far, 285 miles to the ferry had taken four days. Hmm ... was this a harbinger of the journey ahead?

After a quick stop to pick up provisions for the overnight crossing, we drove out to Tynemouth for the long wait to see if there was room for us on the ferry. Our names were eventually called, embarking with about 10 minutes to spare.

From that point, our confidence in reaching Norway on schedule was boosted by the fact that Ernie was safely loaded and stowed in the hold. After watching the coast of England ebb away into the distance, we settled in and engaged in the pleasurable pastime of people watching. That led to the first bet of the trip. Bets and card games inevitably ended in who would fix the next meal, with the loser scoring the honour.

So it was Des's comment, "Bet he's a Kiwi" that tapped into our competitive spirits. It turned out to be a sucker bet; I was unaware Des had inside knowledge. He won only because of the open-knit, action-gusset, black shirt our fellow passenger was wearing. Who, but another Kiwi, would have known that the open-knit, action-gusset Bob Charles shirt was so popular that it could have held the status of being part of New Zealand's national dress for men? Bob Charles was the country's celebrated golfer who won the British Open in 1963. Charles did everything right-handed but played golf left-handed. Go figure. It was one of many quirks I would learn about New Zealand and New Zealanders over the months ahead.

That evening in our sit-up seats was spent reading, eating, downing our cans of Newcastle Brown, planning our route through Norway, and settling in for the overnight crossing of the North Sea on the Bergen Line ferry, TS *Leda*.

Until the TS *Leda* arrived in Bergen at 11.30 a.m., we passed the time in conversation with an American woman while I created elasticised wrist and ankle bands to help keep out wind and moisture. Des and I felt clean and refreshed after our respective long showers taken earlier, motivated by the thought they could be the last for several days. Then, not wanting to miss any scenic moments of the remaining nautical miles, we headed to the deck and chatted with the couple of 'Bet-he's-a-Kiwi' fame.

As the ship entered the fjord, there were many pictures to be taken, and my mind clicked the shutter to tattoo the views in my memory. Back then, film and processing were costly, so there were many times when savouring scenic moments didn't involve a camera.

We admired the busy harbour, the brightly painted wooden buildings along the waterfront, and the tall wooden houses stretching towards the mountains forming the backdrop to this coastal city, the second largest in Norway. Nowhere else on earth are there more fjords than in Western Norway. For this reason, the region is commonly referred to as Fjord Norway and Bergen as its gateway. The fjords were formed when glaciers retreated, and seawater flooded the U-shaped valleys to create long, narrow waterways of incomparable beauty. In effect, they're nature's own work of art, masterpieces showcasing some of the most magnificent and spectacular scenery in existence.

We were eager to make our way to fjord country as quickly as possible. I'd briefly visited Norway during the summer of 1972, when it left a powerful impression as one of the most beautiful countries I'd ever experienced. After docking, we slipped through passport control then down to the wharf to watch Ernie being unloaded, hopefully with great care, by crane. The TS *Leda* was built before the age of roll-on-roll-off ocean-going vessels, so every vehicle had to be unloaded over the edge of the ship.

On the wharf, Des posed for a photograph as Ernie was lowered to terra firma. A split second after my camera froze the image for posterity, the crane operator let Ernie free fall the last metre or so. Des and I rushed to his aid, brought him to a standing position, and reviewed the damage. Ernie was shaken but seemingly intact. Now that the three of us were on Norway 'soil,' it was time for the European adventure to begin.

London, UK to Bergen, Norway

Chapter 3:

Norway

Des Molloy

"When writing the story of your life,
don't let anyone else hold the pen."
Unknown

Arriving in Bergen heralded the start of the real adventure. Droning up the UK mainland was nothing but a dull dress rehearsal. Now, there was a frisson of excitement; we were to start the real deal. *Let the Games begin!* was the silent cry.

There was a bit of bureaucracy to be complied with before we finally hit the road, fully legal. We had a rough plan to head northwards to Trondheim, about a third of the way up Norway and only three degrees south of the Arctic Circle. Then, we wanted to cut over to Sweden and across to Helsinki in Finland to rendezvous with Anne's friend Monica. We had a desire to meet with some of our London crew and enjoy some hedonism in Munich at the Oktoberfest in late September, but otherwise, nothing was locked in. We wanted to wander free and loose, and not be beholden to an itinerary. Heading away with a soaring heart, I couldn't picture a more perfect time. The sun was shining, and the views were biscuit-tin perfect. Already Anne was proving to be a good pillion. Yes, the introductory ride to Newcastle was not challenging, but I could sense she was relaxed and trusting on the back. A tense pillion upsets the balance and oneness needed for a loaded moto to perform to a safe and enjoyable level. Finally, we had corners she needed to lean into with Ernie and me as we climbed away from Bergen through fir forests.

Norway's landscape has often been described as very similar to that of New Zealand. Quickly, I saw the similarities, but also the differences. We, too, have beautiful sounds and fjords (anglicized to 'fiords') but in nothing like the quantity or scale of Norway's. That first afternoon treated us to a sampling of what was to come. We rode along the shores of four fjords, the sea shimmering blue under a clear sky, steep escarpments overlooking and defining the view. Each fjord was stunning in its perfection. Completing this perfect day was the sight of an idyllic, water-fronted camping spot.

The ride already had incidents to be remembered in our personal folklore. Between the fjords were often climbs and sometimes tunnels hewn through the hillsides, unlit and challenging.

The balance of a bike depends significantly on your vision. Take away that vision, and your balance wavers. Entering an unlit tunnel from bright sunshine presents a problem. You can see the exit as a near circle of light at the end of an inky blackness in which you can't see anything. Immediately, your balance is compromised. If you don't focus your eyes on the bright light of the distant outside environment — you will do as we did — start wobbling and randomly zigzagging your way to hitting the side of the tunnel.

Upon impact, which wasn't at any significant speed, Anne toppled from Ernie without too much trauma. Once she had found the side of the tunnel with her outstretched hand, she jogged along to safety. Ernie and I did our best to follow her murky figure without compounding the situation by running her over. It was all a bit of a blow to my ego, as I had always prided myself on being a safe rider. My days of trying to impress girls by scaring them whilst on the back were well behind me. With the resilience of youth and our composure regained, we carried on. However, about 10 kilometres further on, we managed a variation of the theme by running into the back of a car that had paused in a similarly unlit tunnel. Once more, Anne slid off the side and onto the tunnel floor. We hadn't yet done a full day in Europe, and already she had hit the deck twice.

"I THINK WE SHOULD FIX THE LIGHTS ANNE !!"

The picture-perfect campsite made up for the tunnel experiences and stuttering progress of the day. With the almost endless daylight hours available to us, we could have ridden on and on, but 120 kilometres felt satisfactory considering the paradisaical spot to overnight. Soon the tent was up and a cooking fire going. We were at Kvanndal near the head of the Hardangerfjord. Two otters were frolicking … entertaining us for some time. This was *National Geographic* stuff. It was so exotic that we could hardly believe it wasn't a show and that someone wouldn't soon appear and ask for our tickets. A stream enabled freshwater, and Anne called across it to two hitchhikers to join us for a brew. It turned into an all-night natter with a Yank and a Frenchman. The young, not-fully adult often can just commune and talk drivel for hours on end, especially when sitting around a fire. We noticed that it finally got dark about midnight when moonlight stippled the surface of the stream with millions of glittering particles. We acknowledged dawn when she peeped up at 3.00 a.m., but it was 4.30 a.m. and fully light before we finally climbed into our little nylon house.

Of course, this meant a tardy start followed. Our little campsite had been one of absolute perfection. It could have graced the cover of a glossy brochure. At first glance, it seemed untouched and completely unspoiled, with no sign of people having paused here before. Yet, upon closer study, we could see black charcoal-burned circles where fires had previously been. There were no rings of encircling rocks or half-burned bits of wood. It contrasted markedly with our experiences in the UK, where often there was litter and obvious despoiling from an uncaring populace. We also removed all signs of our fire and were happy to leave the spot as nature had provided it.

Unfortunately, the day that followed was not the idyll experienced the day before. There was a strong wind coming off the fjord, making our preparations for leaving unpleasant. We broke out the waterproofs with the expectation we might need them.

Coming off a short ferry crossing, we briefly interacted with Sue and Tony Collins, a Kiwi couple I'd read about in a New Zealand Automobile Association magazine. They were touring the world in a 1926 Chevrolet truck converted into a camper. They sat up front in a semi-open cab and slept in the back. The side of the truck offered a canvas for recording data on their travels, and we noticed Norway was the 17th country on their trip so far. I admired their ambitious adventure. Disappointingly, they had no time to dally with us; they were being loaded onto the ferry for the next departure. Decades later, I again admired their wooden-spoked old truck, this time in New Zealand's premier collection of vintage vehicles in the Southward Car Museum just north of Wellington.

It was a prudent move to don the rain gear. By the time we reached the old Viking village of Gudvangen and the adjacent Nærøyfjord, the heavens had opened up and sheets of rain sluiced from the sky. The Nærøyfjord is an arm of the 17-kilometre-long Sognefjord, Norway's longest and deepest.

After a steep 1-in-5-hairpin descent and picking up a few potatoes at the bottom, we caught a ferry at 5.00 p.m. The two-and-a-half-hour sail took us out of the Nærøyfjorden. It was stunning, but it must have been even more spectacular during good weather. The exceptional natural beauty is highlighted by the narrow and steep-sided crystalline rock walls that rise as much as 1,400 metres high and extend 500 metres below sea level. The sheer walls of the fjord have many waterfalls that add to the phenomenal beauty of the area. We cruised into Sognefjorden where more stunning scenery awaited us. It would have been breathtaking on a sunny day. It was almost a sensory overload. Soon after 8.00 p.m., we found a camping spot in a small orchard beside the fjord near the tiny settlement of Kaupanger.

We'd enjoyed a respite from the rain and whilst the day hadn't been the massive success of the previous one, we were pleased with the 160 kilometres or so managed. Around 9.30 p.m., an explosion rocked the tranquil spot as I experimented with petrol to start a fire using wet wood.

I chuckle as I think back to my youthful South Island moto loop where my mate Andy twice achieved near-immolation. After the first whoomph and blood-curdling shriek, I ran to his aid from where I was collecting firewood. "I don't know what happened!" he stuttered, "I was just pouring some petrol on the fire like this." I then got the full replay as he poured petrol from an old can we'd found. Of course, the fire then shot up the poured petrol-fall and into the can. Once more, he shrieked in surprise and terror, scattering flaming fluid in all directions as he threw the conflagrating can in the air.

In my case, I took a bit of stick from Anne, but singed eyebrows aside, no harm was done. I took it as another of life's learning opportunities.

The next day, we caught the ferry across the Sognefjord to Balestrand, a gem of a village that has been a tourist magnet since the 19th century. We thoroughly appreciated the Norwegian authorities' philosophy that if there is no road to your destination and you need to use a ferry, it is free because you have not been provided with a road.

The mountains across and behind the fjord were arranged in layers, like theatre curtains framing one fantastic vista after another, all in differing hues. It was still raining, and in a low-level state of misery, we resolutely pressed on. I was impressed with Anne's resilience. Any complaints were good-natured. We were as wet as two shags on a rock and feeling the cold because our gear was proving to be inadequate for the conditions. After arriving at the tiny village of Moskog, we walked a bit to warm up our feet. Anne picked some wildflowers and attached them to Ernie's handlebars, hoping this somehow might entice the sun to shine. It didn't, so we pushed on.

When almost to the summit on one of Norway's classic hairpins, Ernie decided he didn't have enough petrol to finish the climb. This prompted us to use a manoeuvre that we subsequently employed many times throughout the trip. The petrol tank straddled the top frame tube. On many motorcycles, the lowest point of each side had an outlet to drain petrol to feed the carburettor. Ernie had a tap on only one side, so to get the trapped fuel over the hump, he had to be tipped almost upside down. The manoeuvre was dubbed 'Arse over Tit' or, more politely, 'A over T.' It persuaded Ernie to finish the climb, and with a stroke of luck, he ran out of steam right outside the summit café. We bought a litre of petrol for Ernie, hot coffee to warm us up, and chocolate to replenish the energy we'd burned shivering.

Further on, we stopped at Skei on the shores of Lake Jølster for supplies of bread, milk, tinned meat, and bacon-cheese spread. We then turned off to take the road along the shores of the lake in search of a camping spot. When we stopped for the night, I persisted with a fire long enough to bake some potatoes and heat the canned meat. Meanwhile, Anne wrestled with the tent, poles, pegs, and wind before bringing in reinforcements in the form of 10 enormous boulders for the guy ropes and numerous others to anchor down the inside of the tent. Thinking we'd be disturbed during the night, either by the wind whipping at the tent or the rising water lapping at our sleeping bags, we turned in around 6.00 p.m. This premature end to the day also balanced the lack of sleep to date on our adventure. Our repose was anything but restful as the rain was soon penetrating the nylon tent roof, creating a fine mist indoors. By morning, everything was sodden. So much for believing in the qualities of the spray we'd applied to the tent back in Leyton to make it waterproof! It was a revealing lesson on the difference between 'water-resistant' and 'waterproof.'

With the new day, we assessed the situation. The tent was sagging in the centre, and it was so wet! Our clothing and sleeping gear were saturated. Inside was just as miserable as outside. The rain was intermittent — intermittently drizzling or intermittently pouring. There seemed to be no other option than to wait it out. Kitted out in our rain gear and enveloped in our sleeping bags, we curled up with our novels, a loaf of bread, and a litre of milk, emerging outside only when nature called.

This would not be good for my down sleeping bag. Already it was a bit lifeworn and fatigued. It had been an expensive and considered purchase two years earlier. New Zealand had little choice in consumer products at the time, but most things were of good quality, albeit expensive. This applied to sleeping bags. We had one leading domestic brand — Fairydown. As a nation, we were immensely proud of it. The famed New Zealand mountaineer Sir Edmund Hillary used one on his historic climb of Mount Everest in 1953

Norway

when he and Nepalese Sherpa Tenzig Norgay became the first people to reach the summit. Hillary's 1957 expedition to the South Pole in Massey Ferguson tractors was similarly outfitted. I'd chosen the Twenty Below version as a balance between price and performance. Clearly, Twenty Below was meant for cold conditions. It was unlikely we'd ever encounter such temperatures, especially as at the time NZ's temperatures were measured in Fahrenheit, and that would be more like minus 30 Celsius. Goose down was still considered the best material for sleeping bag filling. There was one proviso — it must be kept dry — otherwise, it will compact and become pretty useless. Useless was indeed the outcome, and subsequent drying didn't return the down's loft.

The day stretched out almost forever, and the night was a similarly torturous struggle. By the next morning, we were ready to concede that the weather had won, and we weren't even a close second.

After a marathon 40 hours, there was no alternative but to get the soaking, saturated, and sorry show on the road. Resolutely, we braved the elements and packed up Ernie. The roll of our tent, sleeping bags, LI-LOs, and towels was heavier, fatter, and wetter than usual. Still, in the urgency of the moment, we moved much faster than usual. Forty kilometres later, our pathetic and pitiful little party was off the road, wetter and colder than before. We pulled into a camping ground in the small village of Byrkjelo and checked out one of their *hytters*. The cost of 30 Swedish Crowns (kr) was equivalent to only a few British Pounds, and when we saw the electric heater on the wall of the cabin, it sold us. In no time, we had transformed the hut into one huge drying chamber with gear draped everywhere and the heater on full blast. Even the tiny hot plate brought in for reinforcement provided the ever-so-welcome hot drinks.

A little later, we walked to the shops and bought a PVC plastic cover to serve as a waterproof fly for the tent. We also bought snacks for a few games of euchre, with the stakes that the loser would cook that night's meal.

After a severe losing streak, I threw in the towel and headed outdoors to commiserate and tinker with Ernie. Off came the carburettor to be stripped and cleaned, followed by an application of Araldite to the magneto. The petrol tank was drained, and unfortunately, petrol spilt over the floor.

With the luxury of a hot plate, Anne cooked up every grain of rice we had. We had been planning to ration it out, but the temptation of a blowout was too much. It also meant enough leftovers for fried rice for the next couple of days. A packet of dried mince was added to give our evening meal a hint of flavour. The result was savoured and enjoyed as though it was something cordon bleu. Life was looking good again. I'd even dodged doing the cooking.

Anne was up at the crack of dawn proclaiming that she'd had the best sleep in ages, whilst I still felt fatigued and jaded. Once the odours of fried rice and egg wafted through the hut to replace the lingering scent of Eau d'Ernie from last night's tinkering, I deemed the day worthy of participating in and emerged from the top bunk.

We decided we needed a rest day to get over the rest day penned in our tent. Most of the morning was spent tending to Ernie's needs. We refitted the petrol tank, and the petrol that hadn't spilt on the floor was poured back into the tank through a sock. The carburettor and magneto were replaced. The mirror was repaired, along with endless other tasks associated with Ernie's well-being. My wire and Araldite, so ridiculed by Read Titan, were both brought into play. Ernie's front pipe had needed wiring back to an engine stud to keep it in place. I'd cursed the shoddy design and cheapskate materials many times. The post-war era was a time of austerity, resulting in the cheapening of componentry that had worked well in the 1930s.

Early in the afternoon, we headed to the village store to buy an entirely new set of PVC rain gear for me so I could return what I had borrowed from Anne.

As the days were almost endless, and there would be another nine or ten hours of daylight, we decided to move on after all. By mid-afternoon, we were successful in getting the dried-out show on the road. Not long after, Ernie needed attention. The gravel roads with the heavily corrugated sections climbing out of corners had caused the panniers to sag alarmingly as the support brackets were found to be inadequate. There was little that could be done at the side of the road, and we were out-of-hours for a suitable artisan to help. Ernie would have to wait until the next town to get it sorted. It was an enjoyable late afternoon ride, and we managed to stay dry. There were many farms in the area, so we obtained permission to sleep in a barn overnight. After wheeling Ernie inside, we rearranged piles of hay to create soft bedding for sleeping. We were enjoying the freedom of not being cooped up in our claustrophobic nylon hutch.

We got off to an early start and spent a significant part of the morning working on Ernie. Just outside Stryn, we found a tractor mechanic who cut, drilled, and fitted two metal strips to lift the back load higher off the wheel. Stryn sits beside Nordfjord, where the majestic mountains and glaciers meet fjord. Many people make their living from agriculture, so it wasn't surprising to find a handy and capable mechanic to fashion a solution to Ernie's sagging panniers. Our riding in Norway had mostly been on quite rough gravel roads, and our gear had been taking quite a hammering. I supposed we had to pay for our pleasures somehow. We were either sidling along the edge of a scenic fjord or climbing through forests to get up and over to another dazzling view. New Zealand's South Island has stunning rides, but hand-on-heart, I can't claim they match what we had been riding through. However, I would assert that we have more vocal birdlife.

For the mountain route over to Geiranger, we adopted the precautionary measure of wearing most of our clothing as the weather felt cool, dreary, and unpredictable. However, never in our wildest dreams would we have expected to come face-to-face with a snowstorm. Enthusiasm was running high as we climbed to the snow level that we had only admired on distant

Norway

peaks until then. Not long after encountering roadside snow, our excitement intensified further when it started snowing.

Yahoos and gleeful cries pierced the desolation. I'd never ridden in snow and found it to be soft and gentle as it fluttered down over us. White flakes silvered the sky, and we were riding over the freshly fallen white mantle that thoroughly covered the landscape. I could no longer ascertain the edges of the road, so I kept Ernie to what I thought was the mid-point between fences or banks and viewpoints. There was no traffic, and we were alone to whoop and holler. The cameras were soon out, and they remained so for a marathon clicking spree. Snow was such a novelty for both of us, especially so for Anne, who had grown up in tropical Queensland. Until then, our exposure to snowy landscapes had primarily been limited to pictures of tranquil scenes on chocolate boxes and biscuit tins, contributing to a romanticized vision of snow. We were oblivious to the dangers and

Norway

inexperienced in riding on roads covered in snow and ice. Compounding the situation was that our clothing was patently inadequate.

The novelty soon wore off, and reality struck. The peripheral regions of our bodies became frozen beyond feeling. We didn't seem to be at the summit of anything and ploughed on, stuck on a seemingly endless plateau. The snow-white surroundings only gradually dwindled. When we were almost at our breaking point, we saw the all-but-deserted settlement of Grotli on the horizon with its welcome Kafeteria sign. Neither of us tasted the cheese rolls we demolished in short order. The two cups of steaming hot coffee proved to be the icing on the cake, generating enough warmth to pronounce the exorbitant equivalent of £1 or so well spent. After writing postcards, it was a 'straight' run (notwithstanding the dodging of sheep and endless zigzags of the road) to the picture-perfect village of Geiranger. We stopped for the occasional snapshot, including one of sheep that interrupted their cropping of the lush grass to stare quizzically at us.

The Ernie Diaries

Geirangerfjorden is a 15-kilometre branch of the Storfjord (Great Fjord) and considered one of the most spectacular in the world. Formed in the shape of an S, nature herself provided the first letter for many of the English language superlatives often used to describe the Geirangerfjord: stupendous, sensational, stunning, and spectacular. The deep-blue colour of the fjord and its elegant snow-covered mountains created one large three-dimensional postcard for our enjoyment. It was easy to see how the Geiranger district has earned the reputation as the crowning pearl of Fjord-Norway.

I was fortunate that with Anne's teaching background, she had access to resources beyond my building sites. It is a hazard of youthful travel that so often you get somewhere, and your mates are pontificating about some world-famous attraction that you passed by in ignorance, back a day or so ago. Not that you would pass by the Geiranger Fjord — it is too big, too dominant, and too overwhelming — overwhelmingly beautiful.

Soon after, an unlocked cabin failed to escape our scrutiny, so we investigated it as a possible overnight haven. It more than met our standards, so we made ourselves at home without disturbing anything and spent the night indoors yet again. The enjoyment of our Norway experience had been dampened somewhat by the poor weather of the past few days. Had the weather been better, we might have overdosed on nature's stunning spectacles. There was a high risk of hyperventilation at some of the scenery we'd ridden through. Being on a moto, we felt and smelled the view. We sensed the enormity of it all. We were in it, our view unrestricted by the frame of a bus or car window. Famed traveller and scribe Eric Newby once said: "If there is any way of seeing less of a country than from a motor car, I have yet to experience it." We fully concurred. Our ride so far had been challenging, but it had been magnificent.

The following day, we were away from our gun club cabin soon after 9.00 a.m. The sky looked encouraging enough, but we would not be lulled into the optimistic belief that we were in for a change of weather for the better.

We opted to wear just about everything we had. Our arrival in Eidsdal in time to see the back end of a departing ferry provided the incentive to check out the nearby supermarket. We stocked up on sugar, coffee, camping gas, postcards, and various odds and ends. Our small butane cooker with its proprietary screw-fit canisters was not proving to be my most prudent purchase. The canisters were punctured by a spike and needed to remain on the cooking unit until empty. A rubber seal kept the gas from escaping when not in use. More than once, we had found that the corrugated roads had caused the seal to ease back and let all the butane out. We also found that a full billy of snow-fed alpine-stream water to make a brew or add to a can of soup would all but use up a canister. Unfortunately, I had yet to discover the practicality of the legendary Optimus 8R petrol cooker.

The next ferry took us to Linge across Norddalsfjorden. We were now in Møre og Romsdal, the most northerly of the famous west coast fjord regions. Because of the many islands and deep fjords, the area has several relatively short ferry crossings of between 10- and 20-minutes' duration. This was one of them, and we arrived in Linge about 10 minutes later. Linge boasts the northernmost fruit farms in Norway (and Europe). It must be beautiful in springtime when thousands of fruit trees are blooming. We were soon going to head away from the fjords, as we needed to get some serious 'kays' under our wheels. There was a more inland route north that promised to be equally spectacular.

We took the Trollstigen Road, also known as 'The Troll's Path,' from Åndalsnes to Dombås through troll country. It twists and climbs through mountainous terrain dotted with waterfalls, fjords, tunnels, and lakes. According to Norwegian folk legend, trolls roam through the mountains of Trollstigen every night, changing to stone when they are struck by sunlight each morning. Clouded in a veil of mist, their stone bodies add a mystical quality to this lunar-like landscape. The mountains encircling the Trollstigen road are enormous. Names like Kongen (the king), Dronningen (the queen) and

Bispen (the bishop) confirm their majesty in this mountain world. An engineering feat in its own right, The Troll's Path climbed 852 metres, completing many hairpin turns while moving up the mountain. It was like a Walt Disney comic-book road up an almost sheer face.

Ernie's single-cylinder thudding exhaust rang out across the vast valley, and we were like proud parents when he finally crested the top. The road is usually closed in October and, depending on snow conditions, opens in May or June for the summer. Paying due respect to the engineers involved in its construction, each curve on the Trollstigen Road is named for someone who worked to create it, an effort that took eight years. When it opened in 1936, the road offered a vital link for farmers, traders, and residents in the otherwise remote region.

We picked up a few supplies in the village of Dombås, and 100 kilometres later stopped beside a stream for the night. It had been a few days since we'd pitched the tent and it looked quite purposeful with the new PVC fly.

We built a fire and cooked mince and rice for tea. Snuggling down in our little tent was like going back to an old routine. It certainly was cosy. Whilst I was disappointed that Anne hadn't yet been overwhelmed by my wonderfulness, there was still time. She probably didn't realise what an easy conquest I would be. We were seemingly a pretty good team though, so I didn't want to rock the boat or upset the apple cart. Anne had been very good at facing the adversities to date. Only our first day in Norway had been as dreamed. The ones that followed were more like an endurance test. The sound of rain on our new tent fly provided the incentive to sleep in. It was more relaxing compared to previous rainy mornings with the added security and protection of the PVC cover.

Roughly 100 kilometres later, we arrived in Trondheim, Norway's third-largest city, situated on an inlet on the south side of Trondheimfjorden surrounded by a ring of hills. The first stop was the swimming pool for hot showers. We both enjoyed our respective stays under the showers, a good four kroner worth. Now that we were in a metric world, I noted that

I weighed 75 kilograms but was unaware of how that related to imperial stones, or how it compared with how much I weighed in London. With 14 pounds to a stone and 2.2 pounds to a kilogram, it wasn't important enough for me to do the calculations. Uppermost in my mind was that it was good to be clean — all 75 kilograms of me. Our personal hygiene had been a little neglected of late, with alpine streams only encouraging a quick splash. Our search for a Laundromat proved fruitless, so we went shopping instead. Anne bought a beautiful Norwegian woollen sweater for 148 kr (the equivalent of £11), posting it to her sister Barbara in Devon. This evaded the purchase tax and avoided the hassle of finding space on Ernie. Afterwards, we treated ourselves to a meal of schnitzel and chips, devouring it in the centre of a pedestrian street. We were not really into cities at this stage of the trip, so didn't make it a stay.

Cleaned, refreshed, and satiated, we left Trondheim around 6.00 p.m. With plenty of light left in the day, we were hoping to make up for lost time and cover a considerable distance before camping for the night. Unfortunately, about 30 kilometres later, Ernie had other ideas. We'd just had a mini-break and were pulling away when he uttered a *chuff, chuff, chuffing* noise. Immediately, I knew this wasn't good, and a couple of exploratory kicks confirmed that there was no compression. It didn't feel like he had nipped up and would benefit from a rest; this sounded terminal.

The spanners were soon out, and with Anne on one side and me on the other, we quickly stripped Ernie's top end. All seemed in order. The cylinder head and valves looked fine, and there was no hole in the piston. Mystified, I knew this meant going further in and removing the barrel. Maybe the rings were broken somehow. Carefully lifting the barrel and blocking off the gaping crankcase mouth with a T-shirt, we gently slid the barrel off the piston as carefully as if we were handling a Faberge egg.

To understand the problem, a person needs to know what each vital piece of the engine does. The explosion in the combustion chamber of the cylinder head forces the piston down the barrel (aka the bore). The crankshaft turns the linear motion into a circular motion linked to the back wheel through gears and chains. The piston must be spaced off the walls of the barrel so it can slide up and down without friction. To fill in the space, thin rings of cast iron are used. They are made so as to be almost a complete circle. They are a bigger diameter than the bore and compressed in order to fit, so they are constantly springing out against the wall of the barrel. These rings are retained in a groove in the piston. In Ernie's case, there were two of these (called compression rings), and a third more complex multi-piece ring to scrape the bore of oil. On the piston, the full-diameter part of the piston between the piston ring grooves is called the land. To my horror, a third of the land between the first compression ring and the second compression ring had broken away. This was allowing the combustion gases to hit the first ring and go behind it into the underside of the piston, and on towards the crankcase without being stopped and compressed.

Of course, Anne expressed concern, and I assuaged it as I quickly assessed our options. The Ciba-Geigy blurb on the side of the Araldite box mentioned its ability to glue wings on jet planes. What was there to lose?

Sometimes, I wonder if there is an omnipotent one above somewhere and she devises little tests to see how resilient and resourceful we are. There are so many things that can go wrong when stripping an engine alfresco. Firstly, you are not in a workshop with a clean floor and bench. Nor do you necessarily have all the right tools and equipment. Removing a piston from the connecting rod (and later replacing it) without losing the sprung-loaded circlip will challenge the most careful. Even removing the gudgeon pin to enable the removal of the piston is a task not to be done outdoors.

Epoxy of the day required at least 24 hours of curing, or an oven to quicken the process. I cleaned everything as best I could and glued the piece of land back in place. I planned to let it harden and give it some warmth on the cooker in the morning. With little energy left to cook and eat, we downed some coffee before a late bedtime.

It was a fatigued and anxious sleep-in while the Araldite set and gained strength. Undaunted by the absence of an oven to speed the process, I set the piston on top of our cooker. We passed the time reading and eating pretty well all the food we had. At 12.45 p.m., we emerged from the tent to start putting Ernie back together. I wasn't all that confident that the Araldite would hold the glued-together piston in one piece. Still, it was best to maintain a confident visage. At 3.00 p.m., Ernie gave every sign he was ready to go. Hopefully, the wings were on the jet plane and lift-off assured. Confidently, we loaded up and crossed everything we had to cross. We pushed him to the top of a rise, climbed aboard, and ran down the other side with the compression-release lever fully in and the engine turning over in second gear. I let him spin over with little or no compression for a bit, then with no throttle but full compression. Then finally, I fed in a bit of fuel and gently applied some throttle. Soon we were purring along quietly. We were both incredulous and ecstatic. Take that Read Titan!

Grateful and relieved to continue our journey, an hour later we stopped at a seemingly unattended camping ground for water and to wash the spuds we'd gleaned along the way. It was then that we spied a communal cooker and moved in. Not ones to pass on a readily available cooking source, we enjoyed fried potatoes for tea. We'd planned to be on our way after the meal, but the owners returned, necessitating our checking in for the night. We'd reason to believe that the rate of 5 kroner included hot showers, but much to our chagrin, showers were extra, so our ablutions had to wait.

With communal cookers at our disposal, it made sense to have chicken soup the next morning for breakfast. We were away at 9.30 a.m. and an hour later realised we were on the wrong road. Scrutiny of the map confirmed the error to the tune of 120 kilometres. We were still heading up Norway towards Tromso and the Arctic Circle when we should have been almost across to Sweden. Apportioning no blame (i.e., both pissed off), we turned around and headed back south towards Verdalsøra and a shortcut across to the E72, the road we should have been on. We passed through Steinkjer, the geographical centre of Norway, for the second time. It was raining cats and dogs, so we stopped for coffee — four cups each consumed over a couple of hours. During our break, we decided to abandon our plan to visit Helsinki and Finland and instead go straight to Stockholm when we reached the Baltic coast. It was a safe assumption that the remaining days of August in Scandinavia would bring more rain and colder temperatures, and it was time to seek warmer climes. There is only so much misery you can take and still say you are having fun.

What were we thinking when we established our original plan to include the USSR??? It was at that moment in Steinkjer that we were grateful to the Soviet authorities for rejecting our application for visas because we were travelling on a motorcycle. Thanks to Ernie, we had avoided many cold and miserable kilometres.

The secondary route to link up with the road we should have been on turned out to be a humdinger, a euphemism for a road negotiable only by those with no respect for their modes of conveyance. Riddled with potholes, it involved weaving acrobatically around and between each Scandinavian crater. Completing the 100-kilometre journey was a true test of stamina. The weather was cold, wet, and miserable, and by the end, we were drained and weakened by the ordeal. Ernie was absolutely marvellous! He didn't get sick, run out of petrol, or throw a tantrum. However, he did get dirty, filthy dirty, the dirtiest so far. After joining the E72, we stopped at the first sign of the crossed spoon and fork. Boosted by a hamburger and egg, and two cups of coffee, we struggled for another 70 kilometres before settling down in a centrally heated stugor (Swedish for a Norwegian hytter). After such a taxing day, as demoralized fugitives from the weather, we deserved the luxury of a cabin. We had crossed into Sweden, but there hadn't been a border crossing to mark the exact spot.

Norway

Chapter 4:

Sweden

Des Molloy

"The struggles we endure today will be the 'good old days' we laugh about tomorrow."

Aaron Lauritsen,
100 Days Drive: The Great North American Road Trip

The comfort of the cabin was a definite impediment to an early departure on our first morning in Sweden. Anne seemed appreciative of my efforts to cobble together fried chips for breakfast and happy to have a delayed start to the day. We were finally away by midday. At the first town, Östersund, I posted a letter to Joe Francis Motors on Footscray Road in London. The company was the only old Norton specialist I knew of, and I asked them to send a new piston and a few bits and pieces to Stockholm. Also, we sent a telegram to Anne's friend Monica in Helsinki to let her know of our change in plans and that we would hopefully see her in Stockholm. Monica was on her way back to Britain from Australia via the Trans-Siberian Railway. We'd been hoping our respective travels would intersect in either Helsinki or Stockholm. Notations in Anne's diary indicated Monica would be in Helsinki on August 28, and Stockholm from August 29 to 31. It was now August 27.

With these tasks behind us, we rode another 200 kilometres until just past Sundsvall on the Baltic coast, stopping only for a few supplies at a supermarket. The going had been pleasant, but without the spectacular grandeur of our Norwegian riding. There were green pastures and small lakes, but nothing to take our breath away. The tar-sealed roads were of good quality.

An early start the next day meant reaching Stockholm should have been easily achieved, as we had only 400 kilometres to cover and 15 or more hours of daylight. However, this depended on Ernie's cooperation, and that failed to materialise. The first 100 kilometres went quickly, but for the next 200 kilometres we were stopping and starting (mostly stopping) to attend to Ernie's various ailments. He began by shedding his exhaust while overtaking a semi-trailer, but we were fortunate to recover it, mostly undamaged. After some minor first-aid treatment, the exhaust was tenuously refitted, only to require several adjustments during the afternoon. A puncture to the back tyre resulted in several delays. Ernie didn't have a centre stand, and the side stand kept breaking off. And, of course, it was no

good for allowing the removal of the back wheel anyway. On the road, we applied the emergency Finilec Instant Puncture Repair sealer, and later, air at a garage. But our troubles weren't over; we needed Finilec, then air again about 50 kilometres later. We eventually stopped for the night about 80 kilometres north of Stockholm, hopeful that we could reach our destination without a tube replacement.

In the morning, Ernie's tyre was almost as flat as a pancake. Ten kilometres later, it was. After more Finilec, we limped another five kilometres before it was flat again. Two police officers stopped to tell us we couldn't stop on the motorway. They suggested we mend the tyre, and they'd return with a pump in an hour.

We lay Ernie over on his side on a steep roadside bank, and after hoicking him up on a rock, I could remove his wheel to replace the inner tube. Several hours later, there was no sign of the police or the pump, so I flagged down

Sweden

a car. The occupants kindly agreed to take the wheel to a service station and return with it inflated. After putting the wheel back on Ernie, it became flat again just a few kilometres later. It was probable that the tube had been pinched during the replacement and inflation. This time, I hitched to a garage with the tyre containing the now patched inner tube. We put in air and hoped for the best, not entirely confident that the roadside patch was as good as needed.

About 40 kilometres down the road, on the outskirts of Stockholm, the back tyre was flat once more. Expletives were once again 'expleted,' but nothing we tried seemed to work. Ernie had already shed his exhaust (again!!) 20 kilometres earlier, so we were growing weary of trying to reach our destination in stops and starts. When we couldn't find a garage that would repair the tyre, we left Ernie on the side of a hill, minus his back wheel, and continued into Stockholm without him. Truth be known, we were a bit over Ernie at that point. We figured some time apart would probably benefit us all.

Our arrival in Stockholm was the same day Monica was expected on a ferry from Helsinki. We found our way to the ferry terminal by bus, but there was no sign of Monica, so we headed out to a camping ground. We weren't missing Ernie, so the separation was working.

Relying on our internal alarm clocks to wake up at 5.00 a.m. the following day to catch the T-Bahn to Ropstein and the ferry port, we hoped to meet Monica. There were plenty of ferries, but again, no Monica. We made our way to the Poste Restante to collect mail and rang Joe Francis Motors to add an exhaust to our previous order, along with various other titbits.

Poste Restante provided a valuable service for travellers. Mail addressed to a person, care of, for example, 'Poste Restante, Stockholm' was all that was needed. We'd let friends and family know when we expected to reach a particular town or city. Then, one of our first stops on arrival would be the Poste Restante counter of the main post office. Communicating by telephone was expensive and invariably involved a pocketful of coins or communicating across a language barrier to obtain operator assistance. Besides, having a static-free connection was never guaranteed. So, the Poste Restante was virtually the only way to receive news from home and our travelling friends. It also provided a critical link for travellers to confirm arrangements for meeting up with each other. Such was our hope regarding Monica. After unsuccessfully locating her at the ferry port, we hoped to find correspondence from her at the Poste Restante. There wasn't, so we made plans to return to the post office the following day.

Always willing to respond to Ernie's every need, we spent the next few hours attending to his back wheel. A new tube was fitted to the wheel that had accompanied us to Stockholm. After getting back to the nearest off-ramp, I ran along the E4, batting the wheel along with my hand like a kid in an old black-and-white movie. We eventually reached Ernie, patiently waiting for us on the hill where we'd left him. After refitting the back wheel, we rode triumphantly into Stockholm with Ernie spewing, spluttering, and backfiring explosive coughs through his exhaust. We parked him in a nondescript and unassuming back street and wandered through the streets and shops of Stockholm. We then returned to the camping ground where we dived into the used Leon Uris novels we'd picked up whilst browsing.

The next day, we spent a good part of the morning with Leon until 11.00 a.m. when we again made our way to the Poste Restante. Waiting for us was a letter from Monica with information regarding her hotel. We stopped by the hotel, but elusively, yet understandably, she wasn't there. We left a message and spent the next few hours divided between a Laundromat and cruising the shops. We headed back to the hotel around 6.00 p.m. with packs of Tuborg and Pripps under our wings. The following six hours were spent watching and listening to Anne and Monica catching up on the last 18 months — telling stories and laughing a lot over a few drinks. Monica hailed from Middlesbrough in North Yorkshire, and as the night wore on and the beer-fuelled discussion became more animated, her Teeside accent became more pronounced, so I was picking up less and less of her side of the conversation. She had been a 'Ten Pound Pom,' a grateful beneficiary of Australia's post-war immigration scheme. A £10 fee enabled a passage to Australia (New Zealand had a similar scheme) in return for committing to spend a minimum of two years working in the country. Monica had stayed three years, teaching maths at the same high school in Brisbane where Anne taught. They became firm friends and had travelled together across Australia from Brisbane to Perth and back again during holidays at the end of the 1970 school year. By midnight, we were in no state to make our way back to the camp. The bedding was shared out. I took the floor and had a night of adequate sleep, undoubtedly aided by the alcohol consumption.

We accompanied Monica to breakfast at the hotel, sliding our trays along the metal runway, feverishly filling them with the morning's offerings. Our presence failed to escape a staff member who spotted a ring-in. With my long hair, beard, and 'sartorial elegance,' I was an exception to the hotel's usual demographic. She approached me and asked from whence I came. "Room 121," I bluffed confidently. Thankfully, such a room existed. She went out to reception (presumably to verify this information), so we dropped our trays and were ready to do a runner when she returned, seemingly unperturbed. Needless to say, we retrieved the trays and packed them with goodies — food we'd dreamed of since hitting the road. We devoured the lot and slipped out while Monica was arguing about having to pay for showers. Our haste was also motivated by the thought of the guest from Room 121 appearing on the scene.

We saw Monica off from the station at 8.00 a.m. For the rest of the day, we adopted the personas of true tourists in Stockholm, starting with an early morning stroll through the medieval streets of Gamla Stan (Old Town). One of the largest and best-preserved city centres in Europe, the narrow cobblestone streets lined with buildings painted in mainly autumn hues contribute to its unique character. We then took a boat trip terminating at the Vasamuseet (Vasa Museum) on Djurgården, an island in central Stockholm. This unique museum is named after the Vasa, a warship that sank in Stockholm's harbour on her maiden voyage in 1628. The museum's crowning jewel is the world's best-preserved historic ship that spent 333 years on the seabed in the Baltic's chilly waters. When the Vasa was raised in 1961, nearly all her contents were successfully salvaged. Seeing the Vasa in all her splendour and learning about the salvage and restoration process was a definite highlight of our visit to Stockholm. On a roll, we dropped by the nearby Nordiska museet (Nordic Museum). Sweden's largest museum of cultural history tells the story of Nordic lifestyle and traditions from the 16th century onward, through its exhibits on topics such as holidays, housing, furniture, fashion, food, and toys.

It was a day of immersion, though somewhat superficial, in a history and culture that was entirely new to us.

After eats and a leisurely stroll back to the T-Centralen metro station, we took the train to the camping area. We were a bit overwhelmed by the Swedish place names, and if we didn't note them carefully, we struggled to find our way around, including getting back to camp. All Swedish names looked the same to us, and often signboards found us peering and mouthing, *Was it 'Urglefulgledup' or 'Flargleuppenlaup,' or 'Uggleflaup'?*

The next six days were fairly evenly split between lazing around the campsite, visiting more of the sights of Stockholm, and readying Ernie for the next leg of our journey. Sleeping bags were aired, and clothes were washed. Amazingly, Anne randomly bumped into a friend from her college days and spent time with her and her sister. Of course, we communed with travellers, sharing lies and adventures. One night, one of the Aussies lent us their jar of Vegemite for dinner. We devoured it with enthusiasm, and both agreed that it was a worthy substitute for what we'd left smeared on an English motorway three weeks earlier.

A nearby apple tree kept us supplied in apples during our stay. Sweden was very expensive, and in the year since our previous European travels, the British currency had fallen dramatically. On a straight conversion, we weren't getting much more than half of last year's money. This meant that treats were rare or contemplated thoughtfully before we lashed out and spent. One day, we couldn't resist the sight of bacon in the supermarket. We matched it with eggs, and back at camp, everything was fried up in our one pan. The sounds and smells of such a delicacy brought almost orgasmic pleasure. When ready, we eagerly and speedily hastened towards our tent area. Predictably, disaster struck. A slight stumble saw the panful of delights suddenly arc through the air and land in a muddy puddle. Aghast, we looked at each other, then acted as one. We gathered up our muddy repast, washed it off with water from a standpipe, gave it a bit more fire, and scoffed it down.

One day, we visited an International Trade Fair. Moving from stall to stall to taste the various samples, we enjoyed sausages, ham, tea, coffee, kiwi fruit, cheese, bread, biscuits, and numerous other treats. Each stand gave minuscule samples, necessitating cruising for a couple of hours to get any sort of feeling of being replete.

In town, we wandered through the NK (Nordiska Kompaniet) department store like yokels from the farm. With the dismal exchange rate, we looked but didn't buy. Purchases of more appropriate clothing would have to wait. We also visited Skansen, the open-air museum on the island of Djurgården in the middle of Stockholm. Founded in 1891 by Artur Hazelius to illustrate life in different parts of Sweden before the industrial era, it housed over a hundred historic buildings relocated from various parts of Sweden. Interpreters in period costume represented craftspeople such as tanners, shoemakers, silversmiths, bakers, and glassblowers, demonstrating their skills in period surroundings. The complex contained an animal refuge featuring a cross-section of Sweden's wildlife. Also, it now has my camera. Perhaps it's displayed as an item used by travellers in the 1970s.

Finally, the parcel arrived from Joe Francis Motors, and Ernie was soon all spruced up, and handsome he was with his new exhaust. Anne had given him a thorough wash, and he shone in the sun, seemingly eager to continue. Sadly, there was no new piston, so we just had to carry on, hoping the wings wouldn't fall off. We were also pretty keen to get back on the road. Our maps showed we'd achieved something, but it had just been a taster. There was a lot more to see and experience. We especially wanted to get south into some sunshine and warmth.

After the hiccup of running out of petrol early, our first day back on the road was a steady and slightly dull ride through featureless countryside. Ernie now had his running-out-of-petrol routine down to a fine art, and Anne and I had become equally adept at performing the manoeuvre to redistribute the remaining petrol in the tank. We stopped 330 kilometres south of Stockholm and with the sun shining brightly, out came the novels. The unexpected warmth of the sun encouraged us to linger longer, and we made plans to settle in for the night. We soon found a spot among some trees near the coast. When the daylight finally faded, we read by Ernie's headlight (yes, Ernie's lights were working again), and had a short *korv* (Swedish sausage) for tea.

We left our camping spot at Oskarshamm quite early, heading down the coast to Kalmar, where we doglegged inland. At Anne's urging, we took in the glass-manufacturing region of Småland province. The region's glass-blowing prowess dates to the 16th century when Gustav Vasa brought artisans to the area from Venice. In the heavily forested region between Kalmar and Växjö are several of Sweden's most famous glass factories, including Kosta (founded in 1742), and Orrefors (founded in 1898). We toured both plants and then stopped at Hovmantorps to browse for purchases, almost buying. I was amazed at the wide variety of glassware. My astonishment at discovering 'it's a thing' to have one prawn cocktail setting for each person made it into Anne's journal. Until then, I assumed that a feed of prawns was presented in one huge communal bowl.

After rounding the lake, we came upon a closed camping ground that was an ideal spot for bunking down. As a bonus, we found a lakeside-changing shed, meaning we didn't need to put up the tent. Bacon and eggs were on the menu for tea. Mud-free, they were delicious.

Once more, we were on the road relatively early, but off again soon after when we spotted a large supermarket. We would soon cross into Denmark, and our small stash of Swedish krona was taking up valuable space in our kitty. The Swedish clogs grabbed our interest, but at the checkout came the discovery that we didn't have enough krona for two pairs. Under the watchful eye of the cashier, we flipped. I called 'heads,' Anne called 'crowns,' and 'crowns' scored the clogs.

With our loaf of still-warm fresh bread taunting our nostrils, we stopped a short while later for sandwiches of sliced meat and cheese. Afterwards, it was time to knuckle down to the serious business of putting kilometres behind us. With a shared agreement to leave Sweden by the end of the day, we did the big roads. The day was overcast and cool, with a cutting crosswind. It was a chore sitting still with little to look at, hour after hour. Gone was the excitement of the fjords, glaciers, and mountains. The dullness of the ride encouraged Anne to settle in low behind me, and I suspected she spent some of the afternoon napping. Ernie was no power machine, and to gain speed and get out of the wind, we pulled in behind a semi-trailer. The slipstream sucked us along, and Ernie needed just a whiff of throttle. From time to time, I moved out far enough to ensure the driver could see me in his mirror. We connected with a thumbs-up. Although Ernie was a 1957 model, the design of his 79 x 100 mm long-stroke pushrod engine dated from 1928. Our paired juggernaut was pulling us along at 70 mph (112 km/h), and after an hour, I decided this was a bit too quick for us and pulled away with a wave.

One brief rest stop was the only interlude before Helsingborg, the commercial and industrial seaport on the Øresund Strait. This ended our time in Sweden. Tomorrow, Denmark, another Nordic country.

Chapter 5:
Denmark, West Germany, East Germany

Anne Betts

> "If we were meant to stay in one place,
> we'd have roots instead of feet."
> Rachel Wolchin

Our departure from Sweden marked an end to the suffocatingly slow progress of the previous four weeks. In precisely 28 days, we'd covered only 2,500 kilometres. The time had come to get the lead out and quicken our stride.

Travelling overland from Sweden to Denmark involved crossing the narrowest part of the Öresund, the sound that separates the two countries. Our ferry took less than half an hour to cover the 2.5 nautical miles between Helsingborg, Sweden, and Hamlet's hometown of Helsingør in Denmark. One of the world's busiest ferry crossings, it had been in operation since at least the 11th century, the earliest known written mention of the route. About a dozen ferries crossed the sound every 15 or 20 minutes.

A ferry service was the only option in 1973. This was well before the architectural marvel comprising a tunnel, the artificial island of Peberholm, and a massive bridge eight kilometres long offered a viable alternative.

From Helsingør, we wasted no time in taking the road towards Copenhagen. We chose the most direct route and battled it out with a steady flow of trucks on the freight corridor connecting the busy port town with the nation's capital. A roadside sign encouraging the use of seatbelts featured a kangaroo, marking our only stop on the busy motorway to capture a photograph. We reached Copenhagen just 40 minutes after arriving in Helsingør, travelling at Ernie's ever-tranquil pace with no mechanical upsets or upheavals. We'd put only 55 kilometres behind us but crossing into another country felt like we'd made progress.

The camping ground in Copenhagen offered the luxury of unlimited hot water for showers. Its other standout was noisy boozing tour groups. It was my first recollection of passing judgement on the way some people chose to experience the gift of travel. These were heady days of feeling like the world was opening up in front of us, and these folks seemed to be squandering the opportunity with their self-indulgent hedonism.

The shoe would be on the other foot within a couple of weeks when Des and I would descend on Oktoberfest in Munich. Reminding each other of this reality, we cut our fellow travellers some slack and turned down the judgement ratchet by several notches. Never mind a couple of weeks — the next day, we were up at the crack of dawn to be at the Carlsberg Brewery for 8.30 a.m. With their 1973 tagline, "Probably the best lager in the world," Carlsberg warranted our first stop.

In Kiwi speak, 'crack of dawn' is 'sparrow's fart,' just one of the many quaint yet subtle distinctions I was to discover between the Australian and New Zealand vernacular. Mostly, our trans-Tasman expressions were similar. Terms such 'togs' (swimsuit), 'shout' (treat), 'tea' (evening meal), 'mince' (ground meat), and 'she'll be right' (everything will be okay) required no translation. Des had already become used to the Queenslanders' use of 'port' for a suitcase and 'thongs' for jandals or flip-flops, but most of the time we were working from the same page of the English language manual. So here we were, off early to explore some of the highlights of Copenhagen. We figured tours of Denmark's top two breweries could be easily accomplished in one day, interspersed with a visit to Den Permanente. In operation since the 1930s, Den Permanente showcased the very best in modern Danish design and craft. It was an illuminating introduction to a blend of the simplicity and functionalism that exemplifies Danish design. Being a combination of exhibit and store meant that admission to Den Permanente was free.

After the Carlsberg Brewery and Den Permanente, our proclivity for seeking out free experiences extended into the afternoon when we fronted up for a tour of the Tuborg Brewery. Beer has been a prominent part of Danish culture for over 5,000 years. The country is too far north to produce wine, but with a climate that supports the production of high-quality malt barley, Denmark has emerged as one of the world's beer-brewing giants. With beer being our bevvy of choice, Des and I welcomed our tasty introduction to the beer culture of Denmark, compliments of these two world-class breweries. *Skål!*

With two tasting-room experiences under our belts, a sobering introduction to a notable era of Danish history was in order. The Museum of Danish Resistance chronicled the struggle of resistance during the Nazi occupation of Denmark from 1940 to 1945. As a result of our visit, I learned that the Danish experience during World War II was somewhat unique. What began as initial cooperation with the occupying forces eventually grew into a resistance movement. It was marked by acts of sabotage and large-scale rescue operations that saved a large majority of Danish Jews. Neighbours helped Jewish families flee to villages on the coast where residents provided shelter, and local fishermen transported them to neutral Sweden. As a result, Denmark earned its place in history as one of the few countries that protected a significant portion of its Jewish population.

Throughout my travels, it was one of many memorable visits to sites shedding light on the Holocaust and resistance to Nazi oppression.

Interest in this slice of history had a lot to do with one semester of my Grade 12 history course. Was it a touch of laziness or a glimmer of brilliance on the part of our teacher, Mrs Wilde? She offered the choice of Asian or European history; I chose the latter. We could choose one of several select epochs and complete assignments based on our research. With no internet in 1966, history classes were mostly spent in the school library on self-directed research. Her approach fuelled my appetite for learning as much as possible about the period between the two world wars that allowed Adolf Hitler to rise to power with such disastrous consequences. Shelved to emerge six years later with my arrival in Europe, I came to realize how much I appreciated her methods.

A quick cruise by the Poste Restante brought us 'home' to the campground and the on-site shop to pick up bacon and eggs for tea. Mixing food genres and switching generally accepted menu items between breakfast, lunch, and dinner marked our approach to meals. Soup for breakfast or cereal for dinner; it didn't matter to us. Our choices were influenced by what was in our pantry or harvested from passing fields. Food was a biological necessity. Regarding it as an indulgence in this part of Europe required a more expansive travel budget.

After two breweries in one day, we slept the sleep of the over-indulged. Our hoped-for early start to leaving Denmark would come soon enough.

The longer-than-anticipated stay in Norway and Sweden meant short-changing Denmark, unfortunately. The opening of Oktoberfest in Munich was just 10 short days away, and it was clear we couldn't continue at a lame snail's pace.

With morning, the engorged gunmetal grey clouds promised inclement weather for part of our 300-kilometre ride to Hamburg. Our rain gear meant reaching the port town of Rødbyhavn without getting too waterlogged. The fare for the one-hour ferry crossing from Rødbyhavn to West Germany cost the equivalent of £4. We pronounced it a little rich by our standards, but it was a sign that the higher prices of Scandinavia might accompany us into West Germany. Our preoccupation with European prices had a lot to do with our British wages. My well-paid teaching job earned £32 a week and the cost of a one-hour ferry crossing, all things considered, cut a not-so-insignificant swath into those earnings.

From Rødbyhavn, our plan was to head south to Hannover via Hamburg, and then east to Berlin to travel through East Germany, Poland, and Czechoslovakia before returning to West Germany in time for Oktoberfest. Given our experience to date, it was a very ambitious schedule.

Who were we kidding? It was roughly 2,500 kilometres, the same distance we'd covered in the first 28 days.

We were curious about the Reeperbahn, the street in Hamburg's St. Pauli neighbourhood renowned for its nightlife and red-light district dubbed *die sündige Meile* (the sinful mile). As with many port towns, sailors would spend a major part of their shore leave in the multitude of nefarious bars and brothels. While those days were long gone, the strip clubs, sex shops, and legalized brothels remained. In the 1960s, it became the mecca of rock music when the Beatles, among others, performed in its many nightclubs. It was where the famous four honed their craft and prompted John Lennon's oft-quoted statement, "I might have been born in Liverpool — but I grew up in Hamburg."

Upon reaching Hamburg, we made a beeline to the city's naughty neighbourhood and parked Ernie on a side street. None of our gear was lockable; our possessions held little monetary value and rarely made decisions for us. We'd park Ernie in plain sight and head off exploring. Occasionally, Des would unstrap the tank-top bag, we'd stuff it with things we couldn't afford to lose (like rain gear), and he'd carry it as a 'man purse.' Ernie didn't have a key. Des explained that no British motorcycles had keys until the 1960s. Riders were an honourable bunch of motoring enthusiasts who wouldn't countenance stealing another's pride and joy. Des was prone to wax poetic when pressed for *any* information about motorcycles. Providing more detail than I wanted or needed, he explained further that when bikes embraced the technology of coil-and-battery ignition, rather than a 'kick-it-and-she'll-run' magneto, Lucas had supplied one simple spade key. The key fitted all makes and models using their equipment. So, every Triumph, BSA, Norton, Matchless, AJS, and any other British models from the mid-1950s until 1967 used the same key; if you couldn't find your key, grab a small screwdriver. I took the information in and nodded in feigned interest with what I hoped was a look of understanding. Yep, Ernie didn't have a key because he was born in 1957.

In Hamburg's cramped corner of concupiscence, we wandered past the bars, brothels, strip clubs, sex shops, and other attractions that made the Reeperbahn famous. Acknowledging that a daytime visit to this den of debauchery would be less revealing than one at night, our introduction to this X-rated side of life was nevertheless an eye-opener. We wandered past women behind windows, beckoning customers to drop in for a visit. Sex-shop storefronts displayed a range of adult toys that left little to the imagination. More entertaining than educational, it tapped into our competitive nature as we pointed out examples of depravity and excess to each other, treating it as a contest.

"That's nothing ... look at this!"

"I'll see your seedy discovery and raise it to this sleazier one."

Our curiosity eventually satiated, we agreed that while the experience had been enlightening, it was as erotic as a stool sample.

We weren't ready to leave Hamburg, so rode out of the downtown area until we spotted a field in which to pitch our nylon hotel. I was keen to visit

Hamburg's Olympus camera repair centre the next morning. As a result, we were up quite early and almost fully packed when the local constabulary paid us a visit, but the language barrier proved impenetrable. We were grateful beneficiaries of the linguistic stalemate when they shortened their stay and moved on. It likely had something to do with where we were camped.

Olympus wasn't open when we arrived at 8.30 a.m., but an edition of the *Daily Express* grabbed our attention. We passed the time by catching up on news of the coup d'état in Chile by the US-backed military junta led by Augusto Pinochet. Our curiosity as travellers with interest in world affairs was tempered by the fact that we were mostly out of touch. Our news was gleaned from other travellers or the headlines of English-language newspapers. When something captured our interest, we'd invest in a newspaper for more information. The coup d'état was one such event. Salvadore Allende had been democratically elected as Chilean President in 1970, and news of his overthrow by a U.S.-sanctioned coup was alarming.

After leaving my camera for repair, our next stop was a bank to collect traveller's cheques. Checking out several photography shops resulted in Des's purchase of a camera to replace the one he'd left behind in Sweden. These tasks consumed the better part of the morning, and just after midday, we left Hamburg, heading south. Given our time constraints, we chose the autobahn for the 150-kilometre stretch to Hannover. West German autobahns were the big roads, built for speed and massive volumes of traffic. What we could see of the countryside through brief glimpses between passing vehicles was uninspiring. But then, at this stage of our journey, we were more focussed on piling on the kilometres than stopping to enjoy what lay in between. After pausing at a rest stop for a quick corn boil for lunch, it was a relatively uneventful trip to Hannover during the afternoon. Before camping for the night, an exit took us a short distance to the outskirts of Hannover to a Grossmarkt to buy five litres of oil and four stretchy cords. After rejoining the autobahn, we left it 20 kilometres later to camp on the sandy shore of a lake for the night.

The next morning, we treated Ernie to an oil change. The new stretchy cords fastened our rearranged belongings that included leftover oil and a bag of corn. Eager to reach West Berlin well before nightfall, we needed to incorporate delays that would inevitably be encountered while negotiating the corridor through East Germany. With just 50 kilometres to the Helmstedt-Marienborn crossing, we wasted no time in taking to the road. During the Cold War, Germany was divided into East Germany (German Democratic Republic) and West Germany (Federal Republic of Germany). East Germany was part of the Eastern Bloc, and West Germany was in the Western Bloc. Separating the two German states was the 'Iron Curtain,' a political, military, and ideological barrier erected by the Soviet Union at the end of World War II. It was designed to seal off the Soviet Union and its dependent states in the Eastern Bloc from open contact with the West and other non-Communist influences.

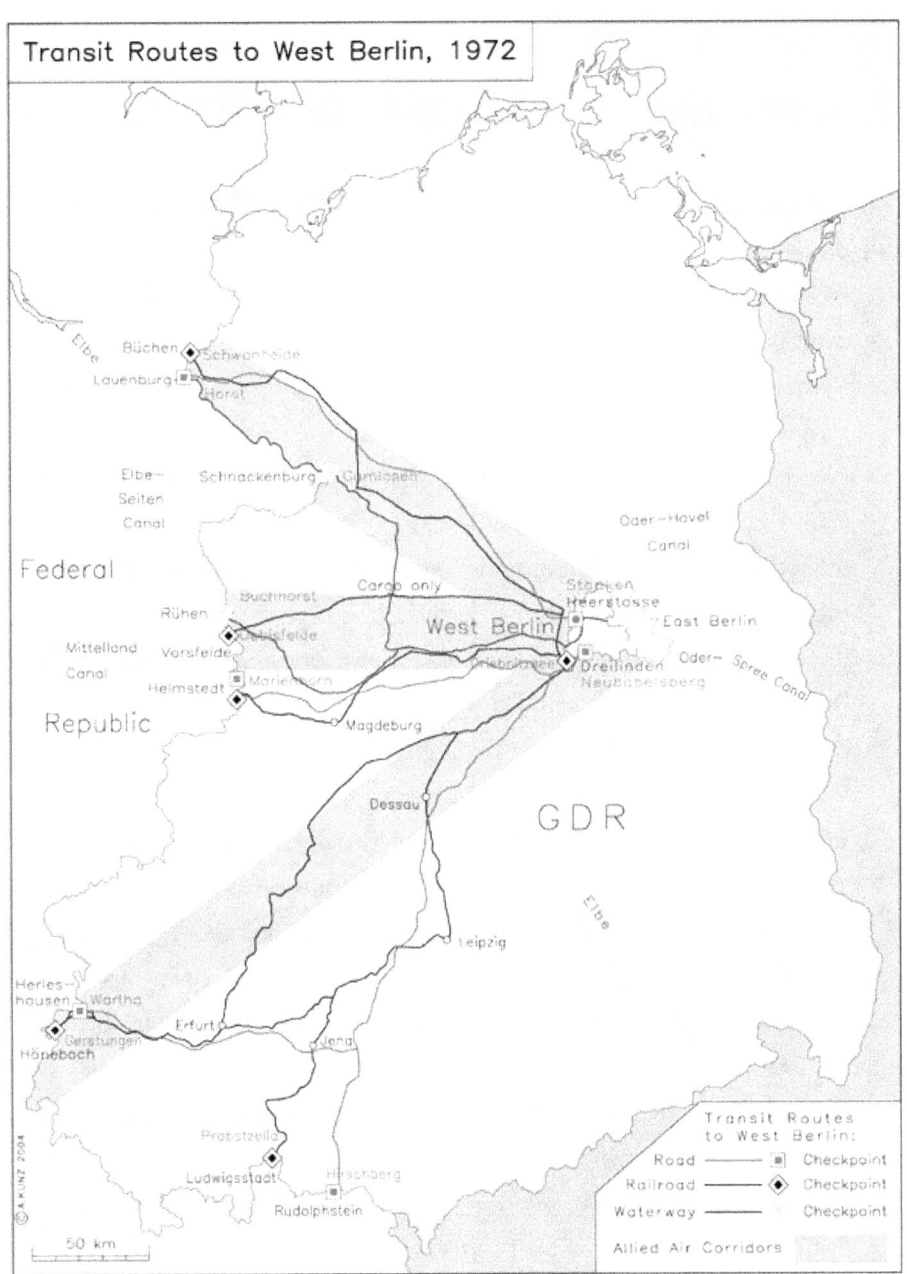

Denmark, West Germany, East Germany

The Helmstedt-Marienborn crossing (named *Checkpoint Alpha* by the Western Allies) was one of the access points across the Iron Curtain. Nestled in a relatively small enclave behind the Iron Curtain was West Berlin, a geopolitical anomaly. It was part of the Western Bloc. In 1945, Berlin was divided into four Allied-controlled zones — the British, French, and US sectors in the west, and the Soviet sector in the east. Reaching West Berlin overland required travelling through a 180-kilometre corridor through East Germany.

Having travelled the route in 1972, I had a sense of what to expect. The van I was in then was stopped nine times by the German Democratic Republic (GDR) authorities for vehicle and passport checks at various points along the corridor. GDR border troops, numbering approximately 40,000, patrolled the inner-German border. Armed guards, boom gates, and observation towers were ever-present reminders of a strong military presence.

Des and I were familiar with the rules — whilst in transit through the corridor, it was forbidden to take photographs or deviate from the highway. Stopping was permitted only in designated parkways.

With a prescient sense of yet another misadventure, we shared these details with Ernie, warning him of the possible consequences of attracting the unwanted attention of GDR officials. Things were looking good, given that he had displayed no incontinent tendencies since Sweden. Unfortunately, our optimism was misplaced as it soon became apparent he'd failed to heed our advice. After running out of petrol, we employed the carefully choreographed manoeuvre that had worked successfully on previous occasions. However, when Ernie came to a halt a short time later, like a grounded falcon with a broken wing, Des announced that Ernie had lost compression. I'd learned that the combination of 'lost' and 'compression' in a single utterance was serious business and a potential harbinger of doom. As Ernie and Des played hide and seek with the latest mechanical cataclysm, my feeble David Bowie impersonation of "Ground Control to Major Tom ... Your circuit's dead, something's wrong" was a weak attempt to make light of our predicament. Finally, waxing philosophical in a manner that would have impressed both Socrates and Plato, Des mused, "I think we're stuffed." Was this the *coup de grâce* that had failed to materialize by such a slim margin in Norway? I quickly surmised that the desperate bodge of our earlier field repair had failed, and the adhesive power of Araldite, and our luck, had indeed run out. Despite Ernie's apparent indifference to the gravity of the situation, Des dexterously set to work. My sceptical façade was shattered when Des's perspicacious talents produced magical results. The roar of Ernie's engine was music to my ears. It was no longer David Bowie's 'Space Oddity' but the rich sounds of an entire orchestra. It was worthy of a spontaneous fist-pump and celebratory dance, but neither of us was a jump-up-and-down kind of person, so we gave Ernie an affectionate pat and continued on our way.

Des wallowed in my admiration of his mechanical genius for a couple of hours, but his conscience eventually intervened. He finally fessed up and admitted that he had done nothing of note, and it was Ernie who had decided to re-establish the needed compression.

Disaster averted, our demeanour was decidedly upbeat for what remained of the corridor. With great relief, we arrived in West Berlin without further setbacks, happy to be back in the pulsing pace of urban life.

In the 12 months since travelling through the corridor the year before, the political landscape had changed. The Transit Agreement of 1972 eased travel restrictions, and the Basic Treaty that came into effect in June 1973 paved the way for the two German states to be recognised by the international community. These significant breakthroughs in diplomatic relations between East Germany and West Germany trickled down to our adventure with Ernie, resulting in our documentation checked just three times while passing through the corridor.

Denmark, West Germany, East Germany

The central part of our Berlin plan entailed visiting my cousin Chris, who lived on Markgrafenstraße with her spouse, Rod, and two children. Before doing so, we made some of our usual urban stops — a bank to cash traveller's cheques, a Laundromat to obliterate the travel grunge from our denim staples, and the Poste Restante to collect mail from home and our 'wanderlusting' friends.

Traveller's cheques were a convenient and safe way to carry money in an age before credit cards, debit cards, pre-paid travel cards, and ATMs. The pads of five or ten American Express cheques were available in different denominations in a variety of foreign currencies. There were two places for signatures, one to be signed at the time of purchase, and the other in the merchant's presence when cashing it. Each cheque had a unique number. We'd record the numbers in a separate place from the cheques, so if they were lost or stolen, the cheques could be replaced.

As Chris and Rod lived a couple of blocks from the Berlin Wall off Friedrichstraße, we visited *Checkpoint Charlie* on the way. *Checkpoint Charlie* was on the busy thoroughfare Friedrichstraße in the US-occupied sector. It was the crossing point into East Berlin for foreigners after the wall was built in 1961 by East Germany. The wall was built to prevent what had become an embarrassing mass exodus of its citizens' fleeing to the West (over 3.6 million by August 1961). The departure of so many people was an ideological blow and a detriment to the East German economy. Many who fled the East in 1961 were much-needed youth; from the beginning of 1961, every second person making a move was under the age of 25.

The Berlin Wall severed the neighbourhood where Chris and Rod lived, creating neglected wastelands within close proximity of the wall on both sides. Hostage to a divided Germany, the area seemed to be waiting for an opportune time to undergo modern urban development or be restored to its former glory. Or, more importantly for Berlin, for the two beating hearts of a divided city to be joined as one.

The waves of change had begun. But it would take another 16 years for the tectonic shift that would see the wall come down in 1989 and pieces gifted or sold to governments, institutions, and individuals around the globe. The reunification of Germany would be celebrated a year later, in 1990.

Many buildings near Chris's and Rod's apartment were still showing the scars of World War II, with their pockmarked facades. There were several vacant lots, presumably casualties of the war and 25 years of cold-war stagnation. Their two-bedroom apartment was on the third floor of an elegant old building in what was likely a less desirable neighbourhood, given its proximity to the wall. The building oozed loads of character. However, it seemed improbable that it would ever achieve heritage status, and we feared it might have a date with a wrecking ball at some point. In 1973, it provided attractive rental accommodation for a somewhat transient Australian family.

Chris and Rod were a couple of years older than we were and managed an antiques business in West Berlin. They were easygoing and gracious and invited Des and me to stay overnight after enjoying their conversation and company over a two-litre bottle of wine. They were thrilled we'd brought a bag of corn, likely because it wasn't sold as a vegetable in Europe. What we called corn was stock-feed maize. Still, it tasted just fine from the pot, and we scoffed it and the wine down with ease.

The following day, our German-style continental breakfast of rolls and copious amounts of coffee lasted until midday. All the while, Chris and Rod regaled us with tales about living in Berlin. They were regular visitors to East Berlin to attend the opera and other events associated with its vibrant arts and music scene. Their description of the ease with which they crossed was reassuring and elevated our comfort level about following in their footsteps. We basked in their company, but unfortunately, Oktoberfest and Munich beckoned, and we felt compelled to push on.

As we were planning to travel to Poland via East Berlin and East Germany, we needed East German mark. Before German reunification in 1990, East Germany and West Germany had separate currencies — the East German mark and the West German Deutsche Mark. The East German government officially valued the East German mark at parity with the Deutsche Mark. In West Berlin, East German currency was available at the considerably better exchange rate of 4:1 compared to what was available across the border at 1:1. The only problem was that it was illegal to import them.

Undaunted, we wrapped our newly acquired 50 East German mark in white toilet paper and buried them in our sugar container.

Today, I cringe at the thought of the risk threshold of our youth. What would have been our explanation had we been exposed for importing illicitly obtained currency? What would have been the penalty? We didn't give either of these questions a second thought; the established value of 4:1 in the West was all we needed to justify carrying it into East Germany.

At crossing points, vehicles were subjected to having mirrors passed underneath, a length of wire thrust into the petrol tank, and contents of the boot inspected. It was challenging for most East Germans to visit the West so to detect escapees, scrutiny was more intense for vehicles travelling from east to west. Restrictions on East German pensioners weren't as stringent. They could visit the West for up to four weeks in a year and allowed to take no more than 10 East German mark with them. The expectation was that relatives or the West German government would support them, and if they remained in the West, so be it. They were no longer contributing to the East German economy, so defections of pensioners were seen as beneficial.

At *Checkpoint Charlie* came the discovery we were at the wrong frontier for transit to Poland. No worries, we adjusted our plans and crossed to spend what remained of the day in East Berlin. Border officials expressed little interest in Ernie and Des and me, and we crossed with no drama.

At each border behind the Iron Curtain, travellers from the West were obligated to exchange a specific amount for compulsory spending based on the predicted number of days of their visit. In the case of East Germany, it was 5 Deutsche Mark per person to cover our 24-hour visa. As a result, we received 5 East German mark each at the official government rate.

After parking Ernie, we wandered around and blended with the crowds as best we could, enjoying people watching and maintaining as low a profile as possible. Control and surveillance were part of the daily realities of life in East Berlin. It was an era when neighbours were expected to report on each other and contact with Westerners was regarded as suspicious. As a result, we mostly kept to ourselves.

Des and I spent our East German mark on food and beer. Having money to burn translated into eating well. We cruised a few shops in search of warmer clothing and possible purchases to trade with the entrepreneurial Turks of Istanbul. But consumer goods were limited in both quantity and variety, and what we saw was of questionable quality.

It had been four days since the September 11 coup d'état in Chile that overthrew the government of Salvador Allende. It was with interest and curiosity that we watched a demonstration protesting these events from a relatively safe distance. While we carried passports of little-known countries that didn't have reputations for interfering in the affairs of other nations, taking part in demonstrations wasn't a prudent choice. We would have loved to protest the role the USA played in the overthrow of a democratically elected government in another sovereign country, but we agreed that participating in these kinds of mass demonstrations was best left to countries where it was safer to do so.

Unfortunately, the repressive Pinochet regime lasted 17 years. After moving to Canada in the mid-seventies, my participation in multiple protests of human rights violations in Chile felt somewhat impotent, though necessary, in the context of what was happening in Chile at the time.

With fading light, we crossed back into West Berlin and covered the two blocks to Chris's and Rod's apartment after picking up refreshments on Friedrichstraße. We were welcomed back with much chatter over refreshments that ran out far too early. After replenishing our supplies from a pub on Friedrichstraße, we returned to the business of making merry, and the chitchat continued over Chicago and Hindenburg dice games. We played firstly for shouts and then for breakfast — corn-on-the-cob or egg sandwiches. The grog and the night ended simultaneously at 1.30 a.m.

The new day started with corn-on-the-cob, coffee, and double egg sandwiches — a tasty compromise. Just like the day before, breakfast lasted well into the morning. It was followed by a Frisbee frolic in the vacant lot next to their apartment building.

A Frisbee and four novels heavier, Des, Ernie, and I bid Chris and Rod farewell and wended our way to *Checkpoint Bravo* at Drewitz for the 150-kilometre ride through East Germany to Poland. Reaching Poland before nightfall was eminently doable, possible only with Ernie's cooperation. But our disinclined friend had other thoughts. Seemingly out of fresh ideas, he returned to old habits, with an opening salvo of shedding his new exhaust fitted in

Stockholm. Running out of petrol followed, and he finished with the flourish of a non-functioning headlight.

At one stop, I retrieved our secreted contraband East German mark from our sugar container, and we gave a young lad from East Berlin our coins. We abandoned all hope of leaving East Germany by the end of the day and stopped at a camping ground at Bad Saarow after travelling only 80 kilometres from *Checkpoint Bravo*. Our cupboard was almost bare, but we were able to scrounge some dry bread from the camp warden to accompany our canned chicken soup. With our purchase of two bottles of beer for the equivalent of only 5 pence, we salivated over our haul all the way back to our tent (over the beer, not the bread). The amber liquid was the hands-down highlight of the meal.

Afterwards, a chat with a guy from Dresden was made possible with the assistance of gestures, drawings in the dirt, and 10 or so words from our 10-or-so-word German vocabulary.

The next day, Ernie was able to travel the eight kilometres to a gas station without a stop once we'd redistributed what little petrol was left in the tank. Obtaining petrol in East Germany was a social experience. It inevitably involved joining a queue for as much as an hour and interacting with others while doing so. People were friendly and curious. One highlight of travelling on an old motorcycle was that perfect strangers approached for a look and a chat. Whenever we'd stop for a rest, folks would come out of the fields to do just that.

Gas station attendants would always try to put a two-stroke mix in Ernie. Motorcycles and cars like the East German Wartburgs and Trabants were of the two-stroke variety, and petrol pumps could be adjusted to produce a four per cent or five per cent oil mix. Des quickly learned to interrupt the process by saying Ernie was viertakt (four-stroke). Four-stroke engines have two separate compartments for petrol and oil and don't require pre-mixing of the two.

After an hour's wait while a tanker unloaded fuel, we drove to Frankfurt an der Oder close to the Polish border to spend the rest of our sugar-coated money. In this part of East Germany, it was a novel experience to be the fastest thing on the roads, passing oxen carts and tractors with ease.

The next major hold up was at the frontier when the East Germans didn't seem too happy about our overnight stay during transit. Their response to such a vexatious revelation was to make a phone call to verify the details, and we were eventually waved through.

Chapter 6:

Poland and Czechoslovakia

Anne Betts

"One thing that I love about traveling is feeling disoriented and removed from my comfort zone."
Sarah Glidden, How to Understand Israel in 60 Days or Less

Crossing borders behind the Iron Curtain was always unpredictable. Agents had the power to search, delay, detain, or generally make life difficult. Their actions might relate to the interpretation of their rule book. Or, it could be rooted in their quest for entertainment or to boost their sense of power and status. Not knowing what we'd encounter was part of the adventure. We relished the unpredictability and basked in the eager anticipation that uncertainty brought. We'd warily roll up to each frontier post, choosing what we thought would be the appropriate amount of obeisance demanded by the situation. We'd relax only with the hefty thud of an entry or exit stamp. Some agents stamped our passports with flamboyance, wielding the stamp like an exasperated judge thumping a gavel, a powerful symbol of authority.

At the Polish frontier, we were told to empty our pockets and show all cash, traveller's cheques, and documentation. No one said anything about money stored elsewhere, so our sugar container remained safely stowed. With no appetite to undermine the agent's moment of authority, we readily complied and placed the requested items on the counter. After buying insurance and changing the 80 Deutsche Mark for compulsory spending for the estimated four days in Poland, we headed east in the direction of Poznań.

Meanwhile, the 'Beast from the East,' a bitterly cold wind blowing across Central Europe from Siberia was gathering strength to welcome us to Poland. It assaulted us with unbridled fury, and Des and I braced ourselves against the steady headwind. Unperturbed, Ernie's reaction was to tackle it head-on, all the way to Warsaw. At rest stops, Des and I scurried for shelter. The cultivated fields along the route stretched out to the limitless horizon, an inland sea of potatoes, corn, beans, apples, plums, tomatoes, cucumbers, and of course, the perennial staple sugar beet in abundance.

Experience is the most unusual of teachers. It gives the test before the lessons. Such was my test in how to recognise a sugar beet plant. My first exposure to sugar beet was the year before when travelling through Eastern Europe with Jo and Rhyll in Fanny, our Kombi. We'd stock up on whatever vegetables could be gathered for our regular diet of stew. Occasionally, we'd splurge on a small cut of meat to toss into the pot. A field of turnips provided the motivation, and a key ingredient, to get the pot on the stove for the evening meal. The first mouthful was a clue that something was amiss, in both texture and taste. Vegetable stew wasn't supposed to have an unpalatable taste with an edge of sweetness. My companions and I had grown up in Queensland where sugar came from sugar cane, not from some root vegetable resembling a turnip.

So Des and I gave sugar beet a wide berth. With 50 per cent of the country's population engaged in agriculture, we speculated that most of them were working the fields in the stretch between Frankfurt an der Oder and Poznań.

Most of the harvest, if not all of it, seemed to be done by hand. With nary any machinery in sight, Poland's rich agricultural bounty appeared to be the result of labour-intensive endeavours. And unlike Western Europe, absent were the privately owned roadside stalls offering an array of produce for sale. Within a 20-kilometre stretch before Poznań, we ran out of petrol three times. With the first two flips of Ernie, we were able to redistribute what little petrol remained in the tank, but on our third stop within sight of Poznań, it was clear the tank was dry. Help miraculously arrived when a friendly local stopped and gave us two litres without charge. Moments like these contributed to what was developing into a steadfast belief in positive outcomes, and the innate goodness of people, regardless of their nationality or personal circumstances.

After staying overnight at a camping ground in Poznań, the next day we passed many more fields prolific with produce between Poznań and Warsaw, including the largest field of tomatoes I'd ever seen. We were travelling through the flat fertile farmlands of Poland's Central Lowlands, where a variety of crops created a lush agricultural canvas stretching as far as the eye could see.

Upon arrival in Warsaw mid-afternoon, we parked Ernie and checked out the prices of footwear and warm clothing. Prices in Poland were such that it was time to upgrade our wardrobe with warmer gear and wade into more adventurous culinary waters. Our 'gnat's-nostril' travel budget easily accommodated our exploration of several traditional Polish dishes — barszcz (Polish red borscht), gołąbki (stuffed cabbage with meat and rice), and pierogi (dumplings stuffed with potato and savoury cheese). It was a welcome gustatory experience after the many less-than-mediocre meals of the previous five weeks.

When the time came to leave central Warsaw for the camping ground, Ernie was nowhere to be found. We had left him within sight of Poland's tallest building, The Palace of Culture and Science, a gift from the Soviets built in the 1950s. Each face of the pyramid-shaped building appeared to be identical, hence our difficulties in orienting ourselves and locating Ernie. Like leaves caught in a swirling eddy, after what felt like several hours of walking in ever-expanding circles of the building, we eventually spotted him standing neglected and forlorn, exactly where he'd been left. We don't know who was happier with the reunion — Ernie, or Des and I. Unfortunately, the search had eaten into what remained of daylight and meant riding to the campground without the aid of a headlight.

We devoted the next morning to becoming acquainted with the private currency exchange process. At the border, the particularly poor official government exchange rate imposed on visitors from countries outside the Soviet Bloc resulted in our receiving a rate that was significantly less than market value. In the Old Town, we advertised ourselves as tourists interested in doing business. We flashed our cameras and sat conspicuously on benches in a large square flanked by four-storey stone buildings resembling towers of aged Lego blocks.

We decided against accepting the first offer of 26 złotych for one Deutsche Mark, so we wandered around the Old Town. We cruised the market stalls in Castle Square where Sigismund's Column proudly towers over the city. From there, we followed the narrow streets, admiring the intricately designed facades of old buildings displaying a rich mix of architecture spanning the previous eight centuries.

With no other offers, we returned to the square, and I discreetly exchanged 50 Deutsche Mark with a young trader. He smoothly intercepted us, quietly seeking our needs as he cut across our bow in a seemingly random way. The process felt as natural as any commercial transaction with a street vendor, attracting no apparent interest from anyone else in the square.

Before leaving the Old Town, Des and I tagged on to the end of a tour group and saw an amazing film on the destruction of Warsaw during World War II and the rebuilding efforts after the war. The Old Town was rebuilt from the rubble using bricks and reusable decorative elements sifted from the debris. The citizens of Warsaw, with the support of the entire country, participated in the five-year reconstruction campaign. Wherever possible, the character and architecture were preserved through the constant reference to what remained of photographs, paintings, and archives. It was a truly remarkable feat. With 85 per cent of the historic city obliterated, it's an outstanding example of a near-total reconstruction of a span of history covering the 13th to 20th centuries. By the 1970s, the Old Town had once again become a thriving hub, a proud testament to the resilience and perseverance of the Polish people and their enormous efforts to recreate what once was. Des and I were fortunate to travel at a time when we could enjoy the fruits of their labour.

We appreciated our brief exposure to snippets of European history. It fuelled our admiration for not only how people had coped with adversity, but their strength in rising above it. It also fostered a deeper appreciation of the fact we'd grown up in countries that had emerged from the Second World War without the mass devastation experienced elsewhere. We had much for which to be grateful.

A visit to where the Warsaw Ghetto once stood was a priority. Our interest in this period of history had been more recently boosted by the historical fiction of Leon Uris. Uris's deep research provided a rich historical context for many places associated with the Holocaust and Nazi oppression. We'd stumbled across *Mila 18* while browsing second-hand bookstores in Stockholm, and *QB VII* joined our reading list as a gift from my cousin in Berlin. *Mila 18* was based on the Warsaw Ghetto Uprising, and *QB VII* was a courtroom drama featuring the fictional Jadwiga Concentration Camp in Poland. Both novels inspired an interest in visiting the Warsaw Ghetto, and Auschwitz the following day.

The Nazis established the ghetto in November 1940 and chose Passover — April 19, 1943, as the day to destroy it. At its height, more than 460,000 Jews were imprisoned there. In the summer of 1942 alone, almost a quarter of a million inhabitants had been deported to concentration camps and mass-killing centres. The residents eventually realised that the daily trains to Treblinka were not transporting them to resettlement camps in the east, but were taking them to a death camp. When the people began refusing to board the trains, the Nazis decided to liquidate the ghetto. It was the only way they could defeat the starved, outnumbered, and outgunned Jews.

The resistance movement, led by Mordechai Anielewicz, was determined to not give up without a fight. It became the largest Jewish insurrection during the Second World War and inspired further rebellions in ghettos and death camps. Nathan Rappoport's Memorial to the Heroes of the Warsaw Ghetto pays tribute to this history. On the front, the sculpture depicts several of the resistance fighters with Mordechai Anielewicz in front holding a hand grenade. On the back of the monument is a line of Polish Jews marching to their deaths in a concentration camp.

In Tel Aviv four months after our visit to the Warsaw Ghetto, I volunteered at a central agency to work on one of the many kibbutzim in Israel. Coincidentally, I was sent to Kibbutz Yad Mordechai that I was to learn upon arrival was dedicated to the memory of Mordechai Anielewicz. There,

in a grove of trees on a hill in front of a water tower damaged in the war of 1948, was a statue of Mordechai Anielewicz sculpted by none other than Warsaw-born Nathan Rappoport. Oh, the wonders of serendipity and travel. Where the Warsaw Ghetto once stood, there was little else to see. The Nazis had seen to that. So Des and I headed into the city to buy warm clothing with my unofficially obtained złotych: a jacket, a pair of sealskin boots, and a pair of woollen socks. The purchases ate up most of the 1300 złotych and a good deal nevertheless — everything for the equivalent of less than £8.

We sampled Polish *kielbasa* and on the way to the campground, stopped by the monument to Polish-born Marie Curie, the first woman to win a Nobel Prize, and the only person to win in two fields: Physics in 1903 and Chemistry in 1911. Unveiled in 1935, gunfire damaged the statue during the 1944 Warsaw Uprising by the Polish Resistance Home Army. After the war, a decision was made to leave the bullet marks intact on both the statue and its pedestal. Perhaps this conscious act was in memory of the patients and staff of the nearby Maria Curie-Sklodowska Radium Institute murdered in the unimaginably brutal attack by the Nazis in 1944.

We collected our camping gear and set off towards Krakow, 300 kilometres away. After a pleasant ride through the forests, fields, and river valleys of the rolling Central Lowlands, we passed through Radom with its gorgeous rows of baroque-style homes from the 16th and 17th centuries. About halfway to Krakow, we set up camp for the night in a sheltered place in a forest where foliage swallowed the tent and hid our presence from passing traffic. We'd become experts at finding concealed dens for our overnight camps.

Around noon the next day, we passed through Krakow, the geographical centre of continental Europe, and rode the 13-kilometre stretch to Wieliczka for a 90-minute tour of the salt mine. In operation since the 13th century, the mine has been an important source of table salt since that time. It used to be one of the world's biggest and most profitable industrial establishments when common salt was commercially the medieval equivalent of today's oil. Consistently a magnet since the mid-18th century, the mine had increasingly become a tourist attraction. One well-travelled French tourist observed in the 18th century that the salt mine was no less magnificent than the Egyptian pyramids. Many appeared to share his enthusiasm as millions of visitors have explored the subterranean world of labyrinthine passages, giant caverns, underground lakes, chapels with sculptures in the crystalline salt, and rich ornamentation carved in the salt rock by the miners.

Heading back to Krakow to take the road to Oświęcim, we had a run-in with police after bungling a left-hand turn. They pounced, seized Des's passport, and created a space in their patrol car for presumably a trip to a police station. My intuition climbed to a level of high alert. If they expected us to comply with obsequious servility, they were in for a surprise. As much a matter of *amour-propre* as self-preservation, come hell or high water, there was no way I was getting into the confined and potentially dangerous space of a Polish police car. I felt more secure on the open and very public footpath.

We were bemused by their reaction, equivalent to squashing a bug with a wrecking ball. It was much ado about nothing, a minor traffic infraction, if that. A mixture of anger and fear propelled us into a zone bordering recklessness. We refused to get in, demanded the return of the passport, and continued arguing with them beside the vehicle. The exchange of

Poland and Czechoslovakia

English and Polish failed to bring about a simple resolution. Meanwhile, a tearful and irate woman had been an unwilling passenger in the back seat. She took advantage of the diversion to slide out, slamming the door on the leg of the officer who was endeavouring to restrain her. She escaped, and we were left with even angrier cops. It was quite the spectacle and not worth more drastic measures to force us into compliance. Eventually, our remonstrations paid off. They returned Des's passport and allowed us to go on our way.

Eager to reach the gates of Auschwitz before closing time, we'd run out of time to explore Krakow, one of the most beautiful cities in Poland, and one of very few to escape major devastation during World War II. Roughly 75 kilometres later, we reached Oświęcim and *Konzentrationslager* Auschwitz, the largest and most notorious of the Nazi death camps. Disappointingly, our late arrival just before 4:00 p.m. resulted in our spending only two hours touring the memorial before it closed for the day. It was worthy of investing much more time.

Unlike my visit to Dachau near Munich in 1972, Auschwitz left the impression that very little had been destroyed or altered since the liberation of the camp by Soviet troops in January 1945. This was due in part to the early intervention of Poland's Ministry of Culture and Art. The authorities sent a delegation of former prisoners to the camp in April 1946 to protect the site and take early measures to establish it as a museum. As a result, Auschwitz is an eloquent yet solemn reminder of the unimaginable brutality and genocide practised by the Nazis and a powerful symbol of the Holocaust. It's estimated that 1.1 million people perished at Auschwitz and its satellite camps.

The memorial's highly moving exhibits pushed emotional buttons and boundaries. Piles of confiscated possessions found in the camp when it was liberated were on display as a memorial to the suffering of the people who were murdered immediately upon arrival, and to those forced into slave labour. There were hundreds of suitcases, many containing the names of their original owners. We saw a heap of human hair several metres high, enormous piles of spectacles and shoes, and a mountainous collection of leg braces and other prostheses. There was a stack of brushes, shaving gear, and other personal items, and pots, pans, and various kitchen utensils. We quietly examined the many photographs and descriptions of atrocities carried out by the Nazis, including the inhumane medical experiments by the chief perpetrator, physician Josef Mengele. The striped prisoner garments, wooden clogs, furnishings, and other items from the blocks and barracks documented the everyday existence of the prisoners. They also illustrated the phenomena of resistance and mutual aid, and how prisoners tried to inform the outside world of the crimes being committed in the camp.

We visited the gas chambers disguised as bathhouses, the crematorium, and the gallows where Rudolph Höss, the camp founder and first commandant, was hanged on April 16, 1947.

My visit to Auschwitz was a sombre and moving experience. It was one of the highlights of all my youthful travels, one that left an abiding memory for decades to come.

Leaving the site, we asked for directions to a camping ground. On the suggestion of the night watchman, we stayed where we were and camped in the parking lot, within metres of the iron gates crowned with the infamous motto, Arbeit macht frei ('work makes you free').

By 7.00 a.m. the following day, the parking area was buzzing with activity, so we quickly packed up and headed for Katowice and then Wroclaw, stopping for a snack en route. At Klodzko near the border with Czechoslovakia, we faced the unenviable dilemma of having to spend 100 złotych, so we filled our shopping basket with food. With złotych left over, I ventured into another shop to spend it.

Ernie thrived on attention and didn't restrict himself to that related to maintenance and repairs. He basked in his ability to attract a crowd and the adulation of an inquisitive and adoring public. He'd been a powerful people magnet in Central Europe, and on my return from shopping, I could see neither Des nor Ernie for the crowd that swarmed around them like a nest of friendly bees. Tearing him away from his fan club was a necessity if we were to keep our rendezvous in Munich.

Our next stop was to squirrel away some Deutsche Mark (that we hadn't declared) in our favourite sugary burial site.

A delay at the frontier was the outcome of camping in a forest and the Auschwitz parking lot. Neither sat well with the authorities controlling traffic at the border. We couldn't prove where we'd stayed, and there was no way for our story to be verified. After a brief harangue in Polish, an hour-long wait was the penalty for our egregious breach of the supposed rules. We were eventually waved through, but their displeasure was painfully obvious. At the post to enter Czechoslovakia, our visas obtained in London were inspected, and entry stamps recorded. Notations were made on our visas indicating a stay of two days for which we each exchanged the requisite

USD 5 for each day's compulsory spending.

We then hot-footed it towards Prague, stopping about 50 kilometres short in a camping ground.

As a baseline, Des and I believed it shouldn't cost money to sleep. Our budget was primarily reserved for things as prosaic as food, petrol, warm clothing, and mechanical bits and pieces to keep Ernie mobile. When we paid for accommodation, it was for showers, security, and shelter that couldn't be satisfied by our tent or viable alternatives. The other exception was when we were flush with local currency for compulsory spending behind the Iron Curtain. What better way to burn a hole in our cache of Czechoslovakian cash by splurging it on a cabin? To our surprise, it came with sheet-clad beds with continental quilts. It all felt deliciously decadent. We hadn't earned it, but we revelled in our posh environment, an ephemeral one night of luxury. With no time to languish in our palatial surroundings, the crack of dawn the next day saw us leap out of bed to the faint sound of poots from the nearby sparrows' nests. We moved with robotic precision to pack up in record time, and in short order, hit the road. Ernie obliged with no mucking about. Eager and ebullient, he could sense a change in mood and seemed to bask in it, behaving impeccably for the entire day. The route took us straight through Prague, taking an hour to get from one side of the city to the other. Anxious to keep our 6.00 p.m. rendezvous in Munich, this magnificent metropolis would have to wait until another day. Rest stops few, we stopped in Zelezna Ruda close to the Bavarian border to spend what remained of our first day's korun on tinned meat. In our rush to get to Munich, we'd crossed Czechoslovakia in fewer than 24 hours, enabling us to change back the 30 Deutsche Mark worth of korun covering the second day of our visa.

Our fervency to reach Munich meant we'd learned less about Czechoslovakia than what could be gleaned from a few paragraphs of any decent guidebook. It was a travesty, and one more missed opportunity at the intersection of circumstances and competing priorities.

Chapter 7:
Oktoberfest, Munich

Anne Betts

"... itineraries are futile; the fun stuff happens when you give them up and go with the flow."
Lois Pryce, Revolutionary Ride: On the Road in Search of the Real Iran

A single boom gate marked the crossing from Czechoslovakia into West Germany. It brought us to a tiny Bavarian village with quaint wooden houses surrounded by lush green fields dotted with grazing cows. People out walking in their leather boots and knee-length jodhpurs did nothing to detract from the tranquillity of the scene.

It was as though Europe had suddenly rolled over, exposing a more appealing world.

The absence of incoming formalities announced, 'Welcome to West Germany,' speaking volumes of the political realities of a divided Europe. There was no interrogation in cold inquisitorial tones, no demands to empty our pockets, and no questions about how long we were staying. There were no unnecessarily ponderous procedures and no compulsory currency exchange at inflated rates. It was as though that single boom gate signalling entry into Western Europe was a curtain made of thin sheer chiffon. It was a stark contrast to the one of iron designed by the Soviets to limit Western contact with the Communist Bloc.

We crossed at 1.30 p.m. with what we hoped would be plenty of time to keep our rendezvous at the Poste Restante in Munich at 6.00 p.m. People were descending on the city for this year's Oktoberfest, the world's largest *Volksfest* or People's Fair. It traditionally takes place during the 16 days up to and including the first Sunday in October. The first Oktoberfest was held on October 18, 1810. It commemorated the marriage of Crown Prince Ludwig (later King Ludwig I) and Princess Therese of Saxe-Hildburghausen, the namesake of the Theresienwiese festival grounds. It was so popular the festival was held the following year, and then again and again and again.

The rendezvous involved quite a few of our mates, mostly flatmates from London, many with roots dating back to our voyage to the UK on the SS *Australis*.

Of the other eight flatmates from our Stamford Hill flat, Jo, Kerry, Kris, and Rhyll were travelling in the Kombi, Fanny. There was also Robyn, Kris's sister, who had left the others in Finland because she didn't have a visa for the USSR. Steve and Graham were also expected, after their trip to the USA with Andy, Donna, and Phil, other SS *Australis* cohorts and flatmates of Des in his earlier Ealing flat. And last but not least, Darcy who was a guide on NAT Eurotours. Naturally, the Oktoberfest was an essential stop on that itinerary. From the Leyton flat where Des and I had been welcomed after the dissolution of our Stamford Hill digs, we hoped to find Michele, Barb, and Marie travelling in their Kombi. And there was Chris, Joan, and Maggie who were on one of the many tours traversing Europe. These were the 603 girls. Everyone had the meeting instructions: Poste Restante, 6.00 p.m. on Saturday, September 22, and then at noon and 6.00 p.m. on subsequent days until we'd all met up.

Besides our mates from the Stamford Hill and Leyton flats, we expected to interact with many others from our recent past. There were passengers on the SS Australis, people we'd socialized with in London, folks we'd met at the 1972 Olympics and 1972 Oktoberfest, and travellers we'd encountered on the road. Whilst living in London, our social tentacles had stretched into the workplaces of our flatmates and the various colonial flats of folks from the SS *Australis*. It was a rare Saturday night when we'd failed to be downwind of a party where we'd connect with people we knew and add others to our ever-widening social circle.

Besides, events such as an international rugby tour (be it the All Blacks or the Wallabies) or cricket tests involving teams from down under meant bumping into folks from back home or those we'd met since leaving. Oktoberfest was a point of convergence for many of us. It was inevitable we'd enjoy a host of expected and unexpected encounters, much like our experience at the Olympics and Oktoberfest of the previous year.

If all went well with no unforeseeable delays (we'd told Ernie how important it was), we reckoned on arriving close to 6.00 p.m. Our eagerness and an elevated sense of anticipation escalated when we saw the first blue and white sign for MÜNCHEN.

For the sake of expedience, we abandoned our earlier pact to avoid the big roads. The autobahn plundered the landscape of any charm but at this point in our travels, enjoying the scenery was low on our list of priorities. We were sucked into a ribbon of glorious movement, streaming towards Munich, mixing it up with cars, buses, trucks, and other motorcycles travelling at speeds we could only visualize in our imaginations. The streaking silhouettes of overtaking vehicles whizzed past, but nothing could dampen our spirits. With a euphoric sense of freedom, we were cruising the crest of perpetual youth, high on energy, like surfers riding into the rip curl of a perfect wave. Our cheerful shouts dissipated into the noise of traffic, absorbed by foliage that blurred into green walls bordering the autobahn. With as much haste as he could muster, Ernie seemed to soak up the excitement. His engine sang in rhythmic pleasure. We passed more München signs, homing beacons guiding us towards Munich, with joy sweeping over the three of us like tidal waves.

Why was this so? What was it about the Oktoberfest that made it such a potent source of excitement?

Firstly, we were returning to familiar territory, a place with fond memories of the year before.

Secondly, we were taking a break from the day-to-day demands of travel to let our hair down and have some fun.

But, most of all, we were reconnecting with friends. Being thousands of kilometres away from home, they had become our support network, with bonds as strong as those that cemented most family relationships. We were keen to obtain news of everyone's more recent exploits, and create fresh memories to add to the heady, halcyon days of our youth.

More and more signs flashed by until we sighted the communications tower of Olympic Park close to 6.00 p.m. We drove straight to the *Hauptbahnhof* (central railway station) and *Postamt München* (main post office opposite the Hauptbahnhof) within 15 minutes. All the while, we kept a sharp lookout for familiar vehicles, nearly wetting ourselves from the excitement on spotting a Kombi resembling Fanny. We leapt off Ernie after parking him conspicuously outside the post office spot-on 6.00 p.m. We had arrived in Munich!!!

We joined the queue at the Poste Restante counter, with our heads on swivels, searching for familiar faces. Notwithstanding the arrangement we had with our friends, Munich was synonymous with bumping into people we knew. However, something felt desperately wrong at that moment. We'd been in Munich at least 25 minutes, and the only familiar sights had been the city's landmarks we'd become acquainted with a year earlier.

We collected our mail — a letter from Kris on behalf of the girls, two from Australia, one from New Zealand, and a postcard from Darcy. I ripped

open Kris's letter, hoping to find details of their arrival. Instead, I found a demoralising opening sentence: "Fanny has finally packed it in, and we're hot-footing it back to London so we cannot keep our rendezvous." Fanny had died in Rome, and they were heading back to London in a car rental funded by Automobile Association insurance. We felt devastated. Then came the realisation that in all likelihood, Graham and Steve wouldn't be coming either. Elation plummeted to deflation in a matter of seconds with the reality that we wouldn't be seeing our friends in Munich (or perhaps for many months ... or maybe years).

That left Darcy and Robyn from our Stamford Hill flat. Would we see them in Munich? Darcy's card revealed that he would arrive at the Poste Restante at 8.30 p.m., so this piece of welcome news lifted our spirits considerably. There was no news from Robyn and nothing from the 603 girls.

With a couple of hours on our hands, Des and I knew just the place to spend them. The Mathäser-Bierstadt on Bayerstraße was a large beer hall we'd formed a somewhat intimate relationship with the previous year. It was an ideal spot for our willkommen Löwenbräu to help pass the time. We each had a half chicken and pommes frites, and half litres shouted by a very

Oktoberfest, Munich

friendly and slightly intoxicated local. We returned the shout and within the next two hours, just about every inebriated Mathäser patron had been attracted to our table. It was Oktoberfest, after all, and the celebratory mood and spirit of bonhomie permeated the atmosphere.

On our return to the Poste Restante, we found Darcy and treated him like a long-lost friend before dragging him back to the Mathäser for more welcome drinks. Darcy had spent the last few months as a tour guide with NAT Eurotours, and his tales of those adventures kept us enthralled.

We continued celebrating at the 'Fest Park or Theresienwiese, an area in central Munich one-and-a-half kilometres from the Hauptbahnhof and the main post office housing the Poste Restante. The word weise is German for 'meadow' (which it presumably resembled back in 1810; in 1973, it was an extensive concrete-covered patch of cityscape). 'Theresa's Meadow' was locally known as the Wiesn that's synonymous with Oktoberfest and the enormous tents that accommodate their beer-loving patrons year after year. We chose the Pschorr tent to continue the conversation that had lapsed only for mouthfuls of that beautiful Oktoberfest bier. It was great to see

Darcy again, and we didn't stop talking the entire night. We were just about the last to leave at closing time and arranged to follow Darcy's tour bus to Campingplatz Thalkirchen, another of our haunts from 1972.

While the NAT Eurotours crowd organized themselves in the bus park, Des and I tried to fix Ernie's headlight, without success. We weren't surprised; his electrical system was finicky and unreliable. We eventually set off, hot on NAT's trail, only to lose them at the first set of traffic lights we came to near the Hauptbahnhof. Our futile attempt to follow a bus that was no longer in sight resulted in our spending the next 30 minutes or so going around in circles.

It was only five kilometres from the Wiesn to Thalkirchen. A trail of breadcrumbs tossed from the bus would have helped. But seeing them would have been difficult without a functioning headlight.

We pulled alongside three pedestrians to ask for directions, so they took us to their basement flat to show us where Thalkirchen was on a map. They were recent university graduates still living in the flat they'd shared while studying at uni. We didn't see a map until two hours later after they'd provided much beer and conversation lasting until 3.30 a.m. We were all of a similar vintage, and they seemed interested in our company and our travels. Perhaps they'd observed others of our ilk partying hardy at previous Oktoberfests while they'd been enjoying the festivities with their friends. It felt like they saw this as an opportunity to connect with outsiders, visitors to their celebrated Volksfest. Des and I took advantage of the situation to find out what it was like growing up in post-war Germany in the shadow of the Nazi era. They obliged by sharing recollections from the 1950s of playing amongst shelled ruins and splashing about in water in the bottom of bomb craters. They described the housing shortages that led to sharing sleeping quarters with several family members and infrequent baths of cold water. As youngsters, they were mostly oblivious to the horrors of the Nazi era. Some of their parents and grandparents had joined the Nazi party, for various reasons, and by doing so had strengthened its power and influence. But, within families, conversations about that period were mainly off limits, and Nazism and the Holocaust were absent from the curriculum in schools. In the 1950s, the war years represented a past that was too recent and too raw, one that most Germans wanted to park in the past. Of greater importance was to focus on reconstructing cities that lay in ruins, rebuilding the West German economy that was in tatters, developing a parliamentary democracy, coping with the effects of the Cold War, and resettling millions of 'ethnic German' refugees expelled from the East. In fact, in the early post-war years, the former Dachau Concentration Camp near Munich housed refugees awaiting resettlement. It became a memorial only in 1965, 20 years after the war. Passing references to 'the Hitler period' and pictures of concentration camps provided clues about the crimes of the Third Reich. But missing from their lives was any meaningful discussion or critical analysis of the era.

Our hosts predicted that ending the long period of silence about Nazi atrocities, and Germany's coming to terms with its unexamined violent and racist history would materialise for their children's generation. They agreed that the much-publicized photograph of West German Chancellor Willy Brandt kneeling at the monument to the victims of the Warsaw Ghetto in 1970 became a powerful symbol of Germany's willingness to seek reconciliation and take collective responsibility for its criminal past.

As I listened to their accounts of the challenges they faced as young children, I gained a deeper appreciation of my own carefree and less complicated experience of growing up in Australia in the '50s and '60s. However, in one respect, I could relate. My father had served in New Guinea during the war when Japanese forces invaded the territory to the north of Australia. It was a topic that was never broached because we, too, knew it was off limits. He would speak briefly of the experience when I quizzed him while studying the war years in high school, but the memories were still too raw and too painful 20 years on.

The time came for us to continue our search for Thalkirchen, and we thanked our hosts profusely for their hospitality and insights. Once outside, they pointed to the first corner we were supposed to turn. But, as soon as we were out of their sight, we were lost again. We passed the same landmarks several times over as we went around and around in more circles. What felt like a monotonous routine was interrupted when we came to a screeching halt, cut off by a police wagon pulling into the kerb. A squad of cops poured out of the van with deafening shouts of "Nicht licht! Nicht licht!"

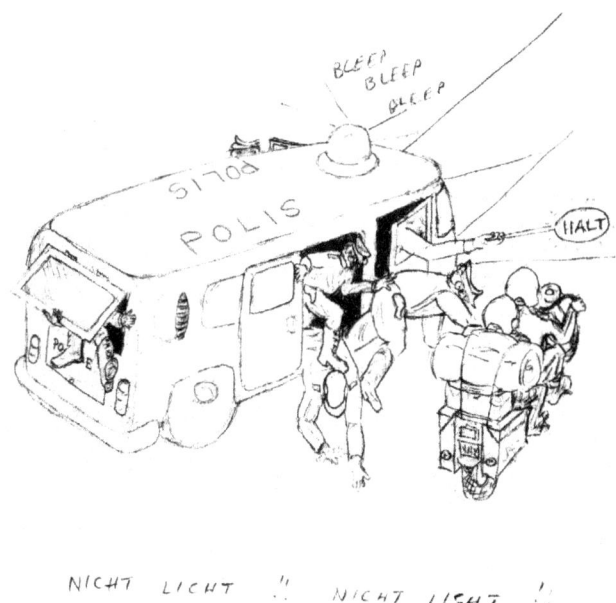

I leapt off Ernie, and Des and I staged an academy-award winning performance. It entailed banging, shaking, flicking, and fiddling with Ernie's headlight, exhibiting utter amazement when it didn't work. The cops circled Ernie, presumably saw the AUS and NZ stickers, and most likely decided that dealing with us would have been more trouble than it was worth. Evidently, they piled back into the van and drove off. My astonishment was genuine when I looked up from my act to find not a single police officer or wagon in sight.

Oktoberfest, Munich

We continued circling inner Munich, periodically stopping beside parks to assess their potential as possible camping spots. Quite by accident, we stumbled upon Thalkirchen. We turned Ernie's engine off (there was no need to turn off his headlight) and surreptitiously slipped inside. The maze of vans and tents was barely visible through the dim light. We had to go well into the campsite before finding a tiny spot large enough for Ernie and the tent. By the time we'd pitched the tent and crawled inside, tendrils of dawn light had awakened the sky. It was 5.30 a.m. and an avalanche of weariness, propelled by Oktoberfest beer, washed over us and sleep took but a few moments to claim us.

Today, I shudder with horror at past societal attitudes towards driving under the influence, and my complicity as a driver and passenger. I count myself one of the lucky ones to have survived and to have done so without harming another person. Thankfully, things have changed for the better to keep impaired drivers off the roads.

The morning after our first night of our second Oktoberfest didn't find us in peak form. However, Oktoberfests weren't meant to be frittered away by lounging around in a tent. Our indolence ended at 10.00 a.m. when we emerged like larvae from the cocoons of our sleeping bags.

Darcy had mentioned the names of several people who were at Thalkirchen, including 'Tassy' from the SS Australis. After freshening up, we went for a wander around the campsite. The only familiar faces in that first tour of inspection belonged to Peter (Steve's mate) and 'Peggar.' It was later that night that we found Tassy in the Hofbräu-Festzelt, one of the largest tents in the 'Fest Park. Tassy was the first Tasmanian I'd ever met, and possibly the only one on the SS Australis from the tiny Australian state. Tassy undoubtedly had another name, but I never knew it, or quickly forgot it. She was easy to spot in the Hofbräu marquee. Waving a beer stein to the beat of the oompah band whilst standing on a chair belied her diminutive stature. Next day, we discovered that their van was parked about 10 metres away from our tent. It had been towed away from a prohibited parking spot the night before and had cost them DM 80 to bail it out of police custody. Des and I left the campsite around 11.00 a.m. to be at the Poste Restante for the noon rendezvous. Unfortunately, we failed to take into consideration the barricaded streets for the Oktoberfest parade. Being the second day of Oktoberfest, this was the festival's second parade — the Trachten-und Schützenzug, the traditional costume and hunters' parade that takes place on the first Sunday of the festival. A noisy affair, it features thousands of participants from hunting clubs, mountain troops, historic costume groups, marching bands, musicians, flag wavers, and decorated horse-drawn carts parading through the city centre on a seven-kilometre route to the Theresienwiese.

We rode around looking for an open route to the post office. Of course, the event had been planned with typical Teutonic thoroughness, and finding a way around the barricades was impossible. To compound matters, Ernie ran out of petrol, taunting us again — the 12th time in six weeks! Our arsenal of invective was reasonably tame at the time, pretty much devoid of obscenities. Our four-letter expletives were as harsh as 'damn' and 'hell' sprinkled with the versatile 'bloody' and 'bugger' that weren't considered swearing in the down-under vernacular. We hurled all of it and more at Ernie as we wheeled him into a parking space. A well-earned break from Ernie fatigue was warranted and thankfully, a subway station was nearby. We headed into the cavernous confines of the underground to take the U-Bahn to the Hauptbahnhof.

In our rush to make it to the Poste Restante on time, we neglected to purchase tickets. If there were ticket machines, we passed by them. When confronted by a plain-clothed ticket inspector, we knew we were having a bad day that got progressively worse when he brought in reinforcements to haul us off the train at the Hauptbahnhof.

Des and I were taken to an office where we were asked for DM 20 each to cover the fine. Our transgression rendered us impotent in the presence of the four representatives of officialdom. Still, we gave it our best shot, arguing and pleading our innocence based on ignorance of the system. Our first defence was that we'd just arrived in Munich and were using the U-Bahn for the first time. That didn't garner the desired results.

When asked for our passports, we indicated that they were back at the campsite (and hoped we wouldn't be subjected to a search to verify this point). We told them we were from London. When we were in trouble, we were never from Australia or New Zealand if we could get away with it. Of course, if we were attached to Ernie with the AUS and NZ stickers on the panniers, this would never fly. We explained that in London, when the ticket office is closed, the fare is paid at the destination. They didn't go for that story either.

It was clear we were flailing in the quicksand of law enforcement with no lifeline within reach. We were then escorted to the police station by four ticket inspectors — four burly ticket inspectors. It was there they gave us an alternative to paying the DM 40 fine in the form of an ultimatum. We would be placed under arrest, spend the night in jail, and appear before a tribunal to hear our case the following day.

Oktoberfest, Munich

While overnight incarceration in a Munich lockup would have been a novel experience, it wasn't one that appealed to us.

Were they bluffing? Probably, but it wasn't one we wanted to call. Instead, we tried another approach, describing how we didn't have any change for the ticket machines (had we known about them). To add a touch of dramatic flair, Des waved around a DM 20 note. Nice move, Desmond Joseph! That lasted in his possession for a millisecond. When I opened a dry kitty purse, four brawny ticket inspectors and one strapping police officer peered inside. It was then that they settled on the one DM 20 note and let us off with a receipt and a warning. We didn't argue any further and ignominiously retreated from our miscreant act DM 20 lighter and with mild contusions to our pride and egos.

It was tempting to blame Ernie for our misfortune. Still, we thought better of it and accepted responsibility for this one. We figured there would be plenty of other times when it really would have been Ernie's fault.

Arriving at the post office a little late because of the delay, we managed to find Maggie and Joan, two of the 603 girls. After meeting up with Darcy the night before, this was our second exciting rendezvous in Munich. Unfortunately, the Mathäser-Bierstadt was packed, so we made our way down to Karlsplatz for pizza and beer. It was another of those reunions when there wasn't a moment when someone wasn't talking. They had news of the other 603 girls and the return to London of Jo, Kerry, Kris, and Rhyll without Fanny. They had seen Graham and Steve on their return from the States and reported on Carol's plans to leave London for Australia in my old minivan that was still going strong. We would have preferred to see all these mates in Munich but having news of them was the next best thing. After our valiant efforts to meet Maggie and Joan at the Poste Restante, we learned that we were all staying at the same campsite. Duh, had we thought about it, Thalkirchen would have made much more sense as a logical place to meet.

Later in the afternoon, we thought about Ernie and his lack of a headlight and petrol, so we set off to collect him before darkness set in. Whilst sitting on the kerb contemplating how to flip him over to redistribute the remaining gasoline in the tank, Brenda Fennel from college days came along. It restored my faith in Munich's ability to facilitate unexpected encounters. I loved how the city could be so large, yet so small at the same time. We yarned with Brenda for quite a while, and after she left, a very kind and considerate local gave us some petrol.

Running out of petrol and driving without a headlight plagued our travels. Why was this so? Here's an explanation from Des:

Ernie's frailties and irascibility were a constant irritation that could have been minimized if we'd been wiser and more thorough in our pre-trip preparations. Sadly, 'wise and thorough' have not been adjectives applied to me in life. It is just one of my small failings — a personal one that shouldn't be shared by Anne. Ernie was my responsibility, and any mea culpa should remain with me.

Oktoberfest, Munich

Motorbikes, until very recently, didn't have fuel gauges. Riders pride themselves as being real motorists with enthusiasm for managing such things like fuel range. In my defence, Ernie should have had a fuel tap on each side of his tank. But he didn't. If he'd had two taps, we could have ridden with one on, until that side of the tank was dry, then we could switch over to the other side to access the petrol on the other side of the frame hump. Our 'A-over-T' operation achieved the same result, but with a lot more effort. Some fuel taps have a reserve position that frees up more fuel, but Ernie didn't have one. When we marry Ernie's limitations with my preference to wait for a gas station on our side of the road, it presents a formula that will ensure regular failings and disappointments. Ernie had a range of 200 miles (322 kilometres) and only in Iran were we to find bowsers further apart than that. So really, we can only put things down to my ever-present optimism.

And our almost constant battle with having working lights? In theory, Ernie's electrical system was simple. However, it was of a design that dated from the 1930s. It was a 6-volt direct-current system from a country and time of imperial-sized componentry. We were, of course, travelling through a now alternating-current 12-volt metric-sized world.

It should also be said that the post-war austerity of Britain had led to the cheapening of products. Coupled with the vibration of a single-cylinder engine, this led to headlight bulbs' blowing with alarming regularity — bulbs that couldn't easily be sourced. It is a little ironic that we could be seen as poster children for the wags among motoring cognoscenti who had labelled Joe Lucas 'The Prince of Darkness.' Lucas was the nineteenth-century founder of Lucas Industries, the dominant supplier of electrical componentry to British vehicles. We never intended to ride at night, so Ernie's lack of illumination was only ever a minor irritation. He had so many endearing qualities that far outweighed such minor foibles.

Fortunately, the ride to Thalkirchen wasn't as long or circuitous as the one the night before. We decided to not go out to the 'Fest Park and had an early night after a chat with two of the 603 girls, Maggie and Chris.

The next day, we were keen to renew our acquaintance with a perennial favourite of 1972: the delectable Hertie's chicken. Hertie was a large department store opposite the Hauptbahnhof. It offered a range of goods at bargain-basement prices, including cafeteria-type food for hungry shoppers. Their roast chicken was affordable and delicious, and the 1973 vintage was better than what we remembered. At Hertie's, we ran into Jill and Max. They were doing the same, and once again, we were impressed with Munich's ability to host surprise encounters.

We'd met Jill the year before at the Munich Olympics. The city had set up a free camping site comprising huge tents and basic amenities for folks who couldn't find or afford accommodation. Or, in my case, for those who saw it as a convenient alternative to accommodation they already had. My travel mate Kris and I had booked bed-and-breakfast accommodation before leaving Australia. Inconveniently, it was in Miesbach, 50 kilometres from Munich, and a hassle to reach by train late at night. Des and his mates were at the free camping site, and Jo and Rhyll slept on the floor of a school on Dachauer Straße, a few blocks from Olympic Park. So, Kris and I ditched our Miesbach digs and alternated between the school and the free camping site to hang out with our mates and more effectively participate in the buzz and trappings of the Olympics. The atmosphere was electric, and we wanted to soak up every moment of its aura.

We had tickets to many events and explored ways to buy, sell, and trade tickets with others. One of the prized events was the men's field hockey final. Kris and I had tickets, and when West Germany earned the right to meet Pakistan for the gold medal, we scalped our tickets and watched one-third of the game from a nearby hill where we could see one-third of the field. Also, we were on the lookout for ways to get into other venues to see more events. Our little gang successfully conspired to make it into the Olympic Stadium on a couple of occasions by continually recycling the same two tickets.

No tickets were needed for the subdued and sombre ceremony in the stadium following the Palestinian attack on Israeli team members in the Olympic Village at dawn on September 5, 10 days after the Opening Ceremony. We were pleased to hear the announcement that Die Heiteren Spiele ('The Cheerful Games') would continue, but they had lost their lustre. Our hearts were heavy, and the increased security and visible presence of armed personnel severely tarnished the celebratory feel of the Games.

We met Jill at the free-camping site. Three weeks later, at the 1972 Oktoberfest, Jill and her friends were eager to unload their Kombi as most of them were heading home to Australia or New Zealand. The closing days of Oktoberfest brought an end to the summer travelling season for many people. It marked the transformation of Campingplatz Thalkirchen from a campground to a used car lot. The price for Sebastian was an affordable £30, so Jo, Rhyll, and I made a spur-of-the-moment decision to purchase him and drive to Istanbul. Unfortunately, we failed to check the oil level, and Sebastian's engine seized two days later near Ried, just over the border in Austria. The silver lining of our neglect was that we hitchhiked the 160 kilometres back to Thalkirchen to invest £90 in our acquisition of Fanny. As time would reveal, she served our antipodean coterie of flatmates and friends exceptionally well for the next 12 months (with regular checks of the oil level).

After catching up on Jill's news since the 1972 Oktoberfest, Des and I wanted to reacquaint ourselves with some of our old haunts. Our ride along Dachauer Straße brought us to the Grossmarkt, where Des bought a pair of boots. We left it too late to visit Olympic Park, given the need to return to Thalkirchen whilst there was still daylight.

That night, we went to the Hofbräuhaus in Central Munich with our Leyton flatmates: Maggie, Joan, and Chris in their Vikings tour bus. There we met Doug (a Kiwi I'd met at the '72 Olympics and briefly went out with), and

Oktoberfest, Munich

Peter, Carl, and Ian from Tassy's crowd. At closing time, I couldn't find the others, so I left with Doug who was staying with a family he'd met during the Olympics. I slept in a real bed with real sheets and ate breakfast at a real table sitting on a real chair. I even had a real bath. Oh my, these were luxuries to savour.

Doug and I returned to the campsite around 10.00 a.m. We chatted with Tassy's crowd for a while, and I recounted the story I'd heard (likely third-hand ... or perhaps tenth-hand) of a vehicle containing a South African that passed through Yugoslavia. In 1973, Yugoslavia prohibited South African passport holders from entering the country, and the van had eight passengers, one of whom was South African. So, the South African hid, and seven passports were handed in at the border. The van passed through without incident, but when leaving Yugoslavia, the frontier appeared before the South African had time to hide. They handed across the same seven passports, but the official counted eight people and only seven passports. Calculating again, this time with the help of his fingers, eight still didn't equal seven. He became very confused (so the story went), and he ended up just waving them through.

"Hey you guys, I've just been told a story about a van of eight people passing through Yugoslavia ... " and the tale was repeated. It was met with raucous laughter, and it didn't take long to figure out I was in the presence of the characters in the story.

After finding Des, the two of us went shopping for cameras, radios, and anything we thought would appeal to the entrepreneurial Turks of Istanbul. We were Turkey-bound and on the lookout for items to sell or trade. At a motorcycle shop, we bought some boot covers and an economy-sized tank top bag. Further on, we chatted with some Americans and then yarned with some Australians. We finally reached Sendlinger Tor to check out cameras. We walked along to Kaufhof and wandered through that store, and then to Hertie's where I bought some warm ski pants. After pizza in Karlsplatz, we returned Ernie to the campsite and parked him outside.

A bus and a tram took us to the 'Fest Park and the Hofbräu-Festzelt once more. We bumped into Phil's cousin Anne, then Phil, then Carl, who took us to Peter who took us to Robyn and Lyn — and the third big reunion of Oktoberfest. Robyn was from our Stamford Hill flat and had travelled with the girls in Fanny until leaving them in Finland. She shared some highlights of their travels, and afterwards after hooking up with Lyn and Peter. She had received a couple of letters from her sister Kris, and we discussed the fate of poor Fanny. Robyn was with a crowd of South Africans in the outside area, so we stayed at their table for the night.

We returned to Thalkirchen in their van and didn't bother bringing Ernie inside for what was left of the night.

The next afternoon was reserved for a visit to the Deutsches Museum, the German Museum of Science and Technology and the largest of its kind in the world. The 603 girls (Maggie, Joan, and Chris) and Des and I left by bus and continued the journey by cab when it started to rain. We spent several hours exploring some of the thousands of thought-provoking exhibits from dozens of fields of science and technology. During a break at the restaurant for coffee, I met Gary Conomos from university days in Brisbane, and once again was very pleased with Munich's magic in facilitating unexpected encounters. With closing time, we walked to Marienplatz and the Hofbräuhaus, where we bought Oktoberfest T-shirts from some enterprising Aussie guys.

That night, Des and I returned to the Hofbräu-Festzelt in the 'Fest Park and joined Robyn's table directly in front of the band. We were among the last to leave and were ultimately bundled out by security. In the melee that followed, Des lingered to finish his beer and missed out on a ride. I caught a lift back to camp in Robyn's van.

Thursday was shopping day. We'd arranged to meet Maggie and Joan at 3.00 p.m. outside the main post office to be followed by a feast of Hertie's chicken. Des and I messed around as usual, and stopped to yarn to everyone as usual, arriving at the post office at 2.55 p.m. — with no shopping done. After devouring our chicken, we went upstairs in Hertie's to buy an automatic watch, and a camping radio with a flashlight, compass, and thermometer that we figured the Istanbul merchants would go crazy over. We left Maggie at Karlsplatz after loading her up with all our gear that she kindly agreed to take back to camp.

Joan, Des, and I headed to the Hofbräu-Festzelt at the 'Fest Park for our last night in Munich. We passed the time mostly with Robyn's crowd and the South Africans, interspersed with trips outside to smuggle empty steins for collection at the end of the night. Clearly, alcohol and the desire to acquire one of these prized mementoes of a special event in our lives had conspired to impair the effectiveness of our moral compass.

After intervening on Joan's behalf several times after she tangled with security, we decided it had been a fine finale to our 1973 Oktoberfest. Peter, Joan, and I headed outside to collect the steins. We searched in all our hiding places, but there was not a single one to be found. We then sneaked back inside to mastermind additional attempts to smuggle out more. By this time, our moral compass had definitely left the building. The security guards were way smarter (and soberer) than we were, and we failed miserably with every attempt. Finally, Tiger smuggled one out for Maggie by adopting a tactic we dubbed 'the three-stein decoy.' It involved two steins in plain sight (that were inevitably confiscated), and a concealed one that passed their scrutiny. Joan had her prized souvenir!

Somehow, we found the Kombi by following people who thought they knew where it was. We squeezed in, and a record 17 people were transported back to camp. Des missed a ride again and had to walk home. We pronounced it an enjoyable night and a fitting finale to our Oktoberfest '73.

The next day was supposed to be departure day. As Des put the finishing touches on the marathon Munich letter to our mates back in London, we snapped a couple of photographs to show off our new Oktoberfest T-shirts. After saying goodbye to the three 603 girls when they left with their Vikings tour, Des and I set upon the epic task of packing up Ernie and leaving as quietly and surreptitiously as we'd arrived. We were ready by early afternoon and had our farewell beer beside Ernie outside the camping ground while chatting with some Americans. Robyn dropped by to let us know they were going to the Mathäser-Bierstadt for their farewell drinks.

It wasn't in the cards to pass up a proper celebratory goodbye to Munich. We found a large table and Robyn, Lyn, and Des left to smuggle in seven Hertie's chickens that were washed down with a second farewell drink. As fate would have it, we continued up at the 'Fest Park after moving Ernie up beside the two Kombis parked outside the Hauptbahnhof.

Being the weekend, locals and German visitors seemed to occupy most of the tables. The passageways were cleared by security, and we were moved outside the tents. It was heavy going to last the evening due to a mixture of fatigue and beer. At closing time, our bacchanalia resulted in staggering back to the Hauptbahnhof in dribs and drabs and flaking in the two vans. The Germans have a name for Oktoberfest patrons who overdo it — bierleichen (beer corpses) — and the label fit us perfectly in our closing hours of Oktoberfest 1973.

The next day, Saturday, September 29, 1973, was departure day — for real. It was tough to get up, and movements were somewhat languid. We said goodbye to Robyn, Peter, Lyn, Brian, and the two Daves — 'Grey Dave' and 'Sunday Dave' — and moved out of the Hauptbahnhof car park very slowly at 9.30 a.m.

Oktoberfest, Munich

Chapter 8:
Munich, West Germany to Dubrovnik, Yugoslavia

Des Molloy

"Stuff your eyes with wonder; live as if you'd drop dead in ten seconds. See the world. It's more fantastic than any dream made or paid for in factories."
Ray Bradbury

It had been time to leave the Oktoberfest. We had spent too much money; we had lingered too long. It had been beguiling. There was fun to be had, and we'd gone with the flow.

As well as the thousands of locals who celebrate this huge *Volksfest* each year, there are large numbers of young colonial travellers who see this as the obligatory blowout before returning to base in the UK or home to the colonies. Many would have spent three to four months exploring Europe in their Kombis. It was almost like a gathering tailored for a specific sub-tribe. These were our people; they were of our ilk. We knew so many of them. It had been a great time of connection and reconnection. It had also given Anne and me space. Our travel had been somewhat solitary, and the Oktoberfest allowed us to fraternize in multiple directions. We'd revelled in this.

Getting to Munich did not find us being part of the swarm of our peers. We'd been behind, given our later departure from London, and not on the main pathways. Again, with our post-Oktoberfest travel plans, we'd not be part of the norm; we were heading south. Finally, on Saturday, September 29, 1973, seven weeks after initially hitting the road, Ernie's wheels turned again in delightful anticipation of what lay ahead.

We chose the autobahn for the 150-kilometre ride to Salzburg, ignoring the exits to the picturesque towns and villages of Bavaria. In our semi-dazed state, we were paying the price for our excesses of the previous week. It was a scenic ride through verdant forests and rolling hills, and a valley bordered by alpine peaks as we neared Salzburg. We both had pleasant memories of Berchtesgaden, Neuschwanstein, and Oberammergau, among others, explored during the period between the 1972 Olympics and Oktoberfest, so we pushed on. Our only stop was for gas and to spend our remaining Deutsche Mark on rolls, cheese, and sliced meat. We had no energy for Mozart and *The Sound of Music*, and besides, we were over big cities, for now, so skirted Salzburg. Mid-afternoon, we found a forest beside the highway where the three of us were quickly swallowed up by tiny trees and tall grass. The day ended earlier and with considerably less fanfare than the day before. As we drifted off to sleep with pleasant memories of Oktoberfest '73, we dreamed of the warmer weather of the Dalmatian Coast of Yugoslavia.

The sound of rain on the tent fly encouraged us to delay our departure until the weather looked a little more promising. Around midday, it stopped raining long enough for us to pack up Ernie and head out. Unfortunately, the rainless interlude didn't last.

We had to get through the mountains out of Austria and over into the Slovenian part of Socialist Yugoslavia. The rain turned to snow as we climbed higher, warranting a stop for hot coffee. My leather gloves proved inadequate, and Anne handed over her woolly mittens. At least she could get her hands out of the wind stream. This selfless act enabled me to grit my teeth and carry on.

Back on the road, we encountered showers of slushy sleet followed by more snow. It was so stormy we stopped for the usual clicking spree to capture what was for us the novelty of falling snow. Interestingly, there was an MGA sports car where we paused for photos.

Munich, West Germany to Dubrovnik, Yugoslavia

It was from the same era as Ernie, possibly the same year, but the inclement weather precluded further investigation. We knew from our experience in Norway that we couldn't dally in the piercing cold of a snowstorm.

It was a slow and cautious descent, given the road conditions. Once we reached lower terrain, we started looking for a barn or an old cabin to provide shelter for the night. There was no way we were going to try to get the tent up in such bleak conditions. We stumbled upon a *pension* — a haven from our misery. We weren't keen on needlessly spending funds, but sometimes comfort is priceless.

Soon we were wallowing in hot baths and the decadence of living inside. The house was heated throughout, and our room had an enormous bed with a continental quilt. It was a novelty for both of us. Coming from a land of wool, I'd only ever known blankets and whilst our house had an eiderdown, it would have been filled with kapok, a silk-like fibre from the pod of a Kapok tree. Of course, with Anne's being a Queenslander, she'd never known cold nights until she had travelled to the Northern Hemisphere. This, however, was the real deal — thick and fluffy, but light beyond comprehension. We couldn't believe it would work, but work it did, and an unbelievable sleep was had.

A double bed was pretty novel for us. Compared to our little nylon cocoon, it was huge and allowed legs and arms to be spread in all directions. Usually, we lay prone like two Egyptian mummies in our sleeping bags atop our LI-LOs.

My aspired-for romance had not eventuated. Anne remained as appealing as ever, but clearly, we were not morphing into 'a couple.' There was mutual respect and affection, but seemingly no overwhelming physical desire aimed my way. We didn't fight or argue; we were a good team. There had been a bit of low-level bickering, but no bust-ups. We both came from work roles where we told others what to do. So, predictably, we might disagree (and occasionally squabble) over minor matters such as where to pitch the tent, hang a clothesline, build a fire, or park Ernie.

I had never spent anything like this length of time with another person, and it was quite satisfying to realise that we seemed to second-guess each other's actions and needs. There was so much I liked and admired about my fellow roadie. The adventure to date had not been a walk in the park, but no matter how hard it was, we always faced the adversities as a team. Neither of us sulked or was the least bit moody, nor overtly pined for another role, place, or situation. Life was good, really good.

Next morning, there was little-to-no incentive to leave the sumptuous bed. We hadn't closed the curtains of the enormous plate-glass windows to allow for the sun to stream into the room. We were hoping the little sunshine fairies would wake us up as they frolicked in the morning light. Unfortunately, such frivolity was not to be. It was raining quite hard, so we lingered in the luxury, revelling in the warmth and comfort, knowing that there would be payback for our decadence. The weather appeared to be resolute and determined to stay inclement. As a result, we clad ourselves in all our layers and went downstairs to find that the Frau had prepared breakfast to our great surprise and even greater delight. Unaccustomed to this type of accommodation, we hadn't realised that breakfast was included. And what a treat it was: steaming hot coffee, fresh rolls, sliced ham, and scrambled eggs. After expressing our approval and gratitude, we were away by 10.30 a.m.

By 10.35 a.m., Anne was soaked through her top two layers. I wore my PVC outer layer that held up well compared to her lightweight nylon. The gently flowing streams had become raging torrents, and our apprehension grew as we thought about negotiating the mountains that were imposingly positioned between Austria and Yugoslavia. This was the Karawanks chain of the Southern Limestone Alps bordering Austria, Italy, and Yugoslavia. Stretching in an east-west direction for 120 kilometres, the summits, slopes, and foothills combine to create a stunning landscape, a paradise for hiking and skiing. On this particular day, the weather masked its beauty and deterred mustering any interest in appreciating it. Visibility was poor, and we were preoccupied with escaping the challenging conditions and the wrath of the rain gods who love tormenting motorcyclists.

The fond memories of the sun-drenched Adriatic kept us focussed and moving in that direction. We'd both travelled up the Yugoslav coast the previous year in our Kombis. It had felt like being transported through page after mesmerizing page of an exotic travel guide, and now we were anxious to catch our first sight of the cover.

At 1,367 metres above sea level is the Loibl Pass. During World War II, a one-and-a-half-kilometre tunnel was built at 1,068 metres. Many of the workers were prisoners of the two satellite camps of the Mauthausen-Gusen concentration camp. Excavation began in 1943, and the first army vehicles entered the very tight tunnel the following year. Military traffic, soldiers, and refugees used it until it was closed in 1947. The tunnel was reopened in 1950 and expanded to two lanes in 1966. We were hoping it would enable us to avoid the tops that we presumed would be blizzard whipped.

We were pleased to find both the road and the tunnel open. Dripping wet, we handed over our passports to the Austrian agent with trembling hands synchronized with the rest of our shivering bodies. We were quickly waved through the entrance to the tunnel. Yugoslavia, winding coastal roads above clear blue water under a hot but gentle sun — HERE WE COME!

We must have passed under the snow and ice we expected to encounter; it was clear when we emerged at the other end. Also, there was no toll. But then, a toll would have assaulted the memory of all those prisoners who suffered or died under the Nazi system of extermination by labour as they struggled under inhumane conditions to build the tunnel. After the liberation of the camps, the survivors' associations tried to prevent the tunnel from ever being used for tourism or commerce. Perhaps the lack of a toll was a legacy to those endeavours. The tunnel was lit, so our previous tunnel problems were not replicated.

At the end, we found the Socialist Federal Republic of Yugoslavia. Although nominally still in the Soviet-dominated Communist bloc of nations and ruled by the strongman leader Josip Tito, it was seen as a bridging country. Whilst still socialist, it was courting the West through tourism and manufacturing. As young travellers, we also loved it because there wasn't a daily charge to be in the country. This set the stage for spending several lazy days camped on beaches once we hit the coast. We couldn't wait! We collected the necessary visas and purchased some petrol tokens. Ernie was from an era of low-octane petrol and had managed okay on the poor offerings of the Eastern Bloc, but we were aware the fuel quality wouldn't improve in the direction we were heading.

Initially, Yugoslavia brought no relief from the rain, and it wasn't until Ljubljana did we see the sun for a few minutes. The change in the weather provided the incentive to go further, and we stopped 30 kilometres from Rijeka, electing to stay in a rooming house to dry our clothes. We were not yet out to the coast, and the area we had been passing through was known as Slovenia. It was verdant and very old-fashioned pastoral. Like other parts of the Eastern Bloc, the roads were poor and fast traffic sparse, which suited us. We'd banked a couple of hundred kilometres for the day, so we were quite pleased.

Water had infiltrated Ernie's magdyno, and in the morning, he was a little recalcitrant about hitting the road. After push-starting him, we stopped in Rijeka to attend to his sticking throttle, another moisture-induced ailment. South of Rijeka, with the sun shining as brilliantly as we remembered, and the Adriatic coast looking as stunning as we recalled, we paused for an exquisite cliff-top view of an inlet township. This was picture-postcard stuff. The sun was warming us up, so we peeled off slightly, and stopped soon after when we saw a London taxi with a NZ sticker. We lingered long enough for a chat and coffee. A short time later, we stopped and talked to two Italian guys on a Moto Guzzi. Travellers were not very common, and we took advantage of the opportunities for interaction when we could. Our attitude was that you never know what you might glean. We were always keen for knowledge, maps, and books. Our day was becoming unexpectedly social.

The sun was gaining strength, and it was a long hot haul (no one was complaining about the warmth, mind you) along the twists and bends of the winding coastal road. This was finally the dream ride I had envisaged back in the cold and dreary winter of London. We were riding through excesses of nature, along a coastline that knew how to flaunt its natural assets. The sea below was a cyan blue that shone at the extreme end of reality, and the sky above was a cloudless blue cover. The craggy rock faces of the landward side of the road stretched up high above us, whilst often there were barrier-less drops of hundreds of feet to the Mediterranean's edge on our side. A bedazzling array of offshore islands punctuated the sea's canvas.

Finally, our riding was exhilarating and fun. The roadside shrines commemorating lives lost in traffic accidents were rushed by, my eyes always focussed on the way ahead. Ernie was cheerfully talking to us, with the occasional backfire on the overrun as we rode into the gullies. He had a delightful crack to his exhaust note as we powered out of the slow bends. We achieved a sensational synergy as we romped along the sinuous grey ribbon of tarmac. Even driving into the numerous short tunnels didn't scare us.

Years later, I penned a piece attempting to elucidate the joy we experience on two wheels:

> Motorcycling is a tactile, almost sensual experience that is both active and passive. Your input and skill immeasurably contribute to the enjoyment. You participate in so many small ways. You put the bike exactly where you want it in a corner by a series of tiny manoeuvres of your body. The moving of a buttock, a knee put out, a dropped shoulder, a weight transfer from one foot peg to another, a twitch of the throttle hand ... all affect where and how the bike tracks. It is your individual skill that does it. You counter steer by pushing your right bar away to turn right quickly. The bike starts to fall to the right, and without realising it, you catch it with a reactive adjustment, and together you glide and swish around bends. It is like a ballet with a machine. With competence gained, it is uplifting. It is an extension of your body, not a vehicle to be guided by remote controls of steering through a transfer box of worm gear and racks, pinions, and the like. You think through bends, and the motorcycle listens to those thoughts and movements reactively.

Smiling, Anne later accused me of thinking I was Ivan Mauger, the Kiwi four-time World Champion of Speedway. I sensed she had enjoyed the afternoon's adrenalin rush whilst also declaring that she felt she had only narrowly escaped a European version of the Acapulco high dive we'd both seen on the way over to the UK. I took her rebuke as a compliment and didn't nitpick that Ivan Mauger was the 'King of Shale.' He slid endlessly around a cinder oval as opposed to dicing with death on road-race circuits like my Kiwi namesake Ginger Molloy who had achieved world champion runner-up status in 1970.

Eventually, we reached the medium-sized coastal town of Zadar in three complete pieces and stopped beside the sea just the other side of town. Scrub separated us from the road so rather than pitch the tent, we used the PVC tarp as a lean-to against Ernie. What a cosy threesome we made!

Next morning, the day was warm enough to sunbathe at 7.30 a.m. Despite the hour, the sun was potent enough to bask in her rays. It was such a change to our lives. We bared an appropriate amount of skin and boiled a pot of seawater over an open fire to wash some clothes. This may not have been a prudent choice, but it seemed a good idea at the time. We also did hot drinks on the fire. We needed to be resourceful as our sources for the little blue gas-cartridge cooker canisters appeared to have dried up. What seemed a great little device in the sitting room in Leyton now looked like being a worthless passenger in Ernie's pannier. The store's enthusiastic urging of "You can get the replacement canisters *everywhere* in Europe!" was now sounding like an empty sales pitch.

Ernie was completely unpacked, and we decorated the campsite cyclone style. All our possessions were scattered about to dry and freshen in the warmth. We paddled around on our LI-LOs and unsuccessfully tried a spot of fishing from the air mattresses. The sea was flat calm, a shimmering deep blue blanket of pristine clarity. Pebbles on the seabed shone like pieces of glitter. The water was invitingly tepid, on the pleasant side of bathtub warm, and lured us in for a dip.

We found the BBC on the radio and, for a novel delight, listened all morning. Early afternoon, we continued our journey in an attempt to at least reach the town of Split. Not too far along, we stopped to chat with an Aussie guy who was hitching, and we passed a few vans heading the other way with GB and AUS stickers. Just north of Split, Anne pointed out a vineyard she'd stopped at the previous year with Jo and Rhyll. We were on a bit of a roll, intent on finding a beach to camp for a couple of days, so purred past Split. Twenty-five kilometres later was Omiš, a small town straddling the mouth of the Cetina River, nestled at the base of craggy cliffs. I recognized that this was where we had stayed last year in our van. Five Kiwi lads wedged in the back of a Kombi was always cosy. We had needed all that shared body warmth as we'd headed north even later in the year when winter was nipping at our toes. Maybe that experience prepared me for the constraints of our little tent this year. Just past Omiš, we found a great little secluded beach. Pines peppered the bank, and we slept under the overhanging branches of a magnificent pine tree. Finding this gem of a camping spot got me some brownie points with Anne, and we were very pleased with ourselves.

We made this a utopian short break. We'd rarely just stopped and stayed. With a bit of bravery, I got Ernie down a steep bank onto the beach, and we made an idle trio for a couple of days. Paying due homage to the sun goddess was not something to be rushed. The lovely weather was still a bit of a novelty, so we soaked up the sunshine for two whole days. The LI-LOs were moved each morning from the bedroom under the canopy of pine branches to the sunroom on the pebbled beach. In between, we passed the time swimming, reading, and doing as little as possible. Occasionally, we interrupted this state of near inertia to walk into Omiš for life's necessities: ice cream, chips, and fresh bread. Yugoslavia was somewhat alien to us, and we appreciated it. There were no tourists in the small towns and almost a total lack of English comprehension. There were no overtly branded products — no screaming Coca-Cola or Pepsi signs, no neon inducements, or commercial spam. Often it took us a while to identify the shops as there was little signage. Many of the trappings of daily life differed from the world from which we came. Horses and carts were still being used in the countryside, and there was no glitz and glamour in the towns. It was very utilitarian and appealed to us.

Ernie had also spent a leisurely two days on the beach paying his respects to his own solar deity. He wasn't too keen about moving on, as we met with considerable resistance when it came to tackling the slope between the beach and the road. It was almost like we could hear him saying: *You expect me to get up there??* Only with some difficulty, we convinced him that the slope, eroded though it may have been, was the only way up to the road. We promised that there would be more Ivan-Mauger riding and that we'd explore more exotic places and meet many interesting people. After a herculean three-way team effort, we finally reached the top.

Our next destination was Dubrovnik, 200 kilometres to the south. Our plan was to catch a ferry from Dubrovnik to the Greek island of Corfu and skirt Albania by sea. Along the road a bit, we chatted with a pommie couple. They put on the coffee; we supplied the biscuits. This stunning part of the coast provided the magnificent cliff-top view. During the conversation, we traded some novels.

We arrived in Dubrovnik late afternoon and briefly explored the traffic-free old city. Starting at the square in front of the Pile Gate, we strolled along the Stradun, the main pedestrian promenade that was once a canal. Encircling the old city were thick medieval walls extending for almost two kilometres. This lofty perch offered a bird's-eye view, with a sea of orange terra cotta roofs on one side, and a dazzling azure sea on the other.

Chapter 9:
Dubrovnik, Yugoslavia to Istanbul, Turkey

Des Molloy

"Sometimes it's a little better to travel than to arrive."
Robert M. Pirsig, Zen and the Art of Motorcycle Maintenance:
An Inquiry Into Values

After finding out that the ferry to Corfu had ceased operating on October 1 (it was now October 6), we adjusted our plans and decided to continue south, stopping at the first beach we came across. Unfortunately for us, this was the one area where there were tourists, and hotels catering to them. They seemed to have a monopoly on the beaches around Dubrovnik. With no apparent place for us to free camp, we pushed on until lack of functioning Ernie lights forced us into a camping area.

Next day, we continued down the coast to the Bay of Kotor. We followed the edge of the bay to the Verige Strait, the narrow waterway connecting the two outer bays of the coastal inlet with the two inner bays. The picturesque

Kotor Bay is often referred to as Europe's southernmost fjord, but it's actually a submerged river canyon. Commanding cliffs offer an epic backdrop to the blue waters of the bay. Its rocky coastline is dotted with sheltered bays and charming medieval towns featuring red-roofed houses and Orthodox Christian and Catholic churches and cathedrals.

We caught the Lepetane – Kamenari ferry across the narrowest part of the Verige Strait, a short five-minute crossing of the 300-metre-wide waterway. After hugging another edge of the Bay of Kotor, we left the coast for about 20 kilometres. Coming back to the coast, from a high point, we could see a long and sandy beach, beneath and a little to the rear of us.

Dotted along its rim were several vans and tents. Although we'd barely travelled 100 kilometres, we doubled back to descend and evaluate its potential as a haven for the next couple of days. We were travelling schedule-free, and this crescent of near-white sand looked ideal for another idyll of idleness. We stopped beside one of the vans and chatted with a Kiwi and two Canadians, and caught up with the news from the Middle

East. The day before, Egypt and Syria had crossed ceasefire lines to enter the Israeli-occupied Sinai Peninsula and Golan Heights, detonating a war in the region. The joint surprise attack took place on Yom Kippur, the holiest day in Judaism. We were on our way to Israel, so the news captured our interest. That notwithstanding, the conflict had all the elements of a serious international crisis involving, among others, the two nuclear superpowers, the United States and the Soviet Union. From that moment, we became news junkies consuming reports of the war over the days ahead.

A Kiwi from the other van, a battered split-screen old VW Kombi, joined us. When we found out he'd come up through Africa and was heading east, we went over to his van to gaze over a few maps and listen to tales of their travels. We stayed with them (Ken and Jill) all afternoon, and returned in the evening for more coffee and more stories. They were of a similar age and ethos to us, so we immediately bonded. They'd had many adventures coming up from South Africa and had their own Araldite story that we enjoyed immensely.

Dubrovnik, Yugoslavia to Istanbul, Turkey

At some stage during their journey, they had approached a stream crossing with gusto, and a rock wiped off the sump cover of the Kombi. Fortuitously, for Christmas, the family back home had sent them a fruitcake in a tin. The cake tin lid was 'Aralditied' on to the crankcase to make a new sump cover, and the adventure continued. Good old Ciba-Geigy, we reckoned, envisaging that we'd soon be poster kids for the brand.

Months later, I wrote to Ciba-Geigy, the manufacturer of Araldite. The response noted that fixing pistons and crankcases were expected uses of their product, and I was urged to purchase their soon-to-be-released Five-minute Araldite. There were no free samples, no names up in lights. Meanwhile, they went back to sticking wings on jet planes and left us to soldier on.

In the morning, ominous grey clouds coated the sky. We'd slept on our LI-LOs on the beach with the tent fly over us, so we pulled the PVC higher over our heads and remained underneath. We enjoyed early morning coffee with Ken and Jill, helped them push-start their van, and then returned to our sanctuary under the PVC. Hopefully, we'd see them along the way. None of us was travelling fast, so it was possible.

A deluge followed, the heavy rain beating down harshly on the plastic. We stayed that way for several pages, simultaneously trying to read and hold down the corners of our shelter. Eventually, the rain gave way to a tiny patch of blue that took all day to inch its way across the entire sky.

A Dutch couple came by to chat, and we exchanged some novels with people in a Yankee van that came onto the beach. Ernie and I went to the supermarket in Budva, a few kilometres away, and returned laden with goodies. We sampled some Yugoslav rough red — very red, and just as rough. At this point in our lives, we weren't big wine drinkers. That was the stuff of foreigners. Aussies and Kiwis were still wed to the hops; grapes were a decade or two away.

Before nightfall, we shifted camp from the beach to back behind a hedge of blackberry bushes. This turned out to be a good move as we had a repetition of the wrath the sky evoked the morning before. The winds lifted the plastic so our sleep was interrupted when we ducked outside to anchor it down. For several hours, the night was rent by lightning flashes and thunderclaps worthy of the omnipotent one. She must have been angry with someone; we just hoped it wasn't us. The precipitation was intense, but our PVC tarp was stout. I was glad to have Anne beside me though, as this was real hell-and-damnation stuff.

The day cracked open like an egg, showing itself as being worthy of remaining behind at our seductive beachside retreat. We were out basking on the LI-LOs quite early, allowing the sun to work her magic and charm on our still-pale bodies. I'm a 'ginga,' a freckly redhead who mainly tans by having my freckles join up. Anne is blonde and tans gently. I sensed she won't ever have the crocodile skin many Aussie matrons display.

The time passed leisurely — reading, eating, and listening to the radio. The BBC had plenty to broadcast, on this the fourth day of the fourth major Arab-Israeli conflict that had acquired the label Yom Kippur War.

Dubrovnik, Yugoslavia to Istanbul, Turkey

Ernie took me shopping again, and Anne noted in her journal that I "returned with a tucker bag full of surprises." Later in the afternoon, a fling with the Frisbee and a paddle on the LI-LOs injected some activity into an otherwise laid-back day.

This motivated us to go for a walk to the end of the beach where we stumbled upon a freshwater spring. As I slurped away at the delicious crystal clear water from a prone position, a young American lad appeared on the scene. "Is that safe to drink?" he uttered as a greeting. I was not sure if he saw me as some sort of water scientist or he just needed another person's assurance. I told him it was great and for him to try some, as it was as pure as could be. He did, wrinkling up his face in dislike. He'd never had water 'from the wild,' and it didn't taste as it did back home. As a city boy, he'd only ever had fluoridated water. Missing the familiar stainless-steel tang and taste of fluoride, he wasn't convinced that the offering from Mother Gaia was any good. Perhaps he saw me as some sort of Robinson Crusoe.

A short while later, Anne and I disturbed two snakes among the rocks. It seems that I had frequently skited that harmful creatures such as snakes, crocodiles, spiders, scorpions, and other venomous and dangerous living things that reside in Australia are totally absent in New Zealand. As such, New Zealand is 'God's Own Country.' As a result of our encounter with what Anne described as harmless snakes, she concluded that the mere sight of any snake turns a grown man born in New Zealand into a quivering mass of inertia. Suffice to say, her assessment wasn't far off the mark. I panicked at the sight of these merciless vials of evil, and it was left to the Amazonian Aussie sheila to come to the rescue and persuade the reptiles to move out of our way. On our return to camp, still shaken from the ordeal, I busied myself around Ernie, while the gloating heroine collected firewood and generally poked the borax at me.

We soon had a fire going on the beach and cooked some soup to help ease the bread through our systems. Our cooker had been kaput for a few days, and we were a little tired of our diet of bread and more bread. I'd cleverly chilled a bottle of Budva bubbly in the sea, but when I went to retrieve it, to my horror, it had been swept away. Fortunately, after a bit of a panic and splash around in the shallows, I was able to recover it intact. It proved to be eminently quaffable and an excellent complement to the meal.

We deemed it time to move and hit the road early in the direction of Skopje. The Dalmatian Coast had been as good as we could imagine, and we digested with delight what remained of the coastal views before leaving the coast at Petrovac for the climb into the mountains. We needed to head inland to get around the mysterious and forbidden-to-outsiders nation of Albania. In 1973, it wasn't possible to continue down the coast through this isolationist country to Greece. The leader, Enver Hoxha, had abandoned Soviet Communism and embraced a close relationship with China and its version of power to the people. He'd also declared it an atheist state.

Soon after expressing our farewells to the coast, we spotted a Roma camp a couple of hundred metres away. At the time, we knew them as 'Gypsies,'

Dubrovnik, Yugoslavia to Istanbul, Turkey

a term inaccurately applied because of the mistaken belief they originated from Egypt. The camp's flurry of activity was not lost on Ernie. With such a captive audience at his disposal, Ernie capitalised on this rich opportunity to replay one of his favourite attention-seeking antics. So, here we were, creating our own busy scene, attempting to mend a puncture to Ernie's back tyre. In pretty quick time, we patched the tube and had the wheel back in place, but we were unable to carry on as we didn't have a pump to inflate the tyre. We'd still not found one to buy and were long since out of Finilec. Meanwhile, the Roma had broken camp, and people, donkeys, and dogs descended upon us from various directions. They all met at the crossroads — *our* crossroads — and in no time, 20 or so helpers offered their assistance, and many others sought donations of our stuff. It was a little overwhelming. Anne sat on all our gear and desperately attempted to discourage the requests of food, dinara, her sealskin boots, sweater, parka, and anything else that was visible. Eventually, after much discussion, gesticulation, and indecision, the tattered convoy moved in a westerly direction (with a baby secured to a donkey with a familiar-looking blue stretchy cord).

Yugoslavia had one of the largest Roma populations in the world. Marginalization, illiteracy, and impoverishment plagued their mostly nomadic existence, compounded by intolerance of Romani people by other ethnic groups. Throughout Europe, Roma had been persecuted or slaughtered since their migration from northern India several centuries earlier. In Jutland (later Denmark), they were prey in a deadly game labelled a 'Gypsy hunt.' In Wallachia and Moldavia (later Romania), they were enslaved. In Nazi Europe, Roma were sterilized, ghettoized, and deported to concentration and death camps. As many as 500,000 Roma perished during the Holocaust.

Our awareness of the tragic history of the Roma population of Europe was minimal, restricted mostly to the period of the Holocaust. Whilst we felt overwhelmed and unsettled by our brief encounter with a group we knew so little about, it paled in comparison to what must have been the everyday challenges of people who struggled to live on the fringes of society.

Soon after, we flagged down a car, and it was fortunate and fortuitous there was a pump on board. We returned to the matter of Ernie's rear end, got some air in, and in no time were back on the road (just one blue stretchy cord lighter). Tentatively, we wobbled our way into Titograd (renamed Podgorica, Montenegro in 1992), to find ourselves off again with Ernie's tyre completely ruined and ripped to shreds. In a town lacking in signage, we spotted a Michelin Man logo. We were now seeing mainly Cyrillic alphabet signs anyway, so the familiar French fat-guy tyre sign was a real score. With what we figured was sadly misplaced optimism, we asked the tyre dealer dressed in grubby overalls if he happened to have a replacement tyre for Ernie's slightly unusual wheel size. European motos have 17-inch or 18-inch tyres; Ernie's were 19 inches. There was nothing brand new, of course, but he led us to a mountain of old tyres of all shapes and sizes, piled up against a wall. He began to climb, throwing the black rubber hoops behind him as he went. Just when all seemed lost, he held a moto tyre aloft. Anne cheered him enthusiastically; I held my breath, as the likelihood of finding a 19-inch tyre was pretty slim. There had been one bike tyre in the whole heap, and we couldn't believe our eyes when it was indeed found to be Ernie's size.

An enthusiastic reorganization followed to put the front tyre on the back wheel and the *new* old tyre on the front. Ernie was treated like royalty when he was jacked up to have his wheels and tyres removed and refitted. This must have felt much better than suffering the indignity of being straddled across the nearest ditch or balanced precariously on the biggest rock we could find.

Returning to the road with the back wheel still wobbling a little erratically, we stopped seven kilometres on the other side of Titograd, behind some bushes in a patch of scrub. I set to getting the tent up in a discrete section of our hidey-hole while Anne headed off in search of water and had her own adventure. It is her story, so I'll let her tell it.

With our water supply exhausted, the nearby stream beside the road offered the potential for replenishment. I could hear the rhythmic lapping of its waters as it flowed gently over rocks, but adjacent cliffs prevented easy access. I was hopeful that at some point the cliffs would magically part and offer a trail descending gently to the water's edge. After almost a kilometre of walking along the road beside the stream, I was on the verge of throwing in the towel when I spotted a house with a group of youngsters playing outside. With the universally understood language of gestures and facial expressions, I pointed to my empty water container. They immediately took me in hand and escorted me around back to their water supply.

Sitting at a nearby table were two guys drinking Pivo, Yugoslav beer. I was immediately ushered to a stool; the top was ripped off a Pivo, and the bottle shoved in my hand. A packet of crackers materialised, and a dish of white cheese was added to the spread. My visit seemed worthy of elevating happy hour to a celebration involving the entire family, as the remaining occupants of the house gathered around the table. It seemed irrelevant that my intrusion hadn't resulted from an invitation, and that I was a stranger to these parts and incapable of carrying on a conversation.

The language barrier was far from being a deterrent. Commonly understood vocabulary in the conversation that followed amounted to no more than a dozen words, and some of these I doubt belonged to any of the languages spoken by humankind. We discussed where we were born, where we lived, our occupations, modes of transportation, ages of the children, languages the children learned in school, and other topics too numerous to mention. We even discussed a possible deal that involved a swap where I would acquire the two guys and Des, my absent 'camarade,' would procure momma and the four 'bambines.' I was offered a second Pivo but at 12% alcohol by volume, I was already a little off centre, so I graciously declined, indicating a need to head back to our camp.

No sooner had I returned to our refuge amongst the scrub, than two people arrived on a moped. One was in a militia uniform, and as he approached, I remarked on the resemblance between him and one of the guys I'd just met. It wasn't until his 'camarade' staggered up the hill bringing up the rear did I notice that he too looked familiar. Our new friends attempted to convey the message that across the stream was a blasting site, and midnight would signal the commencement of blasting. Grabbing a few props in the form of rocks to illustrate the gravity of the situation, they gave us a horrifying preview of what would happen to the tent, Ernie, Des, and me by throwing the rocks into the air with accompanying sound effects of *boomba boomba*. Their obvious concern for our safety was endearing, and their suggestion that we camp at their place offered a feasible alternative to being blasted into oblivion at midnight.

Of course, we packed up Ernie and in the dark, rode tentatively along, using the camping radio's light for illumination. We finally arrived at Anne's mates' place to find that the guys had gone into Titograd. It was with some difficulty that we told momma of the new plan, and we pitched the tent in their windy field.

A cold day followed, with some of it spent negotiating the best mountains southern Yugoslavia has to offer. The roads were narrow, unprotected by barriers, and included several long and dark tunnels to make things a little more challenging. On the road at 8.00 a.m., the first stop brought us to a fantastic blackberry patch teeming with berries. The next stop was when Ernie's silencer fell off — again! We then followed an Aussie van for a considerable distance and made use of their lights to guide us through several tunnels. After parting company with our helpful fellow travellers at

Kosovska Mitrovica, we pushed on to cover the 110 kilometres to Skopje before the sun slipped behind the mountains of Albania.

En route, we stopped to cash a traveller's cheque. Whilst Anne was away doing the money stuff, I counted 38 in the crowd that had gathered around Ernie — mostly kids. We stopped a couple of kilometres up the road to devour the goodies she'd bought, and more kids descended upon us. I gave away a few foreign coins, and they posed for a photo. We were always amazed at how we would stop in a secluded spot, and almost immediately, we were surrounded by a throng of kids, interested shepherds, or farm labourers from a field hundreds of metres away. My flaming red hair and Anne's blonde locks were also attractants; we'd long since passed lands where our colouring was common.

These mountains of Yugoslavia pulled back a memory from the previous year. Driving standards had appalled the boys and me in some of the Balkan States and Turkey. Still, our most graphic example of what fatalistic societies tolerate came in these very hills. Making steady progress up a hill in our

heavily laden 1200cc VW Kombi, we'd passed a tractor pulling a cart, just as we came to a blind corner. We were okay because there was a bit of a shoulder, and the tractor was keeping over as far as was practical. Just at the crucial point of passing, a light truck pulled alongside *and* a small sporty car swept around us all. There we were ... four abreast going around a blind corner with us in the Kombi all shouting "NO!" Amazingly, we all lived to tell the tale. Sadly, it was not the last time I would see this sort of driving.

In Skopje, we checked into a camping ground, showered, and wandered into the centre of the city. Eighty per cent of Skopje had been destroyed in a devastating earthquake that killed over 1,000 people just 10 years earlier in 1963. Most of Skopje's historical architecture was damaged or demolished, replaced with modern concrete buildings and cityscape. The roads and footpaths were packed with people, so we weaved our way through the multitudes to window-shop and find a place to have a snack. Anne ordered a flaky pastry filled with cabbage and white cheese but could only eat about half as the taste was just too foreign and not to her liking. It was rare that we ever left a scrap of food, especially something we'd bought. We had a bottle of Pivo and wandered back to the campsite after stopping to chat with the occupants of some Aussie vans along the way.

We had a plan to sell our blood in Greece. It seemed a bit mercenary, but we were keen to eke out our funds as long as we could. On this trip, we weren't planning to head down to Athens and on to the Greek Islands. Appealing as it was, we'd both done that, and our intention was to head to Turkey and, if possible, on to Israel.

We wanted to arrive in Thessalonika in time to catch the blood bank open, so we were away early, aware of the stares from fellow campers as Ernie roared and backfired his way out of the campsite. It was a good thing we weren't committed to a surreptitious exit. After we solved the problem of how to get out of Skopje with the aid of a helpful police officer, we drove slowly towards Greece through heavy fog.

The day brightened considerably as we sped through tobacco, cotton, and sunflower fields towards the border with Greece. While enjoying a brief respite with a load of grapes obtained on the way, I was propositioned to sell my leathers. In many ways, my one-piece racing leathers had been bloody annoying, but they had kept me from the cold and, of course, offered protection, that I'd hoped we'd ever need.

The Greek border caused no problems. In Thessalonika 80 kilometres later, we stopped by a sign displaying a red cross, only to find it was a pharmacy. We met a Kiwi van full of guys who were also interested in selling blood. All of us must have looked a strange sight, pointing to the inside of our forearms as we asked for directions from passersby who couldn't understand us, nor tell us where the blood bank was.

We thought it would be easy. In Athens the previous year, we had been handed promotional materials encouraging us to 'donate' blood for top prices with easy-to-follow directions to our choice of blood banks. Oh, how 'bloody' convenient it would have been to have one of those handy cards.

We were eventually directed to a building that didn't open until 8.00 a.m. the following day. Faced with a choice, we pondered our next move over a terrific feed for 58 drachmas, which wasn't much, given the rate of 71

GRD to £1. Heading out of town by following the coast, we found a closed camping area where we were permitted to camp on the waterfront at no charge.

The following day, we found our way back to what we expected to be the blood bank, but it turned out to be a clinic. The receptionist wrote the name of a local hospital, and we walked several blocks, stopping to show people the piece of paper and ask for directions along the way. We eventually arrived and on the footpath were greeted by three people who escorted us inside. They stayed at our side, attentive entrepreneurs engaged in the profitable business of blood.

Comparing notes afterwards, we agreed that the doctor who extracted the fingertip sample wasn't the gentlest, nor was the nurse who rammed a needle in our veins. After donating 300 millilitres, we were escorted to a resting place and given orange juice. One of the three men who had been hovering around like vampires paid us 400 drachmas each. We then went to a nearby park to rest some more, before catching a bus back to Ernie.

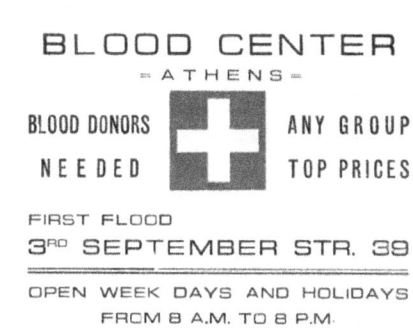

FREE REFRESHMENTS

YOUR BLOOD
MIGHT SAVES SOMEONES LIFE

BLOOD CENTER
= ATHENS =

BLOOD DONORS NEEDED   ANY GROUP TOP PRICES

FIRST FLOOD
3ᴿᴰ SEPTEMBER STR. 39

OPEN WEEK DAYS AND HOLIDAYS
FROM 8 A.M. TO 8 P.M.

We treated ourselves to souvlaki and Coca-Cola for the equivalent of 12 pence each and then stopped by a Laundromat with our pile of dirty laundry. It was a good and successful day. If our daily spend stayed the same,

Dubrovnik, Yugoslavia to Istanbul, Turkey

we'd just gleaned about a week's worth of food with the £11 or so added to our kitty.

Excitedly, we pointed Ernie in the direction of Turkey, and he said, *Righto!* Later, when we encountered a passing storm, it became an opportune time to stop for souvlaki. We were on the road soon after and pulled over among some trees to pitch the tent before we lost daylight. With darkness, the rain came back, and the dry interior of the tent became a haven for creepies and crawlies seeking free lodging for the night. We experienced heavy rain during the night but came through it quite well.

Back on the road, the first 100 kilometres passed reasonably quickly. When the sun graced us with her presence, it was hard to resist the temptation to bask in her soothing rays. A 30-minute fix was just what we needed. It's hard to sit on a moto and then sit some more. Regular breaks are the secret to enjoying the ride. We were pretty hardened after all the miles and kilometres we'd put beneath us, but we still revelled in our stops. We paused in Kavala for bread, milk, cookies, and petrol, and turned off to a beach to take in some more sun. With the northern summer barely a memory, and the northern winter rapidly approaching behind us, we felt a need to take advantage of every pocket of sunshine that came our way.

Back on the road, we managed just over 100 kilometres before we needed to drag out the rain gear in the face of a heavy, grey sky bearing down on us. We stopped 30 kilometres from Alexandroupolis, the last town of note in Greece when we found a perfect camping spot amongst scrub. We knew from experience not to pass up a delightful spot in the late afternoon. Sod's Law means that you'll usually ride on into the dark without ever matching it if you do.

A fierce electrical storm during the night meant that most things needed drying out in the morning. This was another tempest with unbridled fury. Once more, I was glad of my resolute companion. Stopping in Alexandroupolis for souvlaki derailed our plan of reaching Istanbul this day. We ran into a Scottish guy who'd been robbed and didn't have any money, so we shouted him a beer and he entertained us with stories. The one beer became three, and we threw in a feed. He'd been with the Special Air Service Regiment and was heading to Australia to join the Australian Army. One of his tales described how he'd received a lift with an Israeli outfit to the front where he was shot at four times by the Syrians as he crossed the border in combat gear. He also spoke of his nine months with Mike Hoare's mercenaries in Kenya, and his not-so-pleasant clash with 'Gypsies' in Yugoslavia. If the truth be known, very little of it was likely true and we'd probably been had, but it was an entertaining way to pass a few hours. I think Anne thought he was a bit of a big-noter, but I must admit that I hung on his lips. We finally left Alexandroupolis at 3.00 p.m., intent on crossing into Turkey before the end of the day.

Most of the countries visited to date acknowledged our entry with a stamp in our passports. At the Turkish frontier, not only was our entry documented but evidence of Ernie's *"GIRIS"* ('entry') as a *"motosiklet"* with the registration number "VAX–964" was also stamped and recorded in Anne's passport.

The next day, we were off to an early start, eager to experience the magic of Istanbul. From our camping spot not far from the border, we rode all morning, pointing out spots where each of us had stopped in our respective vans the year before. On one of our rest stops, 60 kilometres from Istanbul, we chatted with Ali Mohammadi, who was returning home to Iran after spending 10 years studying in the USA. As a result, he was able to import, duty-free, the brand new Ford Mustang he was driving. He spoke of Iran with pride and encouraged us to visit his homeland. As the war in the Middle East was still raging, we gave serious consideration to such a prospect, and thus delay our trip to Israel, hoping relative peace would return to the area. Ali invited us to look him up and provided us with his address and telephone number.

When we were nearly run off the road, we realised we were among Istanbul drivers and on the outskirts of the city. Engulfed in a torrent of vehicles, we endured the increasing cacophony of horns and hooters and space-invading cars and trucks, gritting our teeth and giving our best. We stopped only when we were finally and safely ensconced among vans and tents at BP Mocamp, relieved to have arrived unscathed. After a couple of quick chats with interested campers, hot showers became our top priority. We were keen to immerse ourselves in the hustle and bustle of Istanbul, just not on the roadways.

Dubrovnik, Yugoslavia to Istanbul, Turkey

Chapter 10:
Istanbul, Turkey

Anne Betts

"Travel opens your mind as few other things do. It is its own form of hypnotism, and I am forever under its spell."
Libba Bray, Rebel Angels

Istanbul's charm never dulls. The more I visited, the more intrigued and enamoured I became.

For Des and me in 1973, it was our second stopover in the city. The bustling metropolis had become the eastern terminus and turnaround point of our 1972 European travels in our respective Kombi vans. We'd both been mesmerized by its unique and effervescent energy and these earlier tantalizing tastes had primed our taste buds for devouring more of its fervour. We couldn't wait to get started.

Clean and refreshed, we walked out to the road to the incessant honking of passing traffic to hail a *dolmuş* that almost ran us over. A dolmuş (meaning 'filled' or 'stuffed') is a shared minibus, an economical means of transportation in Turkey and a much safer alternative to riding Ernie in the madness of Istanbul traffic. Our interest in staying alive was stronger than the need to experience any more of Istanbul's frenetic traffic on two wheels. We climbed aboard and squeezed in with the 20 or so other passengers packed in like sardines.

Istanbul traffic was a cacophonic web of tangled bedlam and venturing into the mayhem felt daunting. Weaving in and out, overtaking and stopping, passing and swerving, drivers seemed to have a complete disregard for traffic lights and pedestrians. Signs dotting the roadsides prohibiting the use of horns were openly flouted, or regarded as suggestions, as drivers blasted their horns at any opportunity. Being immersed in the experience was both frightening and exciting, in equal portions.

Thankfully, five times a day, the omnipresent honking of horns and obtrusive blare of traffic drifted into the background when the haunting intonations of the call to prayer echoed across the city.

With its quintessential clusters of glistening mosques and shimmering minarets dominating the skyline, Istanbul is an intoxicating concoction of melding worlds. Straddling the Bosphorus, a strategically significant strait connecting the Black Sea with the Sea of Marmara, the city spans two continents, the only one in the world that can claim this distinction.

"If one had but a single glance to give the world, one should gaze on Istanbul," said the French poet, writer, and politician Alphonse de Lamartine

(1790–1869). As a capital serving as the epicentre of the Byzantine, Roman, and Ottoman Empires, Istanbul has long captivated the interest of the rest of the world. Another well-known Frenchman, Napoleon Bonaparte (1769–1821) suggested, "If the earth were a single state, Istanbul would be its capital." Though no longer a capital, Istanbul is the cosmopolitan heart of the Turkish Republic, its financial centre and most populous city. Byzantium, New Rome, Constantinople, Old Stamboul — its name has changed, but the allure endures.

A metaphorical and geographical meeting place of east and west, Istanbul sits at the crossroads of human history, a timeless bridge between Europe and Asia. It's one of the most historically diverse cities on earth. During the 3,000 years of its existence, the influences of both continents have created a huge open-air museum brimming with activity and vitality on every street corner. It's a cultural kaleidoscope, a huge multicultural buffet of titillating sights, sounds, and smells that reflect its heart and soul.

We loved Istanbul.

And we adored Turkish food. It was cheap and delicious — and fresh, with meat, seafood, and vegetables in abundance. Earning pounds in London and spending lira in Turkey facilitated a foodie foray into Istanbul's gustatory offerings. One of our favourites was *döner kebab*, seasoned ground lamb broiled on a vertical rotisserie and served with onions, tomato, and flatbread. We were also partial to *şiş kebab*, marinated chicken or lamb on a *şiş* (skewer) grilled over an open fire. Another favourite was *lahmacun*, a thin disc of dough topped with ground lamb or beef mixed with chilli, onions, and seasonings. We especially enjoyed the steam-table restaurants where an acceptable approach was to pick and point at attractive looking options. We enthusiastically took advantage of the endless opportunities for culinary escape, at prices compatible with our budget.

We were intrigued by the hamals, human beasts of burden with their stubby padded backpacks carting an unlimited variety of cargo, from crates of chickens to giant pianos. Bent over under loads of all shapes and sizes, often with legs barely visible, they moved at a steady pace. It was incumbent on others who shared the streets and footpaths of the Eminönü district to have an ear tuned to the shouts of their presence. To be oblivious or distracted could have severe consequences for both pedestrian and worker. We would pause with amazement at the sight of what we imagined was impossible for any one person to carry.

One of our many favourite haunts was the labyrinthine Grand Bazaar. Opened in 1461, the *Kapalıçarşı*, meaning 'covered bazaar' is one of the largest and oldest covered markets in the world. Off the main arcade are innumerable alleyways, each devoted to a category of merchandise such as jewellery, pottery, spices, leather, clothing, or carpets. It represented an ageless milieu of commerce older than the bazaar itself, with its roots dating back to the trade routes of the Silk Road.

It's a market popular with visitors to Turkey. Hence, merchants all seem to speak several languages. Many have the uncanny ability to identify the country of origin of customers and framing a greeting in the relevant language. We met one man who could not only distinguish an Australian from a New Zealander (something I can't do) but he could mimic the distinctions between the two accents with proficiency.

From the brightly illuminated shops, merchants called out to passersby:

"Hey lady, you wanna look in my shop?"

"You want to buy a nice leather coat? I have the best quality, and to you, I give a very special price."

"Best price here in all Istanbul. Come and look in my shop."

"Can I help you lady ... bracelet, ring, watch?"

"Look at my good quality carpets."

The merchant who successfully enticed a customer into his shop immediately provided a chair and a choice of *çay* (tea), coffee strong enough to float a spoon, or Coca-Cola. This was considered a sign of friendship and hospitality and an essential feature of Turkish culture and commerce. The ritual continued with a close inspection of the merchandise, and the inevitable lesson on its background, historical importance, or how it was produced. A volley of suggested prices invariably took place before the parties agreed on an amount. Bargaining could take several hours or be conducted over multiple visits.

On our first day in Istanbul, Des and I headed to the Poste Restante in the Sirkeci quarter, a couple of blocks from the Istanbul Gar, the European railroad terminus of the famous *Orient Express*. Finding the Grand Post Office closed, we walked up to Lale Pastahanesi (the Pudding Shop) in Sultanahmet, the part of the Old City hosting many of Istanbul's historical gems such as Hagia Sofia, Sultanahmet Mosque (Blue Mosque), and Topkapı Palace.

By this time, we'd decided to travel to Iran with the possibility of leaving Ernie in Istanbul, so we were on the lookout for alternative means of transportation. The Pudding Shop, located opposite the Sultanahmet Mosque, was an ideal starting point. Opened by Idris Çolpan and his brother Namik in 1957, during the sixties, tourists made the Pudding Shop famous. It became the meeting place of travellers heading east or west on the so-called 'hippie trail.' Its notice board with advice, mail, messages, and advertisements for lifts and merchandise, offered the potential for us to find a ride. We were aware of the means to stitch together cheap public transportation, but we were more interested in taking a circuitous route and sharing costs with other independent travellers in their own vehicle. After scouring the notice board, we hung around until 9.00 p.m. chatting mostly with Americans over a few beers.

The taxi back to camp cost just two Turkish lira (TL). This was the equivalent of only six pence.

Committed to the new plan to visit Iran, we were up early the following day to take our passports to the Iranian Consulate by 10.00 a.m. The next stop was the Poste Restante counter to find three letters from Jo, Kerry, and the 603 girls. Our excitement at receiving news from our friends necessitated sitting on the steps of the post office, devouring their welcome news.

Next on the itinerary was the Grand Bazaar to unload the radio purchased in Munich a few weeks earlier. It didn't take long for interest to be expressed.

"Hey, you want to sell that radio?"

"Yes, you wanna buy?"

"May I look?"

"Yes."

"How much?"

"One thousand five hundred Turkish lira."

"Wow, you make a joke. That is very expensive."

"It's a very expensive radio. It has a light, compass, thermometer, three

frequencies: SW, MW, and FM."
"Yes, yes, I can see, but it is still very expensive. What is your last price?"
"My last price is 1,450 lira."
"Ooh, you big capitalist."
"Well, what is your price then?"
"I give you … 500 lira."
"Now you're making a joke. I'm not interested. I will keep my radio." (We take the radio and leave.)
"Wait, Mister ... 550 lira."
"Ha! You're still joking!"
"Okay. Okay. Wait."
We return with the radio.
"Okay if we visit my friend who knows all about radios?"
We follow the merchant and the radio for consultation with the expert. The expert examines the radio followed by several moments of deliberation and a few words in Turkish muttered to the potential buyer.
"My friend say radio no good. I give you 550 lira."
We take the radio and leave.
And so it played out, the exchange repeated with few variations several times that day. The flash camping radio we thought the Istanbul merchants would fight over was carted all the way from Munich for the expected sale of the century. We were sadly mistaken, with the radio fetching barely what we paid for it in Germany. We eventually sealed the deal with a handshake in a blouse shop for TL500 and eighteen of the infamous 'Istanbul blouses,' colourfully embroidered cotton shirts. Pleased to be rid of our superfluous possession, we now had 18 others to deal with!
A few steps later, Des sold his watch for TL75.
Afterwards, it was back to the Pudding Shop and the van park by the Blue Mosque to continue exploring the possibility of catching rides heading east.

Unsuccessful, we bought a copy of the *Daily Express* to catch up on the news of the hostilities in the Middle East and headed back to camp around 6.00 p.m. After a couple of beers up in the bar area, we wrote some letters and yarned with a few Aussies and poms.

On our third day, after cruising the camp asking about rides, Des and I wandered down to Londra Camping, a hundred metres from BP Mocamp. It was another well-known spot on the overland route to India, where travellers traded information and news. We chatted with a couple of Canadians, but the prospect of grabbing a ride eluded us once more. A dolmuş took us to the Sultanahmet van park, and then to the Pudding Shop notice board. Coming up empty on our quixotic quest to secure a ride was a stinging slap of disappointment that severely dented our morale. On the spot, we decided to take Ernie to Iran and abandon what had become fruitless, time-consuming efforts.

As luck would have it, this decision turned out to be one of the best of the trip. Little did we know at this point that we'd just escaped a yawning abyss waiting for us at the Turkish-Iranian border.

So here we were at the Iranian Consulate in Istanbul to collect our passports. From there we went to the Poste Restante and then to the Grand Bazaar where we spent several hours buying slippers, puzzle rings, gloves, and evil-eye necklaces. Some of our purchases would end up in a mailing box to either Australia or New Zealand; others were to enhance our comfort on the journey ahead.

One merchant remembered me from the previous year and treated us to *çay* and a bite to eat. It was another example of Turkish kindness and generosity extended to us over several hours of interesting conversation. The hospitality was one thing, and the ease with which it was offered was another. It was all so seamless, so natural, worth so much more than the cost of the food.

The thought struck me that travel can be a great unifier. It wasn't an original thought, but it was one that surfaced with reoccurring frequency. When foreigners come from far away and return for subsequent visits, it surely had a validating effect on the people we met. Our presence could be interpreted as expressing interest in the people and their ways. Asking questions and complimenting them on what we observed perhaps reinforced pride in their country and way of life.

From our perspective, our brief glimpses into another culture meant we were able to better appreciate the similarities and differences of our shared humanity. These types of encounters expanded our minds and stirred our souls.

Our fourth day in Istanbul was spent hanging around BP Mocamp. I cleaned out Ernie's panniers and gave him a thorough wash to erase the patina of dust and road grime. Des removed the shock absorbers for the trip to a machine shop. A kilogram of fish cost TL4 (12 pence) at a local market for our meal of fish and chips and beer for tea that we prepared in the cookhouse while chatting with other travellers.

The Topkapı Information Bureau was our first stop the following day to collect maps and brochures on the route we were roughly planning to take through Asian Turkey. There was a glaring absence of travel guides for this part of the world. We stumbled across cyclostyled sheets of the publication *Across Asia on the Cheap* published in February 1973, a precursor to the Lonely Planet Guides written by co-founders Tony and Maureen Wheeler. It was a helpful resource for travellers on the entire hippie trail and a worthy investment of USD 1.80. With Iran as our planned point of turnaround, it wasn't a match for the type of trip we were on, so it was mostly irrelevant.

From there we toured Topkapı Palace, an immense compound where the Ottoman sultans lived and governed in opulent resplendence for almost four centuries. Initial construction started in 1459 under the direction of Fatih Sultan Mehmet, conqueror of Byzantine Constantinople in 1453. During the long reign of Sultan Süleyman the Magnificent (1520–66), the empire expanded its borders from Iraq to Tunisia and even to the gates of Vienna. At the height of its existence as a royal residence and seat of government administration, it was home to as many as 10,000 people with mosques, a hospital, bakeries, and a mint.

Topkapı Palace gradually lost its importance at the end of the 17th century, as the Sultans preferred to spend more time in their new palaces along the Bosphorus. After the end of the Ottoman Empire in 1921, Topkapı Palace was converted to a museum in 1924.

The innumerable rooms and chambers housed lavish costumes, ostentatious furnishings, impressive calligraphy, and jewels from every corner of the empire. It was all designed to overwhelm visitors with the empire's immense power and unfathomable wealth. The architecturally magnificent Imperial Harem was an eye-opener, featuring intricate Ottoman tile art and built-in cubicles in the walls shaped to accommodate turbans.

Istanbul, Turkey

Our visit lasting two hours barely touched the surface of the immensity and opulence of this extraordinary complex.

One of our favourite vantage points from which to admire the impressive view of the Bosphorus, Golden Horn, and part of Anatolia (Asian Turkey) was the rock wall of Topkapı Palace. It was possible to sit for hours and soak up the scenery. We observed the hurried life of the waterfront where beauty flirted with chaos. We watched the ferries that ploughed back and forth, and the tankers and cargo ships travelling up and down the narrow strait, leaving soapy bubbles and foamy white streaks in their wakes.

The palace wall was a perfect perch for enjoying döner kebab and Coca-Cola. As we absorbed the superb view, it felt as though the gods of the many religious communities that had shaped the urban landscape of Istanbul created this panoramic vista for our viewing pleasure. Perhaps Alphonse de Lamartine was sitting at this very spot when he made his famous utterance. A brief visit to Hagia Sophia consumed the next couple of hours. For close to a thousand years, it was the largest cathedral in the world before serving as the principal mosque of Istanbul for almost half a millennium. In 1934, Mustafa Kemal Atatürk, the founding father of the Republic of Turkey, converted it to a secular museum. The design of Hagia Sophia was so unique that it was reputed to have changed the history of architecture. While it wasn't built as a mosque, it was widely admired in the Islamic world.

Its architecture heavily influenced the design of many Ottoman mosques. Hagia Sophia has undergone many changes over the centuries, having survived earthquakes, pillaging, and other damage wrought by the ravages of time. Despite these challenges, it continues to loom over the Istanbul skyline as a symbol of the various religious communities that have shaped the history of the city. The remarkable interior is just as impressive with its massive dome, an expansive upper gallery, Islamic calligraphy, and glittering mosaics. Istanbul has so many treasures, and Hagia Sophia ranks up there with the best. We were pleased we found the time to experience it.

The shock absorbers were collected on our way back to camp, and Des and the American camped next to us refitted them on Ernie. The local market sourced the steak, capsicum, leeks, and chilli peppers that we mixed with rice for tea. Our first faux meal after leaving London — the unappetizing stodge of rice with chicken flavouring was but a dim memory as we enjoyed our salubrious feast consisting of fresh Turkish ingredients.

For a couple of hours, I chatted with a Malaysian camper from a Malaysian-US van. As a general rule, we associated travellers and their modes of transportation with the occupants' countries of origin. Hence, the 'Malaysian-US van,' 'German van,' 'Aussies in the pop-top camper,' or 'Italian guys on the Moto Guzzi' became the identifiers until we established relationships more substantial than passing encounters. In any case, Hon-Chi (we would stumble across her and her travelling companions in other parts of Turkey) lent me some material on Asian Turkey that required remaining in the illuminated cookhouse for a couple more hours making notes.

After our satisfying binge feasting on some of Istanbul's top tourist sites, we awoke with thoughts of departure. However, when Des broke out the Araldite, I knew from experience that the two-tube epoxy usurped all other plans. As a result, the leisurely day was devoted to allowing the Araldite to set and getting organized for departure.

Brunch comprised eggs and chips. On the way back to the tent from the cookhouse, we stopped by the Aussies from Tasmania in the pop-top camper and chatted for a few hours over several cups of tea. We later traded novels with an English couple. Soup made it on to the menu for tea. Afterwards, over a couple of beers, we chatted with the Americans who'd arrived on three motorcycles.

Des was quite envious of them. Not only were they travelling on modern bikes, but they had real riding gear, not just cobbled-up stuff they had on hand. Here's his recall of the minutiae of the moment:

> They were wearing multi-pocketed Belstaff or Barbour waxed-cotton riding gear. Sometimes known as Japara and promoted as thorn proof, the products of the two rival British brands were de rigueur apparel for the riders in the English magazines I devoured as a young would-be enthusiast. At that time, I'd never actually seen this type of motorcycling clothing up close and was amazed to learn from the riders that the gear was comfortable and 100 per cent waterproof. I now chuckle at the interaction, and with gained knowledge am fully aware that at best, while freshly waxed, they will keep most of the water out for a limited period. The gear has a traditional tough look and my current riding jacket that I've had for decades has been a locally made replica.

We were serious about making Monday, October 22, 1973, our departure day from Istanbul. During the six days spent at BP Mocamp, we'd enjoyed countless hot showers, and washed every stitch of clothing we'd packed. The many illuminating conversations with other travellers allowed us to forge connections with like-minded souls and gather valuable intel for the journey ahead. We'd taken advantage of the free cookers and the cheap meat, fish, and produce from the local market. However, the time had come to retrace our steps slightly, then venture into brand new territory across the water to Asia. It was terra incognita, and an exciting prospect to contemplate. We couldn't wait to experience it.

We bade farewell to Jennifer of the 'honest Aussies' from the pop-top camper and gave her our precious package of Istanbul blouses for delivery to the Leyton flat in London.

Ernie was pointed west to connect to the road to the Dardanelles, one of the great arteries of history, the narrow but significant strait separating European Turkey from Asian Turkey.

Istanbul, Turkey

Chapter 11:
Istanbul to Anamur, Turkey

Anne Betts

"I am not the same having seen the moon shine on the other side of the world."
Mary Anne Radmacher

A few kilometres after leaving Istanbul's BP Mocamp, Ernie shed the Araldite-bonded conglomeration at his back wheel cush-drive. Not prepared to stop to administer first aid, we wobbled for the rest of the day. A couple of additional stops were needed to refit Ernie's chain. As we foxtrotted our way to the Dardanelles, we questioned our decision about not leaving our friend behind in Istanbul.

Once we'd escaped the bustle of Istanbul traffic, the road followed the northern shore of the beautiful Sea of Marmara, with views of the water for part of the way. After leaving sight of the sea, we found a pungent pine forest 60 kilometres from Gelibolu that presented itself as an ideal overnight camping spot to satisfy our reclusive needs. We opted not to pitch the tent and built a nest for ourselves in a mound of pine needles. It was a beautiful night for sleeping under stars that winked at us through the branches. Whilst whispers of wind caressed the trees, we watched the needles and cones dancing in unison, lulling us into a blissful sleep.

As night merged into morning, the twinkling stars had disappeared and the clouds wept, bringing our pleasant alfresco slumber to an abrupt halt. The first tears sent us scurrying for the PVC tent fly for temporary protection from what we hoped was a passing shower. Our wishful thinking soon evaporated, and the blanket of wetness forced us into putting up the tent under the dripping branches. Climbing into our wet sleeping bags in our wet clothes, we dug in until the weather improved.

So far, weather had been the train that had gone off the tracks to derail previous plans, and it was seriously impinging on the present. While cooped up in our nylon prison, the day passed with the pace of a sloth as we read our novels in amicable silence and grabbed nutrient-deficient sustenance in a packet of cream biscuits. After a meal of tinned fish and rice, darkness came early, and the inside of the tent became as black as a Norwegian tunnel. Even the weather was reminiscent of Norway.

It had stopped raining by the morning of the following day, so we didn't surpass our Norwegian 40-hour record confined to the tent.

A short while after setting off, Ernie needed attention. By the time he was ready to go, several youngsters helped push-start him up the road.

Our brief stop in Gelibolu, site of the earliest Ottoman shipyards and navy headquarters, was for a quick bite to eat. Eager to visit the battlegrounds, memorials, and graveyards of the Gallipoli Peninsula, just before Eceabat, we peeled off to take the road to Anzac Cove.

This was the site of the Australian and New Zealand Army Corps (ANZAC) landing on April 25, 1915, and the main Anzac base during the campaign. The offensive was designed to capture the Dardanelles to open a route to Russia through the Black Sea and hopefully engage Germany on another front.

Several hours were spent visiting one of the beaches where the British forces landed. Later, we wandered around Lone Pine, site of one of the most ferocious battles of the campaign where Australian and Ottoman forces suffered fatalities of over 2,200 and 5,000 respectively. The lone tree that stood there in 1915 didn't survive the battle but two Australian soldiers retrieved cones for planting thousands of descendants throughout Australia. On a nearby hilltop, we stumbled upon Turkish trenches and a faded information board and memorial to Mustafa Kemal, commander of Turkish

forces who later became Kemal Atatürk, President of Turkey. The spot offered panoramic views of the battlefields and the Dardanelles.

It's not possible to leave the area unaffected by the tangible reminders of the eight-month-long Gallipoli Campaign and reflect on the heavy casualties suffered by Allied and Ottoman forces. Exact figures vary, but it's possible that the ill-conceived and mismanaged invasion resulted in as many as 150,000 deaths. Ottoman troops suffered the heaviest casualties, with 86,000 lives lost. Other figures on fatalities include 41,000 British, 4,000 Irish, 10,000 French, 8,000 Australian, 3,000 New Zealand, 1,300 Indian, and 50 Newfoundlanders.

It's fitting that both Australia and New Zealand chose April 25 as their 'memorial' or 'remembrance' day to recognise those who served and died in all wars, conflicts, and peacekeeping operations. April 25, 1915, marked a tragic event in history, never one to be glorified. The classic 'And the Band Played Waltzing Matilda' eloquently captures the suffering and senseless loss of life at Gallipoli, and futility of war in general. Scottish-born Australian singer-songwriter Eric Bogle wrote the song in 1971. At the time, young Australians were dying in the jungles of Vietnam, and Bogle had experienced his first Anzac Day march after emigrating to Australia. It remains my favourite anti-war song of all time.

Like all young Australians and New Zealanders, I'd taken part in the annual

Anzac Day services. They paled in comparison to the sombre experience of visiting Gallipoli. I was certain our visit would have a long-lasting impact, etched in my consciousness for years to come.

Hungry for the unknown that was Anatolia, we watched European Turkey fade behind us, reaching Asian Turkey late in the afternoon by ferry across the Dardanelles from Eceabat to *Çanakkale*. It was a short crossing of approximately 30 minutes, and we stopped about 25 kilometres later to camp amongst scrub not too far off the road.

For our 300-kilometre ride to Izmir the following day, the weather wasn't at all co-operative, unleashing its venom as a debilitating wind sweeping angrily off the Aegean Sea. Like a caged beast, the gale discharged its energy with fury, hitting us with hammer blows and creating crosswinds broadsiding us with shuddering blasts. The maelstrom walloped us from all sides and staying upright was a struggle. Ernie's speedometer registered a top speed of only 35 mph. Turning our heads from the teeth of the wind and leaning sideways into the changing directions of the crosswinds, we experienced a taxing day's ride, tiring to the point of exhaustion. Kudos to Ernie, our admiration was well earned and well deserved. With self-assured complacency, he met the challenge with aplomb. He seemed determined not to let some wussy Turkish wind (or maybe it was Greek ... the dreaded Meltemi) dictate unplanned stops. He was perfectly capable of masterminding those on his own.

A typical Mediterranean climate prevails in the Aegean region, with hot, dry summers and mild, wet winters. It was late October, and the rich red colour of tomatoes ripening in the small family-run farms grabbed our attention. Unable to resist, we stocked up on bread and freshly picked plump sun-ripened tomatoes at our next stop. The thick juicy pulp unleashed a delightful sweetness with a hint of acidity. When combined with crusty Turkish bread and a few sprinkles of salt and pepper, the prosaic yet delicious staple offered tasty sustenance after our buffeting ordeal. The meal would

be repeated many more times over the days ahead.

In Izmir, stumbling across the Malaysian-US van from Istanbul's BP Mocamp necessitated a well-earned stop to catch up on their news over tea and biscuits. When stopping to chat with other travellers, mining 'their news' invariably involved obtaining a description of their route, what they saw, what they learned, where they were headed, and their likely next stops. These types of encounters were the social tinder that helped inform our travel plans and allowed us to tap into the perceptions of others about what they were experiencing.

A crowd gathered, and a young guy produced a skull and crossbones sticker, applied it to my trusty orange helmet and then posed for a photograph.

After Des and I stopped for a feed of kebab and salad, another 75 kilometres brought us to Selçuk. The town is near the ruins of the magnificent ancient city of Efes (Ephesus), the best-preserved Roman city in the Mediterranean region. We set up camp a few metres from the main gate of the archaeological site. When it became dark, the night security officer tried to move us on. We were able to get the message across that Ernie didn't have a functioning headlight, so he allowed us to stay. We barely had the tent up when he returned with his co-worker and a can of insecticide to spray the inside of the tent.

They invited us to join them in their security hut inside Ephesus for *çay*, and the four of us nibbled, sipped, and conversed over the next three hours. We were offered tea and apple slices, followed by three beers. They showed us the intricacies of one of the handguns they carried as security officers. The conversation didn't lapse for a single moment despite the fact we didn't understand Turkish, and they didn't understand English. One of them spoke German. Des and I had acquired a *very* limited vocabulary from our visits to Germany, so that became our common language, along with many gestures and diagrams. Despite our mutual linguistic shortcomings, it was just one more example of what I was learning about language and communication in a travel context. The existence of a common language was secondary to the role that hospitality, kindness, generosity, and a willingness to communicate across cultures played in forging relationships and appreciating people who are culturally and linguistically different.

Istanbul to Anamur, Turkey

Just before midnight, we were escorted back to the tent by torchlight and were quickly swallowed by the darkness inside. Our contented sighs were in unison, along with complimentary comments about how much we'd enjoyed the evening. We'd basked in the generosity of people who didn't know us from a bar of soap and accepted their magnanimousness for what it was — kindness and hospitality in its purest form.

Next morning, we were taking down the tent just as Hüseyin, our friend the night watchman, came pedalling down the hill on his bicycle. We arranged to meet him inside, where he gave us a guided tour in German. We strolled up and down the ancient streets bordered by the ruins of Greek, Roman, and Byzantine architecture that included temples, churches, courtyards, fountains, terrace houses, and statues. Some structures were under reconstruction and restoration, including the magnificent Library of Celsus. We understood very little of Hüseyin's commentary, but we could feel his passion and just being in this extraordinary city of antiquity was a rich experience. Most impressive was the Great Theatre, a huge open amphitheatre with a capacity for 24,000 people. With unbelievable acoustics, it had been the venue for performances, elections, public announcements, speeches, philosophical discussions, and gladiator contests.

After our tour lasting a couple of hours, we followed Hüseyin the three kilometres into Selçuk. For part of the way, we gave him and his bicycle a tow. The three of us then adjourned to a café for kebab, beer, and wine. After coffee at a coffeehouse next door and a confusing dice game with some patrons (that I was to discover later was backgammon), Hüseyin gave us another guided tour. The Ephesus Museum houses some of the best archaeological finds, such as statues and ancient coins excavated from the open-air site at Ephesus. It was a perfect complement to our tour of the ancient city.

Late in the afternoon, we set out for the House of the Virgin Mary, eight kilometres from Selçuk. Hopeless without Hüseyin, we couldn't find it;

Istanbul to Anamur, Turkey

perhaps the beer and wine were contributing factors.

After reflecting on the experience with Hüseyin, I realised my mind had grown a couple of sizes. He epitomized the kindness, generosity, and hospitality of the Turkish people we'd met. It was all offered unconditionally, with no expectation of something tangible or some form of material gain in return.

I was falling in love with the country and its ways.

Our interaction with Hüseyin pointed out an advantage of independent travel. It was one more example of those countless casual encounters and serendipitous travel experiences that are rarely afforded to participants in mainstream tour groups.

Leaving Selçuk and the Aegean Coast, we headed inland in an easterly direction for Denizli, 200 kilometres away. On fading light, as the sun dipped towards the horizon, our shadow lengthened. The incarnadine embers of the spectacularly fiery sunset glowed in the west, reflecting in Ernie's rear-view mirror. As the day bled into dusk, we stopped 75 kilometres short of Denizli and slept under a bridge with the main highway above us. Our sleep was disturbed by a steady stream of sheep trailing past our humble camp, followed by a shepherd who pestered us for a cigarette, which of course we didn't have. The thought struck us that perhaps we should have carried a packet for those occasions when a gift would have been appreciated. However, we couldn't get our minds around our abhorrence of cigarettes and the industry that peddled them.

Our departure for Denizli was later than expected because of Ernie. Despite several withering glares in his direction, he refused to start. Des and I were yoked to our capricious companion, and without his cooperation, we were grounded. The entire morning was invested in finding a cure. After his carburettor and magneto had been cleaned, and his timing reset, Ernie finally acquiesced with a kick-back indicating he was ready to continue the journey.

At this stage of our travels, time didn't feel like a sparse or precious commodity. We had time for anything and everything, and plenty to spare. So, in one respect, Ernie's assumption that serving his every need was our life purpose was less aggravating than it had been on previous occasions.

In another respect, Des was a perfect travelling companion for this type of adventure. He accepted Ernie's curmudgeonly temperament with nonchalance and equanimity, tackling both minor and major maintenance problems head-on, with an imperturbable steadiness. Whether repairing a puncture or piston, refitting a shed exhaust, cleaning a carburettor, resetting the timing, aligning the wheels, or tightening a chain, Des did so mostly without giving a thought to the inconvenience of it all. It was as though he was hard-wired to do so. Given his penchant for old motorcycles, I assumed it came with the territory.

By this time, I'd learned to roll with it. Des's sanguine attitude and matter-of-fact phlegmatic approach to responding to Ernie's ailments had tempered any irritation I felt, my waspishness fading away to acceptance that the two of them would eventually sort things out and we'd be on our way.

Istanbul to Anamur, Turkey

Just 20 kilometres north of Denizli is Pamukkale, site of the ancient Greco-Roman city of Hierapolis. Nature's gifts to Pamukkale are the hot springs and limestone deposits that combine to create a fairyland of dazzling white petrified cascades. Tumbling over the plateau's edge, they create a fantastic formation of stalactites, cataracts, and basins. My eyes devoured the sensory banquet, its unique beauty washing over me like a benediction. At the periphery of my imagination, I couldn't have anticipated such an unbelievable sight.

We rode up to the plateau past the brilliant white cascades of petrified limestone. It was there we discovered the German van we'd met at Ephesus, so we pulled alongside and chatted over a cup of tea and biscuits. Soon after, we were joined by our now friends in the Malaysian-US van.

A scramble over the cascades followed, resulting in a pleasant couple of hours sitting among the swirling waters that gently descended to the valley below. The thermal spring waters, used since Roman times for their therapeutic powers, are laden with calcareous salts. The soft caressing movements of the liquid warmth that flowed around us, combined with the sun's heat, felt as close to utopia as we could get.

A group of nomads had arrived on the slopes above Pamukkale. Our curiosity prevailed, so we rode down the dusty road through the remains of the necropolis (ancient cemetery) and up part of the slope just short of their camp. Wansen and Steve from the Malaysian-US van were there, and several of the nomads and their children had gathered. Lollies were retrieved from one of our panniers and distributed to the youngsters.

These were the Yörüks, Turkic nomads who migrate to the pastures by the coast for the winter. In the spring, they leave the parched vegetation of the coast for the mountainous plateaux and valleys where there is sufficient grass and fodder for the animals until the autumn rains regenerate the coastal pastures.

We cheerfully accepted the invitation to venture into one of the black tents woven with goat's hair, with the cooking source consisting of a fire burning dry camel dung. Beautifully woven kilims were laid out for us to sit on, and water was poured from a goatskin bag into a silver kettle with a long, curved spout. Tea was served, along with light bread and white cheese, presumably made from goats' milk. The Yörüks struck me as a proud, resourceful, and resilient people who had embraced the ancient practice of living life on the move and valued their self-sufficient traditional lifestyle. They were convivial hosts, gracious and generous beyond measure. It all seemed so natural, as though it was their Tao of human interaction, and I was totally wrapped up in such an extraordinary experience. It was a moment of pure travel pleasure. One reason I wanted to travel was to be somewhere else, see something different, and experience something unfamiliar yet unique to that specific place. Enjoying the hospitality of the Yörüks personified that goal. The encounter widened my lens and expanded my worldview by several degrees.

The camels returned to the camp from their grazing lands later in the afternoon. They were huge animals, with one hump. The shepherds, with their enormous sheepskin coats, brought their flocks of sheep and herds of goats to the confines of the camp for the night. With so many fine animals, to my Western eye and privileged perspective, the Yörüks appeared to be quite affluent by local rural standards.

In the evening, Ernie was parked among the ruins of the necropolis with the German and Malaysian-US vans, and we all participated in a giant curry cook-up, Malaysian style.

The necropolis was one of the most extensive and best-preserved in Anatolia with its tumuli, sarcophagi, and house-shaped tombs dating from the late Hellenistic period to early Christian times. It was quite large, spreading out on both sides of the road for about two kilometres.

Our approach to free camping resulted in our being both thrifty and enterprising at the same time. The tomb Ernie was parked in front of was austere and unembellished, and met our needs perfectly. It held three elevated slabs, just the right size for three bodies. Dan from the Malaysian-US van joined us, and within the penumbra of candlelight, we chatted until the candle melted. Surprisingly enough, despite Dan's wealth of spooky stories, it was a warm and peaceful sleep.

We were realizing that the best discoveries are rarely what we plan and are more often the result of serendipitous encounters. Such was our interaction with the nomads. They fascinated us, and we were eager to reconnect with them the following morning. As the sun began its leisurely ascent, leaking light and colour across the slopes, Des and I hiked towards their camp to mingle with the shepherds. They were tending to their animals that included sheep and goats, a few cows, and donkeys. They indicated that the camels were grazing in the surrounding hills. By this time, Ingrid from the German van had joined us, so the three of us climbed up the slope hoping to find them. The area was deserted, and the camels weren't in sight, but we stumbled across huts and shelters made of rocks, mud, and branches that we presumed had been built by settled and sedentary peoples.

We descended to the necropolis via various tracks etched by multi-generations of animals to find Spanish rice cooking in the German van. After a successful search for the Malaysian-US van, we bought nine bottles of beer to complement the Spanish rice. Afterwards, Des and the Yankee guys went swimming, and I ventured into Denizli with the two Malaysians to pick up supplies.

Later in the afternoon, Des and I ran into Ken and Jill Duncalfe, the Kiwi couple we'd met back in Yugoslavia. We grabbed a beer at the local motel to catch up on their news and invited them to join us back at the necropolis. With Jill and Ken joining our little international coterie, it had grown to three vans, one motorcycle, and 11 people.

The warm tomb where Des, Dan, and I slept on the first night had grown in popularity with the result that Hon Chi from the Malaysian-US van replaced Dan for the second night.

The next day, we decided to leave Pamukkale and return to the road. After washing a few clothes in warm water collected from the thermal stream, Jill, Ken, and I went to the motel that provided non-guests with access to their pool. It appeared to have been built amongst the ruins of the ancient city of Hierapolis, as segments of columns and chunks of stone blocks littered the sandy floor. The thermal stream had been channelled through the pool, and the warm water was so invigorating it was difficult to tear ourselves away.

It bears mentioning that 40 years later, I travelled to Selçuk and Ephesus, but I couldn't bear to visit Pamukkale. The evocative memories of 1973 had left an indelible impression. They were so profound that my interest in preserving them was stronger than any curiosity I could muster to explore present-day Pamukkale. I feared that decades of tour buses and countless human footprints had surely tarnished the landscape, forcing the authorities to impose restrictions on access to the natural phenomena that were one of Pamukkale's greatest gifts. I pictured the descendants of the nomads no longer tending their herds, but selling kitschy souvenirs, useless baubles, and pointless ephemera to the hordes of tourists. I knew I'd be disappointed discovering nothing approaching the magic of 1973, so I chose to stay away and keep my memories intact.

We left Pamukkale bound for Antalya, 250 kilometres away. Ken and Jill followed us, but after a much-needed hot coffee stop 100 kilometres later, positions were reversed with Ernie, Des, and me behind the van. This enabled Ernie to use their slipstream for protection and relief from the wind. We stopped late in the afternoon, just 40 kilometres short of Antalya, where the four of us enjoyed a cook-up of stew and rice.

We were destined to spend more time with Ken and Jill. When we first met in Yugoslavia, after dispensing with the banal preliminaries of where we were from, where we'd been, and where we were headed, Ken, Jill, Des, and I instantly bonded, slipping quickly and seamlessly into a comfortable and easy-going relationship. We were of a similar age, and they represented the familiar faces of home, an incarnation of childhood friends we grew up with, the kids next door. Our shared vernacular meant conversation flowed smoothly, and it was inevitable we'd have long discussions about travel. Des and I voraciously devoured their tales of past adventures, especially their south-to-north journey up the entire continent of Africa in their Kombi. In addition, their company offered Des and me a welcome respite from being encapsulated in our two-person bubble by injecting much-appreciated variety in conversation and social interaction.

Now, 40 kilometres from Antalya, we wiled away several hours enjoying their companionship and conversation around an open fire. The atmosphere was felicitous. We'd long since graduated from the mundane placeholder questions that dominated first encounters. Under an incandescent moon-ruled sky, the conversation ricocheted between tales of high adventure, perseverance, missteps, averted disasters, and places not yet seen. Our stories were sprinkled with embellishments that were a storyteller's prerogative to include. Among the four of us, Des ruled when it came to hyperbole, inflated statistics, and exaggerated anecdotes.

The next day, the ride to Antalya required just one stop to replace Ernie's shed muffler. After picking up hot bread, tomatoes, and grapes in Antalya, Des and I ˚celebrated seeing the sea again by enjoying our purchases overlooking an enviable view of the Mediterranean. The day was warm and sunny under a cloudless blue sky, and the sea sparkled like a blanket of turquoise-coloured sequins. Ken and Jill came along just as we were about to leave, so lingering a little longer wasn't a tough decision to make. This was the south coast of Turkey, the 1,600-kilometre Mediterranean shore known as the Turquoise Coast. The Taurus Mountains form a dramatic backdrop along much of the coast, often dropping steeply into the sea. The coastline is blessed with beautiful beaches, ancient sites, attractive coastal villages, fertile alluvial plains, and a climate that supports the cultivation of ... bananas!

But that wasn't the only surprise. When we stumbled across stands of eucalyptus trees, as straight as pickets on a wrought-iron fence reaching for the heavens, it all felt just a bit like home. The winding section of paved perfection seduced us for several kilometres through air heavily scented with the delightful aroma of eucalyptus caressing our nostrils.

As Des twisted the throttle and with our knees dipping close to the pavement as Ernie leaned and rolled with the contours, we flitted through patches of sun and shade created by the gum trees. Their shadows wove veils of grey and purple across the road. Ernie wasn't capable of breaking any speed records, and this was a good thing because it meant enjoying the ride and the view. As Des manoeuvred Ernie around each bend with steely concentration, I selfishly soaked up the scenery. Such was one of the infinite pleasures of a pillion.

It was one of those roads and days for which motorcycles were invented.

Approximately 130 kilometres later, we took a break at Alanya, a favoured seaside resort of the Seljuk Turks 800 years ago. Built on a promontory jutting into the sea is an imposing fortress constructed in the 13th century by the Seljuk Sultan Alaaddin Keykubat. However, its foundations date to the Hellenistic period (323 BC to 30 BC). Surrounded by a 6.5-kilometre-long wall, the fortress boasts 140 towers, and inside are several old structures such as brick cisterns, baths, and Byzantine churches. It was one more example of the rich history of Turkey's past.

Back on the road, we had trouble purchasing petrol at the next four gas stations. There was not a drop to be had. Eventually running out and for the first time in many weeks, we flipped Ernie over to redistribute what little petrol was in the tank — a tactic that usually bought us enough kilometres to reach the next station. Des gave Ernie a slight whiff of throttle to conserve the remaining fuel, and it seemed like he was running on fumes. When we ran out again, we began to push and cruise, and in the distance spotted a Kombi towards which we ran and pushed and cruised some more. The two Germans from the van sold us some petrol that enabled us to reach a gas station where we could finally fill the tank. We stopped not long after, only to be joined a little later by Ken and Jill. As it was close to the end of the day, we all parked under the branches of an enormous tree that allowed small trapezoids of remaining sunlight to bathe the sand underneath. Des and I tested fate once more by sleeping under a lean-to against Ernie.

The next day we passed many banana plantations. The climate around Anamur, a short distance of 100 kilometres across the sea from Cyprus, is very hot and the only part of Turkey that can sustain the cultivation of bananas. I was incredulous that bananas could be grown in this part of the world.

Travelling through this region of Turkey brought an elevated sense of awareness of a life being changed by what I was seeing, experiencing, and feeling. Here I was in what felt like a separate universe from my roots, travelling through banana plantations and forests of eucalyptus similar to those I'd grown up with in Queensland. But this was different. With wheels turning both figuratively and metaphorically, a pillion's perch offered plenty of time and space for reflection and introspection. The familiar taste of home was wrapped in a different mantle. With each new glimpse of the stunning coastline, every visit to historical sites, and every encounter with locals and other travellers, I realised that "I am not the same having seen the moon shine on the other side of the world."

Istanbul to Anamur, Turkey

Chapter 12:
Anamur, Turkey to Tehran, Iran

Anne Betts

"Adventure should be part of everyone's life. It is the whole difference between being fully alive and just existing."
Holly Morris, Adventure Divas: Searching the Globe for Women Who Are Changing the World

History and nature converge along this spectacular stretch of coastline where magnificent waterfront fortresses hold court with nature's own palaces of unrivalled beauty. So as the Mediterranean stretched calm and delightful under the morning sun, we toured the impressive Mamure Castle. With its moats, turrets, and 39 towers, the ancient fortress is nestled between two curving beaches close to Anamur. One of the best-fortified castles in Turkey, it was initially built by the Romans in the 3rd or 4th century AD, and later enlarged by the Byzantines and the Crusaders. Rebuilt to its present form in the 13th century after being captured by the Seljuks, it was extensively repaired, and for this reason acquired the name 'Mamure,' meaning developed or improved. What a grand and imposing place it must have been all those centuries ago. I couldn't help but wonder what tumultuous events had been

The Ernie Diaries

thwarted by those massive walls, and what life had been like behind them. Back on the road and with our rain gear confidently stowed, we basked in the pools of dappled shade the trees cast across the pavement. We were riding through pine-clad mountainous terrain that spoiled us with stunning views over the mountain flanks and adjacent cliffs and coves edging the sea.

Down to our last nine lira, we spent it on petrol in the hope it would enable us to reach Silifke, where we were fairly confident we'd be able to change a traveller's cheque.

After changing money and stocking up on food and petrol in Silifke, we spotted a beach worthy of dissolving ourselves in its beauty, and pausing long enough to enjoy delicious tomato sandwiches. With the sun bathing us in glorious late afternoon warmth, we pressed on in search of Ken and Jill. Ernie's magneto needed treatment and Ken had wanted to give their van an oil change, so the four of us had decided to find a suitable spot to camp for a day or so.

They were parked on the beach, the only campers at a campground not far from Silifke. We bargained with the camp manager and obtained the two nights for TL10 (30 pence). Des broke out the Araldite and set to work on the magneto. Lo and behold, we were soon distracted by arms making vigorous semaphoric movements from the Malaysian-US van passing on the road above. They pulled in, followed soon after by the German van from Pamukkale, then a Norwegian van the Germans had met along the way. They all unsuccessfully tried for the same rate we'd negotiated. Standing stoic and inscrutable, with one hand resting on his forehead in a sun-shielding salute and the other smoothing his curved opulent moustache, the camp manager refused to budge. As a result, the prospective customers decided to drive on in search of cheaper pastures.

We were to learn from the manager that their flash vans were a detriment to securing the lower rate. His comment, "They can afford it" exposed his view of when to negotiate and when to stand firm. Ken and Jill's Kombi was old and battered, with a stoved-in front from hitting an animal in Africa. Ernie? Ernie was … well, Ernie. If that wasn't enough to lend credence to our perceived lack of affluence in the eyes of the manager, our sartorial standards were such that it was clear Des and I hadn't stepped off the cover of Vogue. He took pity on our indigence, and we scored the discount. In the face of the more expensive vehicles, he maintained his dignity, despite missing out on the additional revenue.

The sea, painted in every shade of green known to humankind, tempted us to dip our feet to see if it was real. It was, but being November after all, Poseidon's playground wasn't warm enough to entice us into taking a dip. A gentle offshore breeze coaxed ripples to roll across the surface, adding texture to the sparkling veneer. Above, wisps of white added slight smudges to the azure streaks of a bright Mediterranean sky. Nature was at her most benevolent and munificent yet seemed indifferent to our admiration.

It was a perfect late afternoon in a perfect setting. Out came the Frisbee, and some locals produced a football. After sitting on a motorcycle for several hours, the exercise hit the spot. When the sun started to fade, we tried to replicate, as best we could with our stove and skills, kebab with onions and chili peppers. Afterwards, Ken and Jill joined us for çay and cream biscuits under the camp lean-to we'd claimed.

The following day at the campsite was a relatively lazy one, spent reading, washing, repairing Ernie's exhaust, and tossing a Frisbee about. Des tried his hand at fishing, but just like in Yugoslavia, the fish had nothing to fear. Our evening ritual enjoying çay and biscuits over conversation was replaced with çay and pancakes, in Ken and Jill's van.

During the night, lightning bolts ripped the sky apart at the seams, followed by a gale unleashing a tempest on our modest little camp. It brought down the lean-to, snatched our belongings, and scattered them along the beach. We collected what we could in the darkness and left retrieval of the rest until morning.

Thankfully, the new day welcomed dawn as it broke through the vaporous mist, offering a pleasant contrast to the wrath of the night before. Ken and Jill were away early, but we needed to refit Ernie's magneto and salvage what we could of our strewn possessions. Two sections of tent poles were missing, as well as my swimsuit bottom and a pair of leggings. Des's visor was half-buried in sand at the water's edge, and the Frisbee had been blown across the water and trapped under a rocky ledge. After recovering the visor and the Frisbee and searching unsuccessfully for the other missing items, we followed the coast to Mersin where we stopped for a new visor for Des, şiş kebab, and a few vegetables.

For 500 glorious kilometres, we'd answered the siren call of the road and followed the twists and turns of the southern edge of Turkey. With the regular heartbeat of Ernie's single piston and his tyres singing on the tarmac, we had thoroughly enjoyed the rhythm and thrill of the ride. It was as though those spiralling ribbons of road had been engineered by a motorcyclist. We experienced feelings of total freedom, immersed in the spectacular scenery as the asphalted snake wound its way around cliff edges and infinite stretches of sandy beaches and sheltered coves.

At Mersin, we left the coast and embarked on the 300-kilometre ride north to Göreme through the Taurus Mountains. Almost immediately, the climatic change was palpable, the cold attacking with the silence of a school of piranhas. On the trip so far, our bodies had registered significant degrees of temperature change as we rode through different microclimates, but this was beyond belief. The plummeting temperature greeted us with a vengeance, sucking us into its strangling embrace.

Roughly 70 kilometres later, we were forced to stop at a restaurant for temporary relief from the biting cold that gnawed its way through our bodies, from the epidermis to the marrow. After a fix of döner kebab that we devoured with haste in case it escaped, we reluctantly left the warmth of the stove. For the next hour or so, the cold was so intense that it felt as though the piranhas had been joined by a flock of carnivorous birds buzzing menacingly around us, ready to strike at any moment. Just beyond Niğde, the sun slipped slowly behind the paprika-dusted volcanic peaks, taking with it any notion of an imagined sense of warmth.

The colours of the setting sun danced with a fiery orange glow but enjoying them was out of the question as we were preoccupied with finding refuge from the bitterly cold conditions. As the day's remaining light faded from the sky, we parked Ernie in a quarry spotted from the road, and shivered and shook our way to the gaping maw of a cave yawning with an invitation to venture inside. It gobbled us whole, and in a corner well back from the cave's mouth, anything and everything that had the potential to provide warmth was arranged for sleeping.

While doing so, I wondered if snakes were residents of Turkey. Without the relevant volume of Encyclopedia Britannica at our disposal, I assumed they were. Given my experience with snakes in Australia, the weather was such that they would be hibernating. As long as hibernation didn't involve a cosy cave, we were golden. And given Des's reaction to a couple of harmless snakes in Yugoslavia, I swatted these thoughts aside and kept them to myself.

After soup and tomato sandwiches, we climbed into the wombs of our sleeping bags buried under the mound of clothing, towels, tent, and PVC plastic fly. It was too cold to read, talk, or even exist but mercifully, sleep eventually came. The night was long and cold, the coldest I'd ever experienced. It was a low point of subterranean proportions.

After a restless sleep, morning brought the dismal reminder that we'd left the favourable climate of the coast and were headed into the uncertain winter conditions of Central Turkey. Des whinged that where the draw-cord of his sleeping bag puckered to create a small opening, it was as though someone had been pushing the sharp point of an icicle against his head throughout the night. It was so cold that his hair hurt. Meanwhile, fog from my breath wafted above my sleeping bag, hanging ominously within the cave.

From our troglodytic den, I ventured outside to find thick white frost on Ernie's protective covering, glistening like an army of malicious white demons.

Continuing to shiver where we were seemed like our best option, hoping it would give the weak sun a chance to thaw Ernie. Meanwhile, back in the cave, my frozen fingers slowly revealed the lid on the water container frozen on its thread. A solid block of ice was floating inside. Even the toothpaste was frozen in its tube. To someone born and raised in the sub-tropical temperatures of South East Queensland, these were definitely new experiences!!

At 10.00 a.m., the sun had failed to surrender her rays, and the expected heat of the new day wasn't forthcoming. There was nought to be accomplished by staying put, so with impatient optimism, we made a run for it. With our frosty breaths expelled in long white blasts, packing up in such brutal conditions required the dexterity of bare hands while the minutes slid past like glaciers.

It was abundantly clear that summer's seasonal successor had well and truly descended upon us, but there were no thoughts of turning back. At least there were none that were articulated. We were in for a penny, in for a pound.

Hypothermia comes quickly on a motorcycle, and I figured I was likely in the early stages by the time we'd travelled 50 kilometres. But I had no body of corporeal knowledge that comes with living in these types of conditions. Where I grew up, we started piling on the layers the moment the temperature dropped below 20 degrees Celsius. Two things were certain — the cold was stupefyingly brutal, and we were fighting an unequal battle with the weather. Actually, there was another — this quandary was largely self-induced and predictable. We'd left our fate in the fickle hands of the elements. Our feckless and shambolic approach to assembling appropriate clothing was outcome determinative; we should have invested more thought, research, and a larger slice of our budget in clothing capable of keeping us warm and dry in the vagaries of a Northern Hemisphere winter.

Thoughts of stumbling across a warm restaurant were bouncing around inside my helmet when we spotted the mirage that was the German van. It was a feast for sore eyes and partially assuaged my frozen state. I was never more happy to dismount. With my legs barely obeying me, in my teeth-chattering misery, I moved at a glacial pace towards it. Ingrid quickly put the kettle on for a cuppa, and my body worked overtime to reheat itself during the hour-long respite in their warm abode.

The day was defined by the cold, and the 300 kilometres from Mersin to Göreme felt like 3,000.

Once again, Ernie's indomitable spirit was a godsend. It seemed like he'd appointed himself as our guardian, with his role to protect us from harm. This uncanny ability to recognise when he needed to step up to the plate

Anamur, Turkey to Tehran, Iran

and safely deliver us to our destination with no unnecessary trauma or delays was his most appreciated feature. At times like this, he was a paragon of perfection.

It wasn't the first and last time I felt closer to the chalice of Ernie. When it counted, he was our saviour. He had an exceptional ability to read a desperate situation like Vasco da Gama could read a map. As we left the warmth of the German van and returned to Ernie, I reverentially caressed his tank as a mark of gratitude for his strength, endurance, and reliability with murmurs of "You beauty, Ernie!" I had the sense he basked in the glow of my adoration and hoped it would inspire him to press on to Göreme as quickly as his wheels would allow. With calm and intrepidity, he rose to the occasion, and within an hour we were in Göreme, in the heart of Cappadocia.

We spied Ken and Jill's van in the parking lot of the open-air museum. They were genuinely surprised to see us, convinced we'd turned back. We treated each other like long-lost friends, and the warmth of the reunion brought temporary relief from the cold. The night before, they'd camped 20 kilometres from us and the temperature in their van that morning had been −16°C. We were somewhat relieved to find that it really had been cold, and we weren't getting soft.

Cappadocia is dotted with volcanic outcrops eroded by wind and water, leaving hard cap rock on top of conical pillars of softer rock. Standing enigmatically like miniature peaks, they fill entire valleys. These 'fairy chimneys' attain heights of up to 40 metres. Earlier inhabitants of the stalagmite-studded landscape realised that the soft rock could be carved out to create houses and churches, and even underground cities.

To take our minds off the cold, the four of us went for a wander around the carved-out churches and monasteries with their faded yet colourful frescoes and coffin-shaped graves excavated into the floor. Unfortunately, the cold brought an untimely end to what would have been a fascinating tour under warmer conditions.

The Ernie Diaries

We retreated to Jill and Ken's van and fired up the cooker for heat. Between that and the measly contribution of our body heat, we were able to get the temperature inside their van up to zero. Thinking our tent would be inadequate for the conditions, at the Göreme campground we asked the manager if we could shelter overnight in the outside shower block. When he suggested we sleep on the restaurant floor beside the wood-burning stove, we wasted no time in accepting the invitation. What a gift!
With daylight came the onslaught of other campers to the stove. I rolled over and peered between the slithering tendrils of melting snowflakes on the plate-glass windows. The ground was draped in a white sheet of snow.

It continued to snow all morning, and we remained close to the stove, contemplating our options.

Between Cappadocia and Iran is the mountainous region of Eastern Anatolia with an average altitude of 2,000 metres. The road passes Ağrı Dağı (Mount Ararat), traditionally associated as the mountain on which Noah's Ark came to rest at the end of the great Flood. At 5,137 metres, it is Turkey's highest peak. We were currently at 1,100 metres, so the prospect of going higher and further in this inhospitable climate wasn't at all appealing. Ken, Jill, Des, and I discussed the possibility of travelling to Iran via Syria and Iraq, but none of us had visas, and we weren't prepared to take our chances at the borders. Besides, Syria was a combatant in the Yom Kippur War, and the whole point of travelling to Iran was to put time and distance between us and the hostilities.

Remaining committed to our recent resolve to visit Iran was looking more and more dubious. However, on the way to Göreme, we'd heard a train in the distance. It offered a glimmer of hope and warranted investigation as a possible means for Des, Ernie, and me to travel east.

After a cook-up of eggs and chips in the campground kitchen, Jill and Ken decided to push on. Des and I sat around the stove reading, and later, Adnan, one of the camp residents, gave us a useful lesson in rudimentary Turkish. Around 3.00 p.m., we injected a modicum of activity by venturing outside as it had long stopped snowing and appeared to be warmer. The novelty of freshly fallen snow had all but dissipated, and thoughts of snowballs and snowmen were as appealing as a case of head lice. After 200 metres, my ears had become frozen beyond feeling. We hurriedly took a couple of photographs and returned to within a warmer radius of the stove.

Like Prague, Cappadocia was one place I knew I would have to return to under more favourable conditions to appreciate its worth and beauty. I'm fortunate I could eventually do both. It would be several decades later that I was able to return to Cappadocia in more welcoming September temperatures, and appreciate its unique landscape via hiking trails, a rental car, and a hot-air balloon.

Confined to the warmth of indoors, I read Harold Robbins' *A Stone for Danny Fisher* until the stove became ours and we crawled into our sleeping bags for the night.

Des and I had our sights on the train as a possible means to escape the miserable conditions. After unsuccessful attempts to telephone the station at Kayseri for information, at 1.00 p.m. the next day we packed up Ernie and rode the 70 kilometres to the station. It was extremely cold but nowhere near as unbearable as the last time we were on the road. Perhaps the delectable idea of a heated train had something to do with it.

At the railway station, our vantage point in a short queue afforded an ideal spot from which to observe the interaction between the ticket agent and the woman in front. To our Western ears and eyes, clicking your tongue at someone displays displeasure. When accompanied by raised eyebrows and a quick upward tilt of the chin, it accentuates disapproval. Not so in Turkey; these gestures mean 'No.' Two clicking-of-the-tongue tut-tuts and two exaggerated upward tilts mean 'That's definitely a no.' Such was the response the woman received from the ticket agent.

A single nod downward means 'Yes.' That's the one we were looking for when we reached the head of the queue. Luck was on our side. The eastbound train was due the following afternoon, and Ernie could travel as baggage. Thanks to Adnan's lesson the previous day, I stumbled clumsily over "tesh-ay-coor-eddie-rim," undoubtedly eliding one or two critical consonants or vowels and totally mangling *teşekkür ederim* (thank you.) The smile in response reflected an appreciation of my efforts. Or perhaps it was a silent indicator of *I have no idea what you just said*. I went with the former, but clearly more practice on my Turkish was in order.

While at the station, we bumped into three English travellers and followed them back to their hotel. After booking in, a place was found for Ernie in a corner of reception. It wouldn't be the only time we could park Ernie indoors as a treasured non-paying guest. It was one of the benign mysteries that made travelling in Turkey infinitely worthwhile. His value as our means of transportation was recognised, and unlike a car or a van, he couldn't be secured in a similar manner. We retired with a packet of cream biscuits and books until the poms came by to invite us to join them for kebab. Des and I tagged along and later headed to a çay shop where one of the patrons attempted to teach us backgammon. At 9.00 p.m., we went to the movies for TL4 (12 pence) and enjoyed two Turkish movies against a background of cracking and munching of sunflower and pumpkin seeds within the audience. Upon our return to the hotel, we were ecstatic to find hot water coming through the showerhead, so after a long and thorough wash, we hunkered down for the night.

The next day was devoted to stocking up on provisions at the Kayseri Grand Bazaar, filling our basket with oranges, apples, grapes, chocolate, and lollies. Des and I each bought a goat's hair balaclava under the watchful eyes of a crowd that had gathered to observe the process. I tried mine on for size, but Des neglected to do so, and we later discovered it didn't fit. After enjoying what was possibly our last döner kebab, we stopped by the hotel to fetch Ernie and set out for the station around 2.00 p.m.

Operated by TCDD (Türkiye Cumhuriyeti Devlet Demiryolları or Turkish State Railways), the section of the Turkey – Iran line between Kayseri and Lake Van had been in service for nine years. While the railway provided the means to avoid many agonizingly cold days on the road, we were looking forward to the experience of train travel in this part of the world.

With a student discount of 50 per cent, we purchased second-class tickets to Van, a town in eastern Turkey's Van Province. Des was asked to drain the petrol from Ernie, doing so under the careful supervision of a crowd that had gathered to watch. When the train pulled into the station, we were told to push Ernie down to the baggage car, the entrance to which was at least a metre above the platform. The conductor's request to hoist Ernie up was easier said than done, but a group of willing helpers materialised almost instantly, and Ernie was effortlessly lifted into the car.

More recently in rural areas, we'd observed a behaviour that might have been considered rude in other cultures. People would gather and stare at us. Perhaps it was our hair and skin colour, dress, or mode of transportation that singled us out as objects of curiosity. We put it down to a natural inquisitiveness that might have involved dialogue had there been a common language. However, one endearing aspect of what we experienced was that at the first indication we needed assistance, help was forthcoming, and, like hospitality we'd enjoyed elsewhere, it was offered unconditionally.

As the guard's whistle shrilled down the length of the platform, the train stretched its spine to accompanying hisses, clangs, and clunks before pulling away from the station. Des and I ran past several carriages to climb aboard before the train gathered speed.

Without too much difficulty, we found the compartment we were sharing with a Turkish family. After tossing our gear in an overhead rack, we went in search of the poms we'd met the day before to chat, and generally enjoy the first segment of the journey together. On our return to the compartment, our couchettes were down. We climbed up, and the soporific effect of the motion of the train meant we were quickly lulled into hypnotic sleep.

By the time the train pulled out of Elazig around 6.00 a.m., it had emptied of many of its passengers. Des and I found a compartment to ourselves for what remained (334 kilometres) of the trip until the end of the railway line at the Tatvan Wharf. The steady roll of the train rationed momentary glimpses of the snow-covered landscape through a thick protective screen of plate glass. As the beauty washed over me, I visualized riding over these lands, with an accompanying involuntary shiver. Basking in what was one of the best decisions of the trip, we savoured the images from the warmth and comfort of the train.

Anamur, Turkey to Tehran, Iran

At 3.30 p.m., the train arrived at the Tatvan Wharf on the western edge of Lake Van, the largest lake in Turkey and the biggest sodium carbonate lake in the world. It has been said that it's possible to wash clothes in its water without using any soap or detergent. We were now at 1,720 metres above sea level, and it was cold enough. What were we thinking when we'd planned to ride Ernie through this region of Turkey???

The next part of our journey involved crossing Lake Van from Tatvan to Van, a distance of 96 kilometres. When the section of the railway line from Van to Iran was built, it was deemed easier and cheaper to cross Lake Van by ferry rather than build a line around the lake through mountainous terrain without a convenient pass.

At the end of the line at Tatvan, passengers poured out of the train like lemmings, rushing through the biting air for the warmth of the ferry. Ernie was hauled down from the baggage car, and we obtained some petrol from Klaus, also travelling by motorcycle. Klaus was a longhaired, bearded German about our age, and his 200cc Zündapp was even older than Ernie. In the event I needed more information, with an enthusiast's glint in his

eyes, Des added that it had a single-cylinder two-stroke engine producing 12.0 horsepower. By this time, I had learned that motorcycle enthusiasts thrived on these types of pedantic details, but I was more interested in the fact we now had the petrol needed to drive down to the western edge of the lake. Needless to say, I was aware of the absence of inter-marque rivalry and grateful for the helping hand that was at the heart of the motorcyclists' creed.

Straight off the ferry after a four-hour trip across Lake Van, we were quickly swallowed by darkness. Back on terra firma that didn't feel very solid, it was completely white, with each contour disguised under a foot of snow. A combination of darkness, snow, and lack of Ernie lights meant that Des missed the road angling off to the right, and we uncontrollably bumped our way down the railway track, bouncing over the concealed rail sleepers. How we'd clamber over the slippery steel rails eluded us for a disturbingly long time. Eventually, Des and Ernie figured out how to reach the road, and we were sucked into a vortex of stimulation, speculation, and trepidation. The seven-kilometre ride to Van was a mixture of discomfort (given the snow and no headlight, not to mention the episode with the railway sleepers), excitement (with the new experience), and apprehension (about whether we would reach our destination and what we would find when we arrived). It was a slow trip as the road was very icy and one wrong turn in the dim light could see our little entourage entombed until discovery in the spring. At the first hotel, we bumped into Klaus and learned that the hotels were all packed to capacity, so Klaus, Des, and I slept on the floor around a coal-burning stove in the reception area.

A jab in the back accompanied by a request to move away from the stove so it could be refuelled at 5.30 a.m. wasn't an ideal way to welcome the new day. We spent the next couple of hours drinking çay before taking a dolmuş back to the wharf for information on the train to Iran. Then, it was back to Van to buy our tickets to Tehran.

We'd arranged to meet up for lunch with several travellers we'd spent time with on the train. Afterwards, we found a hotel that could accommodate us all. By this time our group numbered eight — John, Peter, and Valerie (English, the poms we'd met in Kayseri), Klaus (German), Dave (American), Michel (French), and Des and me. We occupied two rooms, four to a room. Valerie and I had a Turkish bath, and when we told the manager the water was cold, he didn't charge us. The rest of the day was spent in the warmth of the hotel, reading and playing cards before heading out for an evening meal.

The next day, we lay about until late morning, chatting with some Australian, Canadian, Dutch, and English travellers who were staying at the same hotel. In the afternoon, a vacant lot provided an ideal location for flinging the Frisbee about. We mixed it up with snowballs and eventually left the Frisbee behind with a bunch of kids who'd joined us. On arriving at the station at 6.00 p.m. for the expected departure of 7.00 p.m., we were disappointed to learn that the train would not arrive before 1.00 a.m. Presumably, it was coming from the border as the gauges of Turkish and Iranian railways differed.

We descended on the local çay house, and I finally picked up how to play backgammon, the great equalizer and popular game known in Turkey as tavla. It was a pleasant evening until I needed to go to the loo. There wasn't one. I ventured outside and found a dark corner in the snow. It was only when I was pulling up my knickers and jeans did I see the guy who had followed me out. As he grabbed me, the bitter taste of fight or flight was immediate, propelling me to do both. It was at times like this that I wished a more imposing and courageous version of myself could miraculously appear as my doppelgänger and remain behind to spar with this idiot. With no help at hand, I threw both feet and hands in his direction as rapidly and forcefully as I could and ran inside as fast as possible. With adrenalin coursing through my veins, by the time I reached the crowded refuge indoors, I was trembling. Our experience in Turkey so far had provided no indication that I needed to fear for my safety or take precautions such as requiring an escort to go to the loo. Unfortunately, the incident outside the çay house was just the beginning. We'd arrived in dystopia.

Our route back to the station was lined with lecherous young men preying on the women. It was like running the gauntlet to reach what we thought would be the safe haven of the train.

Anamur, Turkey to Tehran, Iran

A carriage had been rustled up for us for the night, and more lechers were lying in wait in passageways to accost the women as we arrived. By this time, most travellers had long passed their patience thresholds, and some of the offending males were forced to retreat while clutching their private parts. The women sought sanctuary in the compartments, and a few guys remained behind to discourage further unwanted attention. The rest of our group went to the baggage car to hoist up Klaus's bike and Ernie. To add insult to injury, on arrival at the station we found that my crash helmet had gone missing. After organizing Ernie, Des made a futile attempt to locate its whereabouts. We then spread ourselves out in the security of the compartment to grab a few hours of sleep.

It was morning before I woke and realized we were still in Van. It was a horrible conclusion to reach first thing in the morning, given the events of the night before. The new day brought some brightness — the lechers of Van were gone, replaced by cold and weary travellers transported across Lake Van on the ferry. Some were trying to find warmth by entering the already full compartments, and the rest remained outside, shivering in the snow, rucksacks heavy on their backs.

It was 7.00 a.m. Departure was 12 hours overdue. The train took an additional two hours to be assembled, and the passengers squeezed inside. The passageways were cluttered with people and rucksacks, and movement to the toilets at both ends of each carriage was nearly impossible. Fourteen hours late, the train pulled out of Van at 9.00 a.m. as cheers echoed down the length of the train. The 60-hour ordeal in Van was over.

I was puzzled by the physically aggressive, sexist behaviour encountered in Van as I waded through the web of bewilderment trying to make sense of it all. It was uncharacteristic of what I'd experienced elsewhere in Turkey. The yahoos of Van seemed to embrace what they regarded as an inherent right to grope women, and I'd hazard a guess: western women. I sensed that Turkish mothers, grandmothers, sisters, and other Turkish women wouldn't have countenanced such outrageous behaviour. I wondered what it was about. It wasn't just the one isolated incident; something more pervasive was at work. Did it have anything to do with the fact that the railway line from Van to Iran had been in operation for only two years? Had this brought an influx of western women who were known primarily by how they were portrayed in films and advertising imported from the West? Did the companionship of Des shield me from unwanted attention elsewhere? In Van, were we perceived as a collection of individual travellers in transit and the women as single, unattached, and available? Whatever the reasons, it was abhorrent, and an unfortunate blemish on what appeared to be an interesting town steeped in a rich and remarkable history.

The more I thought about it, the more envious I became of the power bestowed on men at birth. It grants male travellers the privilege of being left alone for the most part, free to wander without having to invest an inordinate amount of energy to avoid being groped and assaulted.

It was at times like this that I appreciated the wisdom of the great Mahatma Gandhi, who said, "You must not lose faith in humanity. Humanity is an ocean; if a few drops of the ocean are dirty, the ocean does not become dirty." By the time we'd reached Iran, the lechers of Van had become a minor blip in the grand scheme of things. My love affair with Turkey was still intact, just temporarily tarnished.

There were delays at both frontiers. As we left Turkey at the Kapıköy crossing, my departure as well as Ernie's ÇIKIŞ *('exit')* *were recorded* in my passport. At the entry into Iran at the Razi border station, Ernie's existence in the baggage car seemed to have escaped the scrutiny of Iranian officials, and his entry into Iran wasn't recorded in either of our passports.

What did all this mean? With respect to Iran, it was a critical omission that worked in our favour. Entering Iran without a record of Ernie's existence stamped in Des's or my passport created an option for us to leave Iran without him, should we be so inclined.

Arriving in Iran without the record of Ernie's entry stamped in one of our passports highlighted the significance of entering and leaving countries like Turkey and Iran with a vehicle. When leaving both countries, if the vehicle didn't accompany the passport holder, a hefty import tax was levied before the person was permitted to leave. Searching for a ride east whilst in Istanbul, we were oblivious to this important fact. As fate would have it, our unsuccessful attempts to obtain a ride worked to our advantage. Had we reached the cold and desolate frontier without Ernie, we would surely have been stranded because we didn't have the desire (or the funds) to pay such a substantial and excessive sum. We had no record of Ernie's value, so some kind of bureaucratic book value far in excess of what Ernie was actually worth would have been imposed. We would have been forced to remain in Turkey.

We were later told of a scrapyard of vehicles abandoned by their owners beside the road at the Turkish-Iranian border. It was littered with the corpses of vehicles that had wheezed their final breaths up to the frontier or had been towed or brought on trucks and dumped once their owners had their passports stamped. Travellers were prepared to go to extraordinary lengths to avoid paying the exorbitant tax.

At the Iranian post, one of the passenger carriages was hauled away from beneath us, and the already overloaded train became packed beyond a reasonable assessment of capacity. With night, most passengers squeezed into compartments, but many unfortunates slept in passageways. Our six-berth compartment held nine passengers.

Despite the lechers of Van and the train's arrival in Tehran 17 hours late, the journey proved worthwhile. We'd met many young people heading for India and beyond, and the almost 2,000-kilometre trip cost the equivalent of £14.50 in fares for the three of us. Des and I obtained student concessions that applied to humans only, not motorcycles. As a result, Ernie travelled at full fare (£5). The train journey proved the warmer method of travel.

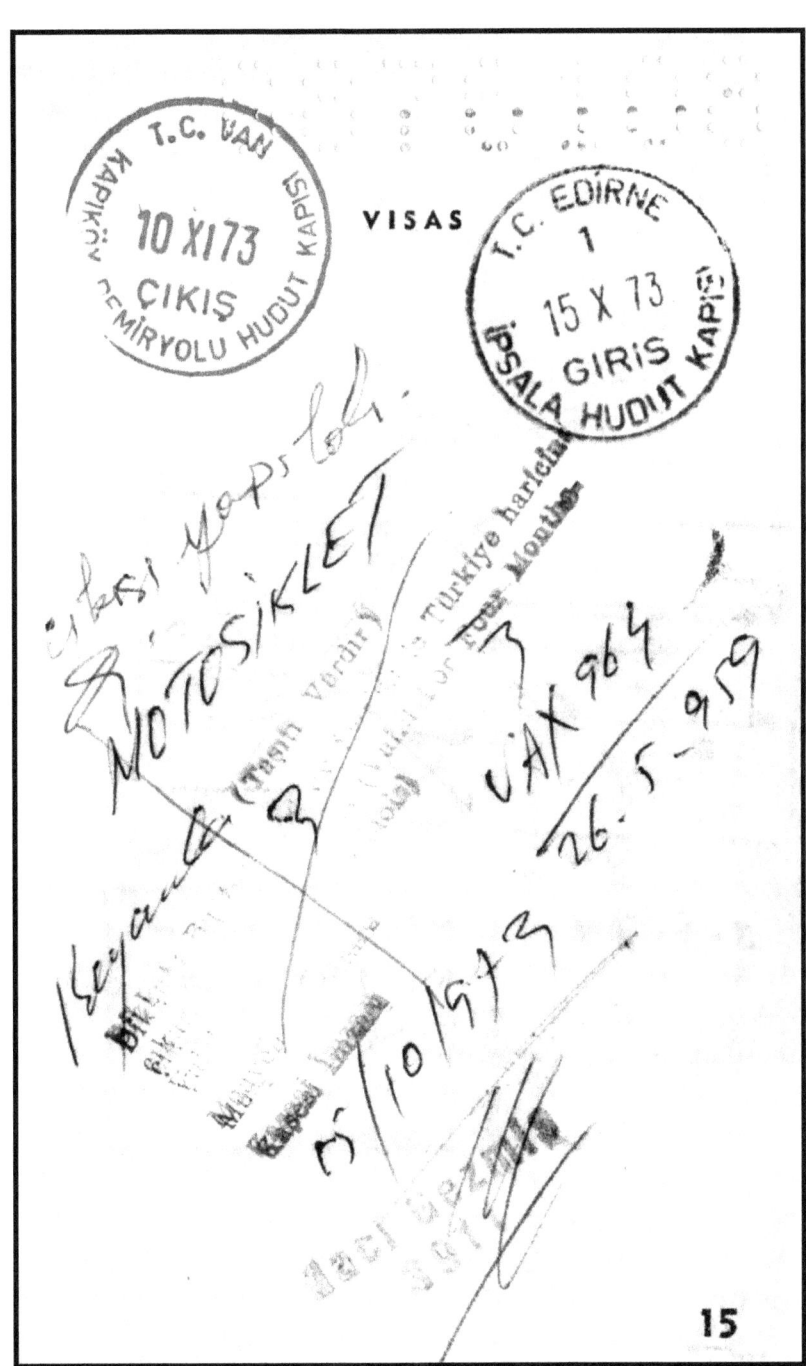

Anamur, Turkey to Tehran, Iran

It was heated, and the road travelled much higher (and colder) than the railway, passing closer to Mount Ararat. In Tehran, we met people who'd experienced −30°C temperatures and no end to the difficulties with freezing of vehicle parts. It's mind-boggling to speculate how Ernie, and Des and I, would have fared. All things considered, the lasciviousness encountered in Van was a minor irritant, and the overcrowding and delays on the train were inconsequential.

When the train overflowing with its human cargo ground to a halt in Tehran to the contented sighs of weary passengers, it was a tremendous relief, bringing to a close our somewhat epic journey across Eastern Turkey and Western Iran.

Anamur, Turkey to Tehran, Iran

Chapter 13:
Northern Iran

Anne Betts

"Travel is about the gorgeous feeling of teetering in the unknown."
Gaby Basora (and Anthony Bourdain)

Life isn't linear, and that's a good thing. It's the detours, the side trips, and the opportunities to go off-map that tend to be the most interesting.

Such was our visit to Iran, an unexpected delight and welcome alternative to our temporarily derailed plans to travel to Palestine and Israel. Our thinking was that our detour to the tune of 2,000 kilometres would provide space for the hostilities in the wake of the Yom Kippur War to subside.

It was a decision pulsing with grand possibilities.

For the most part, our plan was not to have a plan. We were prepared to slow our pace, incorporate a degree of randomness in our movements, and linger when circumstances warranted. At the mercy of Ernie's whims, we'd take to the road whenever the mood struck. With a blend of spontaneity and lethargy, we would cruise on the confidence that Iran would present an unexpected opportunity to savour all that lay ahead.

Little did we know at the time that our 10 weeks in Iran would lead to a serious case of Persophilia.

Our first 20 days were spent in Tehran. We stayed at the Gol-e-Sahra (Flower of the Desert) camping ground in South Tehran, 10 kilometres from the city centre.

On arrival, we were thrilled to find Ken and Jill. After saying goodbye to them in Göreme in Central Turkey, while hopeful, we doubted we'd be meeting up again. That was the thing about making friends on the road. Just when you expect never to see folks again, you run into them at a later date, more often than not in a different country.

So it was a joyous reunion in Tehran, with many tales to trade. After hearing their descriptions of −30°C temperatures and difficulties starting their van in Eastern Turkey, we didn't regret our decision to take the train. They told us of sleeping in a kind stranger's double bed after their van lost power because of the cold. They became mobile only after putting their cooker under the brakes to thaw them, and under the gearbox so it would turn over.

At Gol-e-Sahra, it cost extra to pitch a tent, so Des and I slept out beside Ernie under the PVC tent fly until it became too cold to do so. We then moved indoors to sleep in the recreation room, at no additional cost. The recreation room epitomized so much of what we had grown to appreciate about being on the hippie trail, the term coined during the sixties to describe the overland route to and from India and beyond. It would end in 1979 when both Iran and Afghanistan became off-limits, the former due to the Islamic Revolution and the latter to foreign invasion by the Soviet Union. In 1973, it was a well-travelled trail of mostly Westerners who were heading in both directions.

Most of the campers at Gol-e-Sahra were travelling in an easterly direction, a trend undoubtedly influenced by the weather and time of year. Some were bound for Nepal in search of adventure and enlightenment, or the beaches of Goa to experience paradise. Others were interested in scoring hash that was strong, cheap, and readily available. Many others were returning home to Australia or New Zealand.

Other than the itinerant travellers passing through the campground, we interacted with an interesting resident family. Initially, it was through contact with the older of the two children. Sadly, their names never made it into my journal. The eleven-year-old son had an excellent grasp of English, so he'd drop by for a chat whenever he saw us 'in.' His younger, shyer sister would sometimes be with him. She was about six or seven. One day when we returned from a trip into town, we saw him happily conversing with some Germans. Next day we asked, "So you speak German as well as English?" "Oh, I speak nine languages!" He then reeled them off for us. "My sister only speaks five ... " he relayed a little dismissively, "... but my father speaks 21!" Thinking this was an exaggeration, we challenged him as to what they were. He listed them, language after language until he reached 17. We were convinced, but he was disappointed in himself and dashed off, returning a short time later with the missing four. Wow! This modest Armenian man, with his quiet, retiring Greek spouse and two polyglot kids, was someone a quick-to-judge outsider might easily dismiss because he was living in a campground and making ends meet by teaching English. It turned out that he was a scholar. At night, we would see him poring over ancient Babylonian texts — just one of several 'dead' languages he could read. We were humbled and in awe of the family's richness.

Unlike travelling in Europe where guidebooks and maps were easily sourced, in this part of the world, pickings were slim. While we could polish the thought of exploring Iran with our imaginations, we tended to rely heavily on the stories and recommendations of other travellers. The colourfully decorated graffiti on the wall of the recreation room offered up its own piece of advice:

>Keep heading east
>It's worth your while
>You'll come back with a permanent smile
>Walk in the mountain
>The steppe and the plain

> Take it all in
> You may not make it again
> Kiss the brow of India
> Nepal, Bhutan, Garwhal
> Have a safe journey
> Good health — farewell.

The recreation room was a popular gathering place where a mixture of languages and accents enriched the atmosphere. The capacious rectangular-shaped space was scattered with tables and chairs that helped facilitate conversation and activity. It was a comfortable environment for people to read, write letters, journal, play cards, watch television, or chat with other campers. A small restaurant sold snacks and refreshments until service ended at 9.00 p.m. In the recreation room we spent a considerable amount of time with Jim Gordon from Seattle, and Ric and Lynn Fink from San Francisco.

Jim was young, maybe 18 or 19, and a recent high-school graduate. His grandmother, in her wisdom, saw venturing out into a world beyond Seattle as the next critical stage of her grandson's education. Her graduation gift provided the funds for Jim to travel, explore, and grow. He seemed to appreciate such a remarkable opportunity and displayed a curiosity about people and their adventures in a way that made him interesting to be with. His artistic streak resulted in the contribution of a few drawings for my journal.

Des and I developed a friendship with Ric and Lynn and ended up travelling with them for several weeks. Their Land Rover figured prominently in their travels, so I'll leave it to Des to share his recollection of meeting them (with the inevitable description of their vehicle):

> To us, both Ric and Lynn seemed huge and exotic. They were slightly older, by a few years. They were travelling in a long-wheelbase Africa-specced Land Rover that they had ordered new from the factory in

Gol-e-Sahra Restaurant Portraits

DJ Jim Gordon

Anne DJ Molloy

Northern Iran

Solihull, UK. They'd arrived in the UK in time to watch it come off the assembly line. New vehicles were so far removed from our own lives that we were impressed by anyone young ever achieving the wherewithal to enable such a huge purchase. Our world was one of beaten-up $100 VW Kombis, or something similar. Ric sported a beard and long hair and had a booming voice and presence. He was a Californian and being from San Francisco, we immediately linked him to the fascinating world of hippies. We were later to learn that he was an expert in computers, another unfamiliar world to us. This was early in the days of computing, and Ric had designed a system that he believed had rich potential. Initially, he had engaged a partner to market it while he and Lynn had their overseas adventure, but ultimately sensed a betrayal was in the wind. He had subsequently retrieved the tapes containing his intellectual property and now had them securely secreted in the Land Rover. Lynn was a 'southern belle,' with an intriguing accent. Tall, blonde, and bespectacled, she was always smiling, and subsequently a good mate and confidante to Anne.

There were many other travellers we interacted with in the recreation room, including one we'd met previously. Here's Des's recollection:

Remember the possibly bull-shitting Scotsman who had bludged a meal and some beers from us back in Greece? In the time since, we had met others who had come in contact with him as well. No one had believed a word of his outrageous stories, and he was seen as a bit of a sad joke. Well, he briefly returned to our lives in Tehran with even more bold tales of derring-do. There were no handouts from us this time, and we faced his chat with a little more cynicism than previously.

I was still only half-convinced he was a pathological liar. Being one who tells the truth, I naturally expect others to do the same. Besides, the levels of outrageousness shouldn't be the arbiter as to a tale's veracity. Someone has to be involved in crazy, dangerous stuff. To no avail, I tried sowing seeds to expose him by steering him towards situations I knew a little about.

One morning, we needed to wake him for some reason. Upon receiving a soft shoulder shake, he spun instantly into a karate stance. He was still in bed, and his eyes were just blinking awake, but his hands were up in a cutting ready-to-attack position.

We'll never know if there was any truth in his life as he portrayed it. The first 20 days in Iran were split between Gol-e-Sahra and excursions into Tehran, a sprawling cosmopolitan city of 3.5 million people. Extending from the base of the Alborz Mountains on its northern periphery, Tehran's tentacles stretched outwards across brown and barren terrain in the other directions. Soon after we arrived in mid-November, the mountains received a generous serving of snow-white topping, giving the dry and dusty city a much-needed lift. Withered with the changing seasons and perishing in colour, the leaves of the trees were covered in layers of dust as hazy as gauze over a wound. Vegetation appeared parched, shrivelled, and thirsty. Swirls of dirt and dust whipped around the streets, and dust seemed to hover everywhere.

At times, Tehran felt like a westernized city with US influences. Perhaps the startling presence of phantom jets overhead helped create such an impression. Or, maybe it was the legacy of the Shah of Iran, Mohammed Reza Pahlavi, and his father before him, who ordered the systematic post-war destruction of historic buildings, believing that there was no place for them in a modern city of wide avenues and tall concrete buildings.

Nevertheless, so much about Iran was unfamiliar. For starters, 1973 was 1352 on Iran's unique Jalali calendar.

Another standout concerned language and script, and the fascinating curls, loops, and dots of the Persian alphabet. Our initial apprehension about our

۳٤٩٥٦
تهـران - ج

ability to decipher it, and decode Farsi numerals, was short-lived when we discovered that English was widely spoken and many signs contained Latin characters as well.

I was intrigued by the registration plates attached to the vehicles buzzing through Tehran's streets. From the relative security of the footpaths shared with other pedestrians and the hazardous mopeds, we practised converting them to familiar units of measurement.

We quickly warmed to the country and its residents. When we heard that jobs were readily available for teachers of English as a second language, we pursued the possibility of staying a while. It was true that jobs were plentiful, but the necessary work permits weren't easily obtained. I found this out after contacting an international school, going for an interview, and securing an offer of employment.

Des and I were still keen to visit Israel, so we decided to get our passports in order in the event we decided to travel overland through Iraq and Jordan. After obtaining our visas for Iraq, it was time to visit the Embassy of the Hashemite Kingdom of Jordan.

It involved two visits to the embassy. Our first was on one of our more enjoyable days in the city. The embassy was in North Tehran, so we took a shared taxi from Tahkt-e-Jamshid Avenue with two Germans who wouldn't allow us to pay for our segment of the ride. At the embassy, we learned that the Consul wasn't in, but I spoke to him on the telephone. He advised us to complete the application forms and return two days later to collect the visas. Mahmut, the security officer, served us coffee and piqued our interest in his homeland by sharing highlights of the best Jordan had to offer. He took us to a local off-licence and shouted us beer and pistachio nuts, then back to the embassy for tea and hot dogs. He shared the names and addresses of his two uncles who were Bedouin sheikhs and urged us to visit them near Mafraq, 80 kilometres north of Amman. Mahmut was a gracious and generous host, and as a result, we were excited at the prospect of visiting Jordan.

By the time we returned to Gomrok to catch our minibus back to camp, the bus station had closed. We made inquiries, but it seemed we were out of luck. Deciding not to cogitate on our dilemma any further, we started walking through the concrete clutches of Tehran to find a hotel for the night. A bus driver had heard of our plight and came to collect us with his bus. Near the turnoff to Gol-e-Sahra, he pulled alongside minibuses and, with the help of passengers, yelled out for them to stop. We were eventually escorted from the bus to a stop where it was possible to hail a minibus heading in the direction of Gol-e-Sahra. Very much impressed with these thoughtful and helpful efforts, and on the heels of our visit with Mahmut, we pronounced it a very pleasant day when the universe had taken care of us once more.

Unfortunately, our second visit to the embassy two days later wasn't as pleasant as the previous one. The Consul was in, and I was ushered into his office. Our application forms and photographs were on the desk where he was seated.

"Good morning," I greeted him.

"Sit down, please!" was the terse reply. He then asked for my passport by barking just one word: "Passport!"

Flicking through page after page, he asked with an accusatory tone, "For how long do you wish to stay in Jordan?"

"About two weeks."

"You say that you are a teacher. It does not say so in your passport!"

With as much authority as I could muster to speak on behalf of the Australian government, I indicated it wasn't the government's policy to include the occupations of passport holders in their passports.

"Have you the money to complete your travels in Jordan?"

"Oh, yes, of course."

"How will you travel?"

"By motorcycle."

"Where will you stay?"

"We hope to stay in camping areas where possible."

"There are no camping areas, and the one hotel is completely booked at present."

I thought this was a rather strange state of affairs for such a large country, so the best I could manage in response was "Oh, are there hostels?" but my question was ignored.

"Have you been to Russia?"

"No."

"You have visited Eastern Europe?"

I was stupefied by his manner and tone. His hedging and prevarication made it difficult to pinpoint where the interview was headed. The trail of my travels through the countries behind the Iron Curtain was well documented in my passport, and I wondered if he was trying to trip me up. Was he looking for a reason to deny my visa application? What was going on? I had spoken to him on the telephone on our first visit to the embassy, and the conversation had been cordial, not at all like this one.

"Yes, I have visited many Eastern European countries but not the Soviet Union."

At this point, the passport was thrown on his desk. He rocked back in his chair while simultaneously pulling out his prayer beads. Singling each bead along its string with measured precision, he was deep in thought until his body language suggested he was ready to make a very important announcement.

Oh, oh, here it comes, I thought.

"You realise, of course, that I cannot give you a visa if your friend is a hippie." It came as a complete shock. The best I could manage was, "I don't know what you mean. He's not a hippie. What do you classify as a hippie?"

"Someone with long hair and a beard, does not take care of his appearance, has dirty shoes, cannot support himself ... "

I was thinking the description fit Des pretty well down to the ground. If there was ever an inopportune moment for him to enter, that was it. Oozing dishevelment, in walked Des, scruffily dressed, covered in hair, and sporting dirty shoes. Even his recently clipped beard, specially trimmed for the occasion, did nothing to destroy the hippie image in the eyes of the Consul. In a disdainful tone that seemed to have been marinating since the Consul first laid eyes on our visa applications and photographs, he barked at Des: "Sit down!!!"

To me: "I cannot give your friend a visa."

This was totally unexpected. Still, it appeared all was not lost. I had the sense that I was still in the running for a visa. I was clearly not a hippie, just in hot water for hanging out with one. I drew on what little currency I seemed to have with the Consul and tried to make a case on Des's behalf.

"Would it make any difference if he cut his hair and shaved his beard? We don't want to offend the Jordanian people by not conforming to your customs. It's the custom where we come from for men to have beards and long hair ... "

"But it is not the custom in Jordan! I am not authorized to give visas to hippies! They smuggle drugs into our country! They bring sexual and other diseases into Jordan and live off other people. They are dirty, and they are not welcome!!"

Whoa!! The verbal torrent denouncing hippies continued unabated. After a pause, a little more discussion, more denials that Des was a hippie, and promises of a haircut and shave, we managed to keep our heads below the parapet and visas were issued. I liked to think the Consul was swayed by my eloquence but if the truth be known, he likely wanted to be rid of us so he could get on with his day.

Each visa contained an endorsement written in red ink: "This visa is considered VOID if the bearer obtains ISRAELI visa thereafter."

Northern Iran

That brief statement got me in hot water with Jordanian authorities a few months later, but that story can keep until another day.

Both visits to the Jordanian Embassy had taken us into North Tehran with its neat gardens, paved footpaths, ostentatious homes, modern shops and shopping centres, and contemporary apartment complexes. This was vastly different from what we had observed in the neighbourhoods of South Tehran. There, the dusty streets buzzed with activity — veiled women washing clothes in roadside ditches, children playing outside mud houses, dogs scavenging through litter, sheep being driven through the dust and rubbish, the doomed chicken with tied legs being carried under its buyer's arm on the way to the meal table, and minibuses pulling off the road igniting clouds of dust.

These were not images that could be superimposed on the neighbourhoods of North Tehran.

The latitudinal divide separating the two disparate parts of Tehran had distinct geographical, socio-economic (and perhaps religious) boundaries. We speculated that the inhabitants of each could be strangers to each other in their shared city.

However, certain characteristics of Tehran knew no physical or social boundaries, threading their way through the neighbourhoods of the entire city.

In Iran, as in Turkey, street vendors used footpaths as their salesrooms to display their wares or provide services to their customers. Barbers cut hair and shaved customers shrouded in long white capes in front of small mirrors fixed to posts or railings. Being November, oranges, apples, melons, pomegranates, potatoes, and onions dominated the fruit and vegetable stands. Steaming hot beetroot, potatoes, gourds, boiled eggs, and kebab broiled over charcoal, were all ready to eat: the 'fast foods' of Tehran. Nuts and dried fruit, lollies and gum, stamps and postcards, cigarettes — the variety seemed limitless. Here, as in all the shops, any quantity could be purchased. Scales with identical bronze pans balanced weights on one and merchandise on the other.

Many of Tehran's streets were separated from the footpaths by deep gutters. In some areas of the city, these storm drains were used for washing clothes and cooking utensils. Often, the water was mixed with the most unusual of ingredients as people disposed of garbage.

The toilets in Iran were of the same type we found in Turkey and some European countries — the 'squat-and-drop' variety with two 'starting blocks' — elevated slabs in the shape of two feet. As in Turkey, toilet paper seemed to be unheard of, but toilets had the obligatory aftabeh or 'toilet pitcher,' a water container with a long curved spout enabling the user to reach behind and trickle water to where it was most needed. Needless to say, our roll of toilet paper accompanied us wherever we went. We occasionally saw men, never women, urinating at the roadside where they assumed a squat position.

In North Tehran, it was common to see women driving cars, and most wore fashionable western clothing. Women who led more conventional lives within the framework of Islam wrapped themselves in an enormous silk shawl called a *chador* (meaning 'tent'). Usually, the woman was completely clothed in this garment, with only the eyes visible or the face completely covered with a piece of thinly woven cloth.

Persian cuisine holds an influential position throughout the region, but to our disappointment, the endless varieties prepared in the home weren't available in the neighbourhood restaurants we frequented. Fortunately, we found an abundance of chelo kabab — broiled kebab (lamb or mutton) on a pyramid of fluffy rice with sumac and a slab of butter to melt throughout. It was served with raw onion, paper-thin bread, and an unlimited supply of cold water.

Apparently, the secret to achieving the exquisite taste of the kabab is in the marinating of the meat in onion juice, and sometimes yoghurt, for a day or two. However, the chelo was an absolute eye-opener — never in my wildest dreams could I have imagined that rice could taste so good. The preparation of Iranian long-grained rice is an art, and the Persians are connoisseurs. After washing the rice several times and soaking it overnight, it's then boiled and steamed at just the right temperatures until a crust is formed in the bottom of the pot. It's exquisite, and easy to see how rice is a staple throughout the country.

Like sommeliers discovering a rare vintage of wine, we savoured the taste of chelo kabab, proving it was possible to become addicted after a few delightful encounters.

The most common type of bread was long and flat. The dough was placed on stone slabs in blobs, and the baker's hands skilfully sculpted them into long shapes about a metre long, with furrows ploughed along the length of each loaf. After being taken from a wood-fired oven with a long wooden paddle, the loaves were hung on long nails and sold for eight rials (about three pence).

Refrigerated cabinets in butcher shops were small and used for storing smaller cuts of meat. The carcasses of sheep were hung outdoors, and cuts were taken at the customer's request. One merchant was selling lamb foetuses arranged on a tin plate on the footpath.

Delicious was the juice squeezed from pomegranates, carrots, and oranges with a juice extractor at the many roadside stalls. After savouring the deep red sweet taste of pure pomegranate juice, we were hooked.

Transportation by bus in Tehran was inexpensive. A journey in a blue or red bus cost two rials (two-thirds of a penny), and five rials in a green bus. Our 10-kilometre ride from Gol-e-Sahra to Central Tehran cost five rials. Where a regular bus service didn't operate, minibuses provided transportation. These had no set stops, collecting and setting down passengers anywhere along the route much like the Turkish dolmuş. After experiencing the tumultuous chaos of Tehran traffic on our ride from the railway station to Gol-e-Sahra, we saw no need to take Ernie into the craziness of such a fearful traffic system.

On most visits to the city, we wandered without intention, soaking up the sights, sounds, and tastes experientially.

While the hostilities continued to rage in the Middle East, our world was filled with peace, pleasure, and potential. After 20 days in Tehran, we decided it was time to explore what lay to the north. We hoped to spend a couple of sunny days beside the Caspian Sea, the largest inland body of water in the world sitting at 25 metres below sea level. Some called it a lake; others insisted it was a sea. We were looking forward to seeing a large expanse of water after spending several weeks in the dry and dusty conditions of Tehran. Des had been flat out like a lizard drinking, working assiduously on a major Ernie makeover with parts dispatched from Joe Francis Motors in London. As a result, we were ready to take the newly refurbed Ernie for a spin.

Any mention of mechanical issues relating to Ernie or references to motorcycles in general and Des can't resist joining the commentary:

> Along with the minor fettling of Ernie, we'd been making preparations for heading off into the sparsely populated hinterland of Iran. The jaunt to the Caspian Sea was to be a dry run for a much longer trip to the Persian Gulf. With a long history of running-out-of-petrol experiences in our wake, Iran was not the place to test fate. Despite being in a land of oil, a glance at a map suggested the frequency of petrol stations might be outside Ernie's fuel range. We could manage 300 kilometres, but we had some 450-kilometre sections ahead. As a precaution, we purchased a couple of sturdy army-surplus fuel cans that appeared to be relics from World War I.
>
> I was also worrying about Ernie's rear tyre. We were almost down to the canvas again, and out of ideas on how we could source another replacement. Although my Catholic upbringing had more or less cured me of religion, I am happy to accept serendipitous offerings from the omnipotent one when proffered.
>
> One afternoon at Gol-e-Sahra, I'd paused my travails and was standing back and looking at, and admiring, Ernie. I was brought back to the present with a start when a voice interrupted my dreamy interlude.
>
> "Easy Two's run 19-inch tyres, don't they?"
>
> It was a young Brit of about my age. For a reason long forgotten, he had been rummaging about over the bank at the far end of the camp. He'd already noted Ernie as a Norton ES2 and fortuitously had known its oddball size of tyre. As a result, he was inquisitive enough to investigate the size of a rubber hoop he'd unearthed.
>
> Eureka! This truly was manna from heaven, and whilst not great, the tyre was better than the one we had. We soon swapped the old and worn for the less old and worn, but were reluctant to discard the old, old. We'd just have to cobble up a way to carry it.
>
> Finding space for the two jerry cans, our new larger water container, and the

new old spare tyre was a challenge. But, I knew just the place to carry my new green helmet, a gift from Jim Gordon to replace the orange one that had grown legs in Van, Turkey. I forget the reason Jim was carrying a helmet, and why he no longer had a use for it, but I recall being a happy and grateful recipient. It's another example of how time has stolen one more precious memory.

With Ernie loaded to the gunwales, on December 1, 1973, he started first kick, answering with a throaty bark that softened to a pleasant purr as we coasted out of the campground. The satisfying hum of Ernie's engine after his Tehran makeover was music to our ears, more acoustically pleasing than Beethoven's *Ode to Joy*. You beauty, Ernie!

As the clouds danced with the mountains on the northern horizon, Des's throttle hand wound on the juice as Ernie climbed tirelessly from Tehran's 1,200 metres through rocky terrain past a dam that was anxiously awaiting rain, judging from the mark left by higher water levels. The rainy season is between October and March, but in the three weeks we'd been in Iran, we hadn't seen a drop. At 3,000 metres, we found the road through the Alborz Mountains covered in snow.

Ernie was running faultlessly, shrugging off his heavier load with no fuss at all. However, our enthusiasm for being back on the road was short-lived when a presentiment of doom accompanied our first glimpse of the entrance to a two-kilometre-long narrow black one-way tunnel. It had been some time since our last experience with a tunnel without lights — way back in Yugoslavia — so our memories had dimmed somewhat.

Nevertheless, the driver in front of us was advised that Ernie's headlight wasn't working, and we'd be following him. Taking our place in the convoy, we moved into position waiting for clearance. Ready, set ... and the leader was off, Ernie hot on his heels, following the dim lights that gradually grew dimmer as the driver hared through the tunnel like a rabbit being chased by a pack of hounds. So much for alerting him of his role in carefully guiding us to the other end!

Ernie quickened his pace to catch up until he hit a patch of ice and weaved over the road, bouncing from wall to wall while two pairs of feet were extended to correct him to a straighter trajectory. One foot became entangled with one of the other pair, and it was just after they were freed that Ernie bounced no more. He crashed into the rocky wall of the tunnel, dislodging his two riders.

The Ernie Diaries

TUNNELS

Northern Iran

I tumbled off my perch and hit the road like a limp rag doll.

Being splattered on the tarmac of an Iranian tunnel is only one of countless ways to reach the threshold of the pearly gates. With a healthy dose of gratitude, I realised my time hadn't come. My limbs and digits were intact, and I had another story to add to what was developing into an extensive list of misadventures.

The cortège of vehicles stopped. Ernie was helped up, Des and I were brushed down, and I was bundled into a car. Des and Ernie went riding off into the darkness once more, between two cars moving very slowly, until a pothole interrupted the momentum. A jerry can and the basket flew into the air and landed on the ground, spilling the basket's contents over the road.

We arrived at the end relatively unscathed, with Ernie the only casualty with a bent footrest. Our nemesis, the tunnel without lights and icy patches from overhead seepage, continued to plague our travels from Norway to Yugoslavia and now Iran.

We reached the Caspian late afternoon, after negotiating terrifyingly steep hairpin bends that spiralled down the mountainside like a nautilus shell. Soon after, we passed through a national park flaunting a dazzling array of autumn colours. Our drive beside the sea (or huge lake, the largest on earth) passed an endless number of orchards of citrus ripening to a golden yellow in the sunshine. Interspersed throughout was a patchwork of rice paddies that had been producing much of Iran's rice for centuries. The air was fresher, the land more fertile, and the area obviously received more rainfall than Tehran. We found a patch of seaside frontage on which to pitch the tent and walked the few kilometres to the nearest town for our ambrosial fix of chelo kabab to satisfy our recently acquired addiction. The nutrient-rich waters of the Caspian are the source of prized Iranian caviar harvested from the roe of its sturgeon, but we had eyes and taste buds only for chelo kabab. Satiated, and with our stomachs reverberating with joy, we returned to camp and flaked in the tent, with thoughts of lingering beside the Caspian in the morning light, stealing some warmth bound for the ripening oranges.

The first weak pitter-patter sounds on the PVC tent fly provided an excuse to grab a little more sleep. By midday, the sky was weeping, shedding its burden in a deluge of biblical proportions, a waterfall tumbling from the sky. There was an intense anxiety to the rain, as though this was its last chance to endow the rice paddies with enough moisture for the following season. We were grounded. Our indolence continued through the afternoon and into the night. As the words of *O Jerusalem* became difficult to read in the fading light, I reached for the matches to find the box wet. To the rescue came Des, who braved the elements to coax Ernie into generating a spark strong enough to ignite the camping-gas cooker that lit the candle. And there was light.

Of course, a couple of torches would have been handy for occasions such as this, and they would have offered a little more security when negotiating dark tunnels, or driving at night with a non-functioning headlight. Torches, like decent rain gear, were regarded as extravagances to a couple of frugal boofheads who weren't the brightest bulbs in the chandelier. Besides, torches were larger, more expensive, and less powerful than today's varieties, and candles were cheap, readily available, and didn't require the additional cost of batteries. As a result, torches weren't part of our kit.

Not much changed with the next new day. With a short dry interlude, we packed up and rode 100 kilometres west beside the Caspian. Racing against the rain proved futile, and we were forced to find shelter inside a row of wooden and tin shacks on the beach.

Given our style and type of travel, accommodation was pretty basic and bare bones. If we had the audacity to ride up to a farmhouse in Norway to ask if we could sleep in the barn, we could certainly take advantage of empty change houses in a closed lakeshore recreation area in Iran. Ernie was parked in one, wet clothes hung in another, and Des and I sought succour in a third along with food and sleeping gear just in case we were in for an extended stay. With rain pounding the tin roof like tiny fists, we made ourselves comfortable, and watched the rain sheeting down outside. Unfortunately, it showed no sign of abating, and what we'd hoped would be an hour or so stretched like elastic through the afternoon and night until morning.

Our hoped-for couple of sunny days beside the Caspian had failed to materialise, and it was time to head back to Tehran.

Treated to a canvas-ready day marked by bright sunshine, we set off for the city, 200 kilometres away. An avalanche of striking colours — brown, yellow, red, and orange, burnt and glowing in the sunlight, greeted us as we left the Caspian and drove up a valley, the road clinging to a stream all the way. This continued until a spot where the stream neglected to carve enough space for the road to continue and 'man' had to build a tunnel. He ultimately built several tunnels, many of which he failed to illuminate.

Because of one dark tunnel, we'd made a conscious choice to avoid the other route for the return trip, the one we'd used to travel north from Tehran. We'd failed to heed the warning embodied in the well-known proverb, 'A bird in the hand is worth two in the bush,' and were now paying the price.

A long black tunnel, a pitch-black chasm, loomed in front of us as we stopped on the edge of darkness. I leapt off and walked inside so Des and Ernie could follow. My trepidatory first steps led me to a footpath bordering the wall of the tunnel.

Whoosh, a car whizzed past, and Ernie gained a few metres by following the light it left behind.

"Car coming behind, Des. Edge a little nearer to the side."

"Get off the road, Anne, on to the footpath."

Beep! Beep! Whoosh. Another car sped past.

Between sounds of passing traffic, I could hear Des's boot tapping the edge of the footpath, echoing throughout the tunnel.

"Des! Where are you? Ouch!!" I bumped into Ernie.

"Here!" The tapping continued, as Des felt his way through the charcoal blackness.

"Crikey, it's dark in here!"

The next whoosh of a passing car was followed by a thud and a few expletives.

"What happened?" Des asked.

Blundering along, I'd failed miserably in my ability to detect obstacles by leading with one leg, using it as a white cane. Climbing out of a waist-deep hole with a petulant announcement, "I just fell down a bloody big hole! I'm not walking along this footpath anymore! A person could disappear in this tunnel and never be seen again! Des, are you still here?"

The only sound I heard was the incessant tapping of Des's boot against the footpath. *Thanks for asking, Des. I'm just fine, thank you.*

After much more tapping, beeping, and whooshing, we transfixed our eyes on a pinhole of light that grew larger until we were finally spewed out of the tunnel's end.

Our state of relaxation was short-lived, as we were soon to discover that this first tunnel of the return trip wasn't the last. At the next extra-long tunnel, we followed the same procedure, but the exit was a challenge to reach as the inky abyss meandered through its length. Fortunately, a car stopped beside us to offer assistance, and we were able to follow it slowly and carefully around the dark and snaky bends to the other end.

The preponderance of Alborz tunnels had the potential to decrease my life expectancy, and I was finding no humour in our 'two-in-the-bush' tunnel experiences. However, Des and I agreed we'd likely laugh about them later. The more difficult moments often make the best stories, ones we'd tell and retell, fine-tuned with the necessary hyperbole. Inevitably, our mishaps would be converted into talking points and embellished anecdotes, rather than negative memories.

The road back to Tehran passed some rugged and impressive scenery. Prior to our descent, we saw from our vantage point the entire city reaching out a hand to welcome us back. Like a yo-yo coming home on its string, we headed in her direction. However, we didn't relax and enjoy the beauty unfolding before us until we were convinced that every tunnel was behind us. After the numerous hairpins and faltering progress through tunnels, Des allowed Ernie to stretch his legs as we cruised towards the outskirts of the city.

Returning home to Gol-e-Sahra with our basket full of oranges, we searched for familiar faces. Ric and Lynn had been trying to get themselves organized to pack up their Land Rover for our departure for Esfahan the following day. They weren't doing too well, so we all agreed a postponement was in order. With the extra time on our hands, Des and I decided to ring Ali, the Iranian we'd met seven weeks earlier at a rest stop 60 kilometres from Istanbul. We'd enjoyed our brief roadside interaction with him and had since discovered that his natural warmth and offer of hospitality was typical of Iranians. Calling on Ali was another opportunity to gain further insights into this irresistible aspect of Persian culture.

We recalled the ease with which Ali approached us. He'd pulled in, driving a new Mustang. Climbing out for a stretch and beaming a wide megawatt grin, he yelled out:

"Hey! You guys speak English?"

"Yeah."

Walking towards us, he asked, "Where are you from?"

"Australia."

"Hey, you're Communist."

"No, you're thinking of some other place. Australia isn't Communist."

"What are you then?"

"It has a democratic government and is part of the western world."

"Oh yeah, that's right. You're from Europe."

"No, maybe you're thinking of Austria."

```
Name     Reza Pahlavy St, Lane of
Street
City     No Paghennar No, 108
Telephone  w/house of Mostaffa
Name                          Sherkat,
Street
City     [Persian script]
Telephone
Name     [Persian script]  10  [Persian script]
Street   ALI MOHAMMADI
City     73 DAHMETRY BARGH
Telephone BAINOLMELAL
Name     AMINDOLLEH KH
Street   TEHRAN   IRAN
City     PN. 753 619
```

"No, it's huge, almost as large as the USA. It's got its own."

"No. It's in Europe."

"No."

"No? Let's see. There's Europe, Africa, America, Asia ..."

"There are more, including Australia. Look (pointing to the AUS sticker on the back of Ernie). That's its shape, and that's a kangaroo, an animal that jumps all over the place."

"What language you guys speak?"

"We're speaking it: English."

"No, which language do you speak in your country."

"That's it! English!"

And so it continued. The conversation wasn't that productive, so we changed the subject to a less difficult topic. We talked about his car, how he'd been studying in the USA (obviously not geography), and why he was now returning to Iran after 10 years. It was a period of economic growth in Iran, with plenty of opportunities for well-educated Iranians to join the professional intelligentsia. As for his Mustang, the combination of Ali's citizenship and absence from Iran meant the vehicle could be imported without the encumbrance of hefty import fees.

"Where in Iran are you from?"

"Tehran."

"We're thinking of going there until the war in the Middle East is over. What's it like?"

"Tehran is a great place, people are very friendly, and it's a modern city. You'll like it. Hey, why don't you guys drop by? I'll give you my phone number."

And we'd met Ali. Clean-shaven with short dark hair, Ali was roughly 30 years of age. He projected a confident air, and his sociable, outgoing approach to interacting with others was reminiscent of other roadside encounters. What made this more interesting was that Ali was the first Iranian we'd ever met. During our stay in Tehran, we hadn't managed to call him until our return from the Caspian. On leaving to meet him the next day, we armed ourselves with a world map to point out the locations of Australia and New Zealand. Ali took us into North Tehran to his sister's house, boasting chandeliers and elaborate furnishings, and bedecked in acres of Persian carpets personifying the Persian proverb: 'Where lies thy carpet, there is thine home.' We sat on a large carpet lined with cushions before an impressive spread of fruit, pistachio nuts, and coffee.

Later, Ali took us out for chelo kabab, and afterwards to meet his younger brother Abdul. Abdul knew where Australia was. He'd heard it was a great place to study, so he enlisted my help to accompany him to the Australian Embassy to obtain more information. Abdul was earnest in his efforts to study abroad, and it was the least I could do to help him in his journey to realise his dream.

This prolonged our stay in Tehran by a couple of days, and after another visit to the bazaar, more chelo kabab, and more messing around Gol-e-Sahra, we were just about ready to leave — with my Australian passport that entitled me to visit Australia without the hassle that others must endure. Not an easy country to enter, I concluded, after visiting the embassy with Abdul. The bureaucratic hurdles felt insurmountable, much like what I would encounter a few years later with my efforts to settle in Canada.

One month and one day after arriving in Tehran on the train, it was December 10, 1973, and an opportune time to explore what lay to the south of the Iranian capital.

Chapter 14:
Tehran to the Persian Gulf, Iran

Anne Betts

"I have no reason to go, except that I have never been, and knowledge is better than ignorance. What better reason could there be for travelling?"

Freya Stark, A Winter in Arabia

The Yom Kippur War had temporarily scuttled our plans to visit Israel and Palestine, allowing us to meander in an entirely unexpected direction. Our lack of research and the general absence of travel guides meant we'd arrived in Iran as blank pages with no mental images or preconceived ideas on what we'd find.

So it was with an elevated sense of anticipation of what southern Iran would reveal that we saddled up for the next segment of our adventure. With his 21 horses champing at the bit to get back on the road, Ernie quickly found his rhythm, devouring the distance like a Pegasus on wheels.

For our journey to Esfahan and what remained of our time in Iran, we would travel with Ric and Lynn from San Francisco, appreciating every moment of their company and every supportive gesture extended our way. Finding compatible travelling companions didn't come easily; not everyone synched.

When travellers gelled, the relationships were worth pursuing, and that was certainly the case with Lynn and Ric.

It was bitterly cold on the trip to Esfahan, the coldest we'd experienced since Central Turkey. Togged up in just about every piece of clothing we owned, we endured a long, hard day, possibly the toughest of the trip to date. Seemingly oblivious to the cold, Ernie barely broke a sweat and revelled in the relaxed canter, behaving flawlessly throughout the 450-kilometre journey.

My inherited helmet came without a visor, so the face-stinging cold generated copious tears that rolled downwards to be caught by my goat-hair balaclava. Thousands of icy fingers tore at our clothing; the talons of the cold clawed at our extremities. With a relentless wind battering us, I took advantage of the shield that Des provided to keep my head and torso out of the windblast. Even with his new Afghan coat over his leathers and under his waterproof jacket, Des reckoned he was at the point of capitulation. We were flotsam, floundering in a frigid sea of misery.

We could barely enjoy the scenery through the narrow slits in our Turkish balaclavas. From what glimpses we could steal, the countryside was arid and sparsely inhabited, with patches of sand whitened by the salt deposits of the Dasht-e-Kavir, the Great Salt Desert.

Just before Esfahan, we had an amusing encounter when some Iranians beckoned us to come alongside their car to receive two oranges. The passing of the gift at 90 km/h marked an entertaining point in a strenuous day, providing both parties with a few fun-filled moments.

It was dark when we finally found the campsite. After disposing of Ernie and our gear, we embarked on a hunt for our favourite dish. Unfortunately, the ubiquitous chelo kabab we found in Tehran initially eluded us in Esfahan. Propelled by the desperate cries of our weakened stomachs, our indefatigable efforts eventually paid off after much walking and many mentions of "chelo kabab" to locals. Despite being tired, we were willing to go to any length to satisfy our cravings for our favourite Iranian food.

On our return to the campground, we discovered that Lynn and Rick had arrived during our absence. The four of us would camp beside each other for the nine nights we stayed in Esfahan.

Tehran to the Persian Gulf, Iran

Over the next few days, Esfahan slowly drew us into her spell, revealing herself as an oasis in the Iranian desert — a place of infinite beauty. Wonderfully preserved and unspoiled, the city is a living museum of Persian history and Islamic art. The vivid turquoise domes and artistically designed minarets endow it with grace and elegance.

The people of Esfahan are famous for their skilled craftsmanship. The variety of beautifully handcrafted items makes it an alluring city to explore. We spent a great deal of time in the Qeysarriyeh Bazaar, one of the oldest and largest in this part of the world.

The hammering of steel on metal would invariably lure us into an engraving shop where artisans were beating out motifs on silver, brass, and copper to create trays, vases, plates, dishes, ġalyāns, jugs, teapots, and more. Initially, we were uncomfortably conscious of the constant hammering, but it quickly assumed more musical tones as we realised its artistic and historical importance to Esfahan. Like so many other artisans creating fine works of art, metal workers had been carrying on these traditions for a very long time.

Women and girls of the many nomadic families of Iran produced the vast majority of Persian carpets, and buyers travelled to the regions to purchase them for sale in the cities. We visited the only carpet-weaving factory in Esfahan, where four carpets were being woven. Young girls sat cross-legged on a padded beam connected to the loom where they followed the patterns displayed on graph paper hanging above them. Six girls were working continuously on each carpet, taking strands of wool of various colours and knotting each piece around the vertical strands connected to the base of the loom. Young girls were employed because their fingers were small enough to manage the very fine knotting required for the best quality carpets. On average, each took about a year to complete. One huge half-completed rug was on display, a three-year task in the making.

A wander down an alley past mud dwellings usually led to intriguing

Tehran to the Persian Gulf, Iran

courtyards and workshops where some kind of activity could be observed. We stumbled upon an area where skeins of wool were being dipped in a giant vat of boiling dye. The coils were continuously circulated by rolling them over a series of wooden rods, each one dipping a different section of wool in the vat. After wringing out, the wool was thrown to a worker kneeling on the edge of the roof where it was hung out to dry in the sunshine.

The buildings were made of a mixture containing mud and straw, caked solid and shaped into house-sized rectangular boxes. The roofs were flat, except for the dome-shaped entrances for sunlight. We went for a scramble over the rooftops, with the colourful patches of brilliantly coloured wool drying on long withered poles that had seen many years of service. Rainfall wasn't a threat to the drying process; it hadn't rained in Esfahan for eight months.

From an adjacent rooftop, we admired the Naqsh-e Jahan Square, or the Maidan, considered one of the most impressive and beautiful squares in the world. Flanked by shops and mosques, the central portion was once the arena for riding and polo, with the marble goalposts still a feature of the square.

Bordering the Maidan is the Masjid-e Shah Mosque, 350 years old and considered the perfection of Persian Islamic architecture. Overwhelming in its scale and beauty, the mosque is completely covered, inside and out, with beautifully enamelled tiles in various shades of blue.

The hand-printing workshop we visited consisted of several rooms overlooking a central courtyard, with the railings and open areas used for drying. The motifs were printed on cloth precooked in the juice of pomegranate skins. I bought a section of fabric with a polo design. We were told that Esfahan is the only place in Iran where cloth is hand-printed. With old hardwood printing blocks, one of the artisans printed two woodcut designs for me on scraps of brown paper for my journal. Des bought a printed shirt.

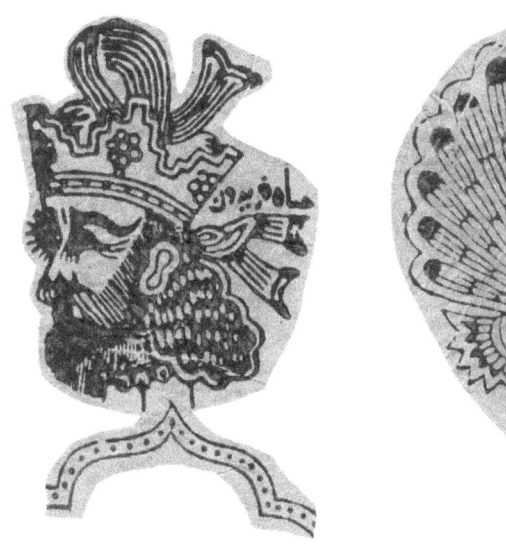

Tehran to the Persian Gulf, Iran

Polo, hunting, camels, smoking the hookah, the Maidan, mosques, the works of Omar Khayam, and many other aspects of Persian culture and tradition were portrayed on the miniatures displayed in shops around the city. Artists painted the miniatures on paper, camel bone or ivory, bordered by ornate frames of wood, camel bone, inlaid brass, or ivory.

Wooden hookah sections were carved using a lathe or a bow, the string looped around the wood and rotated manually. Hookahs were available for smoking in teahouses. In a blur of ġalyān smoke, patrons who indulged seemed to be very relaxed as they puffed away.

There wasn't a single kitschy souvenir to be found. Everything we saw in Esfahan embodied the pride of generations of artisans invested in their craft. During our stay, we bumped into Mustafa, a young independent carpet merchant. Ric, Lynn, Des, and I were wandering through the bazaar searching for 'the camel,' and Mustafa offered himself as a helpful guide. He led us to the spot where a camel moved in a circle rotating a millstone roller that crushed herbs to create spices and dyes. On that day, cumin was being ground. While the process was fascinating, we felt for that magnificent beast whose existence had been reduced to trudging around and around in a never-ending series of circles.

Without a hint of pushiness, Mustafa offered to take us to his rug warehouse, where he tempted Ric and Lynn with two rugs. Two days later, the rugs were posted off to San Francisco.

Mustafa's interaction with us seemed a little clandestine. He wasn't an official bazaar trader and probably shouldn't have been mingling with us openly. He seemed to work on the edges. The British might call him a 'wide boy' as he cruised the market looking for opportunities to engage with shoppers. He had to be discreet, so the traders who paid for a stall didn't spot him touting for business. It felt like being in a mystery movie as Mustafa led us in a zigzag pattern through a labyrinth of alleyways, always looking to see that we weren't being followed. We learned that his nickname was

'Shaking Minarets' because of a distinctive affectation when he spoke, his head wavering significantly. In Esfahan, the name is readily recognised; it applies to the Monar Jonban monument covering the grave of *Sufi Amu Abdollah Soqla*. The shaking movement relates to the ratio between the height and width of the minarets and the width of the *iwan* (vaulted space used as an entrance). If someone climbs one of the minarets and vigorously bounces back and forth to shake it, the other minaret will shake in unison. Hence, shaking minarets.

Mustafa regaled us with descriptions of his visits to the various nomad camps to purchase the much-coveted carpets to sell to his customers. The smaller prayer rugs captured our interest. Typically, a betrothed young woman would spend a year or so making one for her husband-to-be. It would be his for his lifetime and only sold after his death. Thus, several rugs we were shown were in the range of a hundred years old. They were in excellent condition, as the usual practice after prayer is to immediately and carefully roll the rug and store it in a clean spot. Muslims have to be clean to show their respect for God; it's considered disrespectful to toss around a prayer rug carelessly, or place it in a dirty location.

Mustafa made passing reference to a motorcycle such as Ernie as an ideal means to visit the nomad camps. With no record of Ernie's entry into Iran in Des's or my passport, Mustafa's comments spawned new possibilities. When we showed interest in some beautiful prayer rugs from the Baluchi nomads, the prospect of a trade involving Ernie took root. We liked Mustafa, and helping enable his dream of having a motorcycle sat well with us. As a result, we left Esfahan with arrangements to strike a deal on Ernie and a couple of rugs on our return from the Persian Gulf.

We were mildly interested that the campground in Esfahan hosted a group of Americans attached to the US Peace Corps. They expressed little interest in us and as a result, us in them. They were staying indoors, and we never quite knew what they did each day. My sense was that they were learning

Farsi and being oriented on Persian history and culture. One person briefly interacted with us on our last morning by the outside tap.

"Why are you filling your container with that water?" an Ivy League type asked Des.

Dismissively, Des stated the obvious," ... for washing, cooking, and drinking."

"Don't you know Esfahan has two water systems, and that one is strictly non-drinking: washing only?"

It was a credit to the robustness of our systems after being on the road for four months that we had coped with non-potable water for a week and a half with no obvious deleterious effects on our health.

After nine days, Ric, Lynn, Des, and I set off for Shiraz, 475 kilometres away. On the outskirts of Esfahan, Des wound on the throttle as Ernie climbed through the gears until he was thrumming along happily at a steady pace. As the winter sunshine danced on the tarmac, Ernie tackled the long ride with ease, the kilometres unspooling beneath his wheels. Pausing for a rest, we were enveloped in a sombre quiet, seemingly empty of all sound except for the click of my camera's shutter to capture the magnificence of Ernie in the Iranian desert.

The landscape wasn't the least bit monotonous as the eroded hills and mountains produced some stunningly beautiful scenery. Where the countryside had been sculpted with an additional tool — a river — the terrain was even more spectacular. It was a geographer's delight, with striking examples of fold mountains, anticlines and synclines, scree deposits, and river-eroded valleys and ravines. The prize for the tallest vegetation all day was awarded to the sagebrush plants, growing about 30 centimetres high until they found themselves defenceless in the path of grazing sheep and goats.

We reached Persepolis, approximately 60 kilometres short of Shiraz, late in the afternoon after spending an hour attending to Ernie's punctured rear tyre. Ric and Lynn were behind us, so they stopped and put on a brew. We were almost finished when a helpful local rode along on his donkey and paused to lend a hand. The donkey liked sugar.

With the decision to devote most of the next day to Persepolis, we camped under the stars in a dry creek bed nearby, organizing ourselves for the morning sun to find its way directly to us. Different intensities of moonlight and layers of darkness within the wide silence of the desert were captivating. As we prepared to bed down for the night, it was so cold that for Des and me, transitioning from daywear to sleepwear was uncomplicated, distinguished by the removal of our boots that were strategically placed by our respective heads.

The tent, used as a blanket, and the newly purchased 'space blanket' warmed us for the second night in succession. However, we didn't solve the condensation problem and again woke with damp sleeping bags. Kohoutek, the predicted 'comet of the century,' succeeded in eluding us once more as we searched the early morning skies for evidence of its visit to the inner solar system.

Des reminded me of an encounter that didn't make it into my journal. Here's his recollection of the event:

> After another frigid night, we were barely up and about when a local gent who had been dropped off at the nearby crossroads, wandered over for a gander at our small encampment. Anne and I had not yet rolled up our bedding; everything was laid out, airing and drying off in the sun. Our curious visitor, who was on his way to a village about eight kilometres away, expressed surprise upon surmising that we had indeed slept there on the ground.

"What about the wolves and leopards?" he uttered.

Involuntarily, our voices became squeaky and nervous. "Wolves and leopards???"

We couldn't even pretend nonchalant bravado — our incredulous faces gave it away. The Finks were nearby, preparing coffee. Being from the US, I think they were familiar with the notion that big cats and canines weren't a novelty. Coming from New Zealand, where we have no animals that can harm humans, I scare easily. We didn't camp out many times after that, but when we did, I was sensitive to any noise that wasn't Anne gently purring away beside me.

Decades later, with the benefit of the internet, we learned that our visitor wasn't pulling our legs. The fauna of Iran does indeed include the Indian wolf, Persian leopard, Asiatic cheetah, Asiatic lion, and lots of snakes!

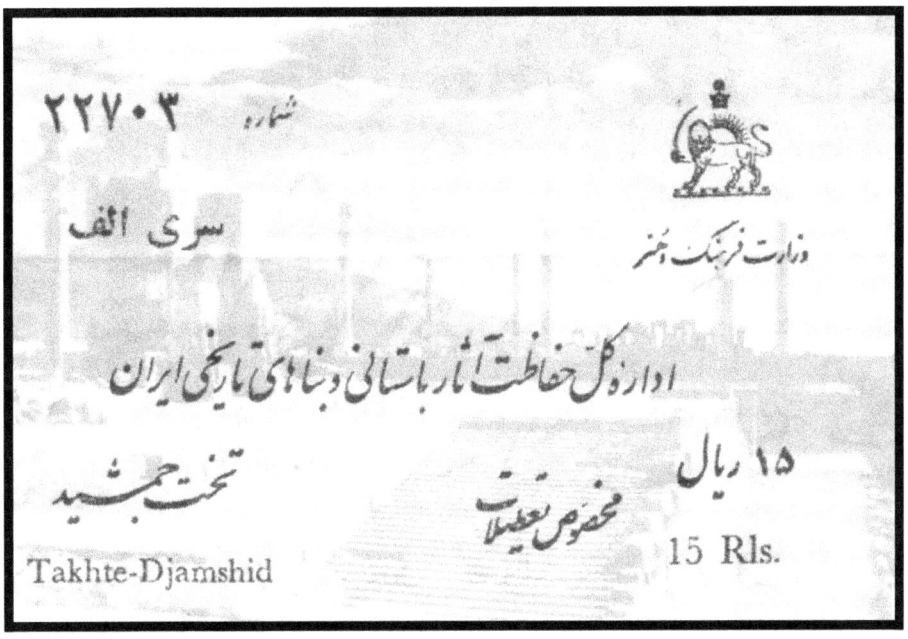

At the intersection of history and heritage, Persepolis is Persia's Takht-e-Jamshid, built by the Persian King Darius the Great around 515 BC. At that time, it consisted of luxurious palaces and elaborate banquet halls for use on occasions of national importance. The entry fee of only 15 rials (five pence) belied the value of such a significant Persian monument. Scrambling over 2,500-year-old ruins, the grandeur of the Persian Empire became evident. As we climbed the terrace with its double flight of access stairs bordered by walls covered by sculpted friezes at all levels, and strolled past gigantic sculptures of winged bulls and remains of large halls, we realised that Persepolis was a remarkable architectural creation. Of particular interest was how it incorporated the best of surrounding regions — tiles from Babylon, precious stones from India, and the contributions of workers from Greece who worked alongside Persians to raise the hundreds of columns to the sky.

Persepolis became the venue of another national event in 1971, the celebration to mark the 2,500 years since the founding of the Persian Empire. Dignitaries from around the world were invited to what the shah labelled 'the biggest party on earth.' Architects, interior decorators, and couturiers from France were hired to design 50 tent-like suites, and chefs were brought from Maxim's in Paris to oversee the catering. Eighteen tons of food was flown in, all of it from Paris, except for the caviar that came from Iran. It was a lavish and extravagant event.

I didn't know it at the time, but as the remainder of the decade would unfold, the decadent affair became a flashpoint for the demise of the Francophile shah whose extravagances didn't endear him to a population growing weary of his excesses and the ostentatious lifestyle of the monarchy. The decade would end with the Iranian Revolution.

Sixty kilometres after leaving Persepolis, we arrived in Shiraz, city of poets and gardens. Dotted with bursts of green, its parks, ornamental pools, and tree-lined boulevards offered a refreshing contrast to the surrounding desert. It had a distinctly different atmosphere from Esfahan. One of my early observations related to clothing. Many of the men wore felt crown-shaped hats and ankle-length outfits that comprised two flaps back and front. The women's dress was a riot of dazzling colour.

The four of us camped at the Shiraz Tourist Camp for four nights. Des and I slept in a huge canvas tent on a tubular steel frame erected on a concrete pad. They were warm nights compared to the one spent camping near Persepolis, and our dreams were free of wolves and leopards.

We'd met Mahmut at Persepolis, where he'd given us his address in Shiraz. When we called on him, he gave us a tour of Shiraz by night — the 'real Shiraz,' according to Mahmut. We saw what he meant. It was a hive of activity as people strolled along the green boulevards looking for a bite to eat, to hang out with friends, or to see and be seen.

We paused by the Nasir al-Mulk Mosque ('Pink Mosque'), where Mahmut suggested we return during daylight hours to soak up the colours of the glass windows reflected on the floor, and the tiles in shades of pink blanketing the ceiling. Then, it felt fitting that our visit to the tomb of Hafez, the revered Iranian poet of the 14th century, was with someone who had grown up with a deep appreciation of his poetry. Within the garden were several young people reciting the works of Hafez, Shiraz's most famous son. As Mahmut left us at the campground, he invited us to his home for chelo kabab on our return from the Persian Gulf. Did he say chelo kabab???

Before leaving Shiraz, I called home to wish the family a Merry Christmas, fully prepared with a pocketful of coins and the exit code for Iran. Following the written instructions on the wall of the telephone box was the first challenge — an impossibility given they were in Farsi. The second challenge involved deciphering the numerals on the rotary dial. Blundering ahead, I was surprised to get a connection.

"Merry Christmas!" I shouted.

It was my mother who answered, "Merry Christmas to you. Who's calling?"

"It's Anne."

To my father: "Jack, it's Anne. Anne's on the phone." To me: "Where are you calling from?"

"Iran."

"Where?"

"Iran."

"Canary Islands?"

How 'Iran' became the 'Canary Islands' had less to do with my mother's auditory perception than the quality of the connection. It was one of several reasons we avoided making telephone calls. They were expensive and somewhat ineffective. Aerogrammes and postcards were our communication tools of choice.

Christmas Eve became our departure day from Shiraz to travel the 300 kilometres to Bandar-e-Bushehr on the Persian Gulf. With evocative memories of Turkey's Turquoise Coast, we were already savouring its warm snug embrace. By this time, we were desirous of some comfort. It seemed like an aeon since we'd removed many layers of clothing. We waddled like the Michelin Man (and the Michelin Woman, if she existed), swaddled in layer upon layer of clothing.

As the outskirts of Shiraz ebbed away, the soaring Zagros range dominated the horizon, in distant layers of brown, purple, and grey. Some were snow-capped, suggesting we'd likely have to endure at least one more cold night before reaching the coast.

The Shiraz – Bushehr Road was built by the British during World War I when they occupied southern Persia. Back then, it would take many days to make the journey by caravan. In 1973, it was a major trucking route to and from the commercial port of Bandar-e-Bushehr, and much of it was paved. It passed through the Zagros Mountains with some dramatic scenery for almost 100 kilometres until it descended to a narrow plain.

Nestled at the base of the mountains, black tents were surrounded by flocks of sheep and herds of goats scrounging among the rocks for food. Camels also roamed the area. Presumably, these were the camps of the Qashqai, Turkic-speaking pastoral nomads. Each year, they travelled approximately 500 kilometres from the summer pastures in the mountains to the north of Shiraz to the lower, and warmer, winter pastures close to the Persian Gulf. Women in brilliantly coloured dress strode purposefully and confidently from the river to their camp with pots and dishes balanced gracefully on their heads. Others were washing carpets transported to the river on a donkey. A section of the river was marshy, and workers were cutting reeds and loading them on a camel. We'd passed several clusters of grass huts, so we presumed the reeds were used to build shelters.

The warmth of the coast beckoned, so we made a conscious choice to push on and postpone interacting with the nomads until our return trip from the Gulf. This was a mistake. We'd failed to take into consideration that their nomadic lifestyle might mean that they would have moved on by then to establish a new camp. It proved to be the case, and we'd lost a valuable opportunity to spend time with an intriguing group of people.

Unfortunately, the sealed road ended soon after, and the bone-grating corrugated surface prompted Ernie to shed several items. Nevertheless, he tackled it with a ferocity befitting his compatriots who'd built the challenging artery several decades earlier. After the jarring ride, my bones felt like the jumbled collection of the skeleton purchased for my university anatomy class five years earlier.

The road, hardly worthy of the name, climbed through the mountains once more. This unpaved section was known as the 'killer road,' the most dangerous in all of Iran. The hair-raising twists and turns were notorious for the number of lives that accidents claimed each year.

On one particularly sharp narrow bend, we came perilously close to teetering on a knife-edge between destination and doom. Ernie and Des ensured we didn't meet a similar fate as the tangled wrecks littering the slopes below, with their wheels pointing towards the heavens.

Slaloming around potholes at a sedate crawl, Ernie fought brief battles with those filled with mounds of fine dust caused by trucks manoeuvring the hairpin turns. With a consistency similar to that of finely sifted flour, the dust was thrown skywards by the trucks before resettling into the potholes and ruts, making the surface appear quite smooth. It was anything but. As Ernie did his best to dodge as many potholes as possible, it kept things interesting. After we'd transferred most of our gear (that hadn't already been shed) into the Land Rover, the now unburdened Ernie tackled the conditions with confidence. His 'sand tyre' (aka bald front tyre we'd retrieved from a

mountainous heap of rejected tyres in Yugoslavia) allowed him to plough resolutely through the dust. It was so fine and extensive that it put the bulldust of Australia's Nullarbor Plain to shame.

We rode through Konar Takhteh dotted with date palms and box-shaped adobe houses with flat roofs, and steps leading up the sides. The sun-soaked mud dwellings appeared golden under the cerulean blue of the Persian sky. As the sun sank below a horizon obscured by the hills, we pushed on down a hairpin descent with the help of the lights of the Land Rover behind us. It was at times like this I was pleased Des had endowed Ernie with the rich colour of McLaren Orange (as close as he could get in a spray can), with visibility approaching that of iridescent papaya.

A narrow rocky stream passed through the valley below. It was tranquil and peaceful, an ideal camping spot to spend Christmas Eve night enjoying several bottles of dust-settling Skol accompanied by shouts of salâmati! ('cheers' or 'to your health'). The amber libation, Iranian Skol, tasted better than any Queensland-brewed Castlemaine XXXX that had ever passed my lips. Lynn popped a plenitude of Jolly Time popcorn to compensate for Santa's certain inability to find us. Des revealed that this was the first time he had ever been part of a 'popping-of-corn' celebration. We cut the young Kiwi lad some slack, accepting his naivety without ridicule. But, when he mentioned that he was 22 years of age before he'd tasted pizza, we couldn't let that one slip by.

The pleasant sounds of the stream's rhythmic lapping of water trickled into the tent on the surprisingly warm December air, drawing us gently toward sleep. That, and copious amounts of Skol, meant that the comet Kohoutek was missed once more.

As we were keen to reach Bushehr in plenty of time to continue our Christmas Eventide celebrations, we left soon after breakfast once I retrieved a journal memento — a label from one of our spent celebratory drinks of the night before.

Back on the road brought more potholes and more dust. A massive pile of it voraciously swallowed the sand tyre. Ernie squirmed like a rambunctious two-year-old, wobbling back and forth and eventually toppling over. The three of us landed in a mound of the stuff. It wasn't as soft as it looked, and our clothing assumed the same earthy tones as those of the road. Our theatrics gave Ric and Lynn something to chuckle about.

Soon after, on a corrugated stretch, we rattled over ruts that had the power to shake the fillings from our teeth. One of the pannier latches gave way, and clothing and books scattered unnoticed over the road. Fortunately, Ric and Lynn gathered them up for us. It was a good thing they were behind us and not in front. With resolute endeavour, Des and Ernie battled with the challenging conditions until we reached the edge of the mountains and looked out on the flat coastal plain. The effort had been more than worth it for the view of groves of date palms unfolding below. As we paused to take in the sight, time stood still for a magical few moments. Our eyes would have swallowed it whole if they could. With our spirits soaring, we began our last hairpin descent. At the bottom, the road weaved among slender date palms standing at parade rest, past nomad tents, camels, and droves of donkeys.

After the cold ride south, it was serene in the extreme. Within sight of the waters of the Gulf, we realised we'd arrived in paradise. The caressing touch of its gentle warmth enveloped us, and we absorbed it like sponges. It shrouded us in its warmth, and we were bound to stay for as long as it took to soak up its aura.

Tehran to the Persian Gulf, Iran

Chapter 15:
Persian Gulf to Tehran, Iran

Anne Betts

"You can't control the past, but you can control where you go next."
Kirsten Hubbard, Wanderlove

For our Christmas meal, we found a seafront restaurant where a friendly and generous local insisted on paying the bill. We graciously accepted, but unfortunately, the night didn't end too happily after our friend paid and left. Later, when we went to leave, we were presented with the bill. Our fierce repudiation of both the bill and the owner's conduct led to a brief argument, and we emerged from the contretemps by paying only for the last round of drinks. The disappointing denouement to our celebration was an unfortunate blemish on what had been a momentous Christmas Day.

Seven days were idly spent at Bushehr, at a picturesque spot in a grove of date palms beside the sea. Sharing it with us were Suzy, Hermann, Hans, and Jurgen — Germans travelling in two vans, and the odd few soldiers from the base who periodically wandered past. It was a social week with tales aplenty. Despite coming from four different countries, we were a covey of

The first and last days were sunny; the rest were sometimes overcast or drizzly. Our layers were discarded, and T-shirts became our garments of choice once more. The sunshine and warmth were gifts we relished, along with the balmy breeze that caressed our skin.

It also meant sleeping out until the fourth night when dark clouds curtained the evening and slowly crept across the sky to swallow the sun. Des and I pitched the tent as rain looked like a probability. 'Rain' turned out to be an understatement, much like calling the Cold War a 'tiff'. In no time, the sky was no longer a warm roof but a cauldron of raging winds and torrential rain. We climbed into the tent during heavy rain that became heavier and the winds more fierce as the night wore on. Our tiny tent endured the worst the Gulf had to throw at it until 4.30 a.m. after reaching saturation point and the limit of its resistance to the winds. The front pole collapsed. Rain swept in, and the wet bodies, sleeping bags, and other belongings soon became waterlogged. Our shouts and curses brought a beam of torchlight from the Land Rover, so we asked to be let in. 'Begged' might be more accurate. On hearing their positive response, we moved like human pistons on full throttle towards the comfort of the vehicle. From the warm refuge, we looked out upon the havoc wreaked by the elements — Ernie on his side, our flattened tent weighted down with rocks, and date palms bent over as they succumbed to the might of the gale. It was dry and cosy in the Land Rover, and somehow, the four of us found space enough to curl up and grab a few hours of sleep.

With morning, the damage was inspected. Ernie was righted and leaned against a tree. Water was drained off the PVC to reveal the saturated rubble beneath. The day produced enough sunlight to dry out most of our gear, and then the mammoth task of rebuilding began. In a new location in a slight hollow, the pegs were driven in with a sledgehammer borrowed from the Germans, and the front pole tied to a date palm. I stitched the torn PVC, and we weighted it down at the base with two lines of the heaviest rocks we could find. Palm fronds that had been blown down were woven horizontally and vertically on both sides of the tent for extra protection from the wind and rain. We were ready for anything. However, the night following the Bushehr cyclone was relatively calm with only light rain and very little wind.

Late in the afternoon of New Year's Eve, Lynn, Ric, Suzy, Hermann, Jurgen, and I went into town to collect supplies and refreshments. It seemed like the entire population of Bushehr was out to greet us and offer any assistance we might need. The Persian New Year, *Nowruz* isn't until the spring equinox, but a helpful local was aware it was 'our' new year and directed us to the beer store. A crowd materialised to supervise our purchases of giggle juice, and in no time a gaggle of curious bystanders surrounded the German guys' van. Those who knew any English practised it on us. Had I recorded it, I would be assured of laughs with every replay. It was one enormous but enjoyable rabble!!

The Germans mentioned that fireworks usually accompanied their New Year celebrations, so the palm fronds from our tent were used to start a bonfire. While the flame danced in the night, Des and Jurgen chopped down what was left of the stump of a palm tree, and this was used to prolong the life of the fire until midnight. We sat around drinking and chatting, and Lynn and I prepared two humongous bowls of popcorn. Five minutes after 1974 surfaced on the Gregorian calendar, thin tendrils of smoke and fading embers of the fire signalled an end to our night of pleasurable jollity. We staggered off to our respective sleeping quarters and slipped into a deep canyon of sleep.

Next day, the debris of empties, camping chairs, and popcorn bowls around the cold dead fire was all that remained of our new-year revelries.

The Gulf had swaddled us in her restorative warmth, and the time had come to leave our nirvana. After tidying up from our merrymaking, we 'got it together' (our new expression picked up from Lynn and Ric), and headed for Shiraz on what was our penultimate ride on Ernie.

The 75-kilometre stretch of unsealed road saw Ernie bite the dust when we attempted to negotiate a recently graded shortcut. The upward slope and the mound of dirt were too much for him, and this time he sent his two passengers in an outward trajectory as he toppled down the slope. Once again, this was rich entertainment for Ric and Lynn who were behind us, and one more episode to add flavour to Des's growing repertoire of hyperbolic tales.

Soon after, the road followed more sedate geography, and nearer Shiraz, the mountains were covered in more snow than before. It was a little colder than before as well. We returned to the Shiraz Tourist Camp, also colder than a week earlier.

While in Shiraz, we spent our time divided between the campsite, visiting

Mahmut, and spending a full day in the bazaar where Lynn and I shopped for fabric for our 'new' skirts. Three days later, we left the colour and vitality of Shiraz after many meals of chelo kabab, and the completion of my skirt for India. It was quite the creation for someone with absolutely no talent in this area. It involved removing the stitches of the leg seams of my second pair of jeans and stitching pieces of fabric in the resultant spaces to create an ankle-length skirt.

Eager to cover the 482-kilometre ride to Esfahan in one day, we were off to an early start on January 6, 1974. It was bitterly cold, this our last ride on Ernie before delivering him to Mustafa, our Esfahan carpet merchant. We rode in stretches of 100 kilometres, stopping at markers 382, 282 (where Ernie fell over in the snow and broke his clutch control lever), 182, and 144. The unplanned stop at Marker 144 was on a sharp bend that wasn't built for fast cornering.

Des and Ernie were both anxious to reach Esfahan to escape the frigid conditions of the ride. In too much of a hurry for this particular bend, Ernie slid along on his side, creating a maelstrom of searing metal, streams of gravel, and clouds of dust.

Des shucked off blame for our demise from both himself and Ernie. He pontificated about hypothermia, and how the body's core cools down, and slowly the cognitive performance lessens, leading to confusion and drowsiness. When he attempted to combine this with a lesson on braking, I was the confused one, so I'll leave the elaboration to Des:

> Although we'd set off dressed fit to assault the geographical Pole, after 300 kilometres we were as cold as is humanly possible. The eyes were open, but no one was home. The road was straight, and we were hunched into a locked, frigid outline resembling Rodin's The Thinker (albeit The Thinker with a shadow).
>
> Motorcycles are an extension of the rider and respond as much to their thoughts as they do to their physical manipulations. Unlike cars, they more or less can only be braked when fully upright and travelling straight ahead. Your reduction in speed is done before the corner is attempted. When a corner was encountered at Marker 144 after such a long straight stretch, there was cerebral confusion. In an

inordinately slow fashion, the options ahead were processed. Brake hard now and stay true and committed, or brake for a short while, then pitch us over in a glorious swoop of the bend with thoughts of road-race champion Giacomo Agostini to the fore?

Like many things in life, to dither is to fail. After finally registering that we were approaching a left-hand corner at some speed, I neither committed to braking or throwing us over to the side like Ago early enough. We braked while going straight ahead for too long to get around the corner safely, but not long enough to scrub off the speed. This meant that when we belatedly heeled over, there was no way we were going to follow the tarmac ribbon that had been guiding us all day. We hit the gravel on the verge, and all adhesion was lost. We slid along on our side in a screeching cacophony of tearing metal. That we were dressed like the Michelin family saved us from shredded flesh. My ego was hurt. This was a crash; our other 'oopsies' had just been falls. It was not what I had promised Anne.

Not one for thinking on my feet with stunning rapidity at the best of times, it took a while to sort through the chaos in my mind. But come to think of it, I wasn't 'on my feet.' After several disoriented moments, measured by a second hand moving as though bathed in syrup, like a stunned mullet I peered through the dusty haze suspended above us. In my befuddled state, my addled brain slowly came to the realization that Ernie needed to be lifted from Des's foot so we could both get him upright. I gradually elevated myself to a standing position and moved Ernie just enough so Des could do the same.

Ernie was a mess!!! He looked like Iranian roadkill. Des and I didn't look much better — like something the cat dragged in. We were battered and bruised, but intact. Everything worked. It was the first (and only) prang of the trip, and for this we were thankful.

After temporary repairs, we pronounced Ernie fit to return to the road.

The Ernie Diaries

"Only one hundred and forty-four to go!" was the enthusiastic cry. With that, we set off for Esfahan, where we limped into the campsite around 5.00 p.m. On this, the last leg of our journey with Ernie, he'd suffered many injuries — a broken clutch lever, bent handlebars, broken pannier lock, bent back-box frame, cracked back box, bent footrest, missing oil cap, and minor damage to both panniers.

At Esfahan Camping, with vivid memories of how cold it had been on our previous stay, Des and I decided against sleeping out, so we asked for a room with a heater. In no time, we were ensconced in an oasis of comfort and warmth. Oh my, it was as warm as a duckling cocooned in its soft vest of down.

Next morning, bleary-eyed, I reluctantly needed to go outdoors when nature called. I robotically opened the door and my half-shut eyes opened wider to see the entire campsite under a duvet of snow. It was still snowing, so I blinked several times to adjust my vision to absorb such an unbelievable sight. What a relief we hadn't slept out.

The camp manager had also been keen for us to sleep inside. Recently, they had lost a couple of folks who had slept in their van with a small kerosene heater running on one of the front seats. The campers had closed the windows for additional warmth, and during the night, the kerosene heater consumed all the oxygen. The carbon monoxide and other toxic gases produced by the heater produced disastrous results.

With so many battle scars, Ernie desperately needed attention. But, given the dramatic change in weather, we opted out of working in the snow. Instead, we stayed in the warmth of the room reading, eating, and chatting with Ric and Lynn around the heater.

The next day was reserved for 'operation Ernie' in an attempt to improve his condition and spruce him up for our meeting with Mustafa. After a few hours of tinkering, Bob's your auntie's husband, and Ernie was ready to put his best foot forward.

The following day, Mustafa brought two friends along to admire his soon-to-be acquired prize. By this time, Ernie was looking less like a wounded war veteran, and more like a two-wheeled wonder machine designed by a creative team of British engineers. Mustafa and his friends inspected Ernie, doing so with a hint of exaggerated respect. We didn't have the heart to taint their image by exposing Ernie's cantankerous side. Mustafa would discover his idiosyncrasies in due course. With so many talented and resourceful workers, Esfahan would undoubtedly provide what Mustafa needed to keep Ernie on the road.

We settled on a price of USD 225 for Ernie. This was a good deal for Des and me considering our estimate of his value in Britain was in the range of USD 100, or £45 in the coin of the realm. We then accompanied Mustafa to his warehouse to select our carpets. With my crash helmet and the tank top bag included in the deal, we scored three prayer rugs. They were all from the Baluchi nomads around Mashad near the border with Afghanistan.

Saying goodbye to Ernie attracted a range of emotions. He'd carried a couple of ordinary travellers to extraordinary places, weaving his own legend into the lush tapestry of travel. It placed us at the crossroads of one journey being irrevocably over, and on the cusp of others about to begin. We were at a stage when the timing and circumstances were right for the three of us to travel separately in search of new adventures. Nevertheless, the finality of the separation was tinged with sadness, and nostalgia for the remarkable journey we'd shared.

Occasionally fractious and obstreperous, Ernie had annoyed me and impressed me in equal measure. He'd been reliable when it counted, and obstinate when it didn't. Despite his many design flaws and an engine that had passed its best-before date, he was clearly a battler, creating many occasions when we'd beamed with pride at his achievements. In the end, the interruptions and inconveniences he caused were a significant part of the journey.

> January 13/1974
> Esfahan, IRAN.
> Dear folks,
> This is one of 2 boxes + 1 rug I am posting today.
> Most of the contents are pieces of 2 sets of brassware.
> A HUBBLE BUBBLE SET of beaten brass (by hand)
> A SAMAVAR (for tea)
> A hubble bubble is another name for hooka (US term) or water pipe. It consists of 3 or 4 pieces, one of these the long snake like section the end of which is inhaled through.
> The Samavar consists of a base to be filled with kerosene) — (it's in the other box) & the next section that is filled with water to be heated. It sits on a tray with a bowl under the tap, & a tea pot sits right at the top. The jug is for fresh water to be used in conjunction with the samavar. I think there is a section of hubble bubble in the other box.
> At home we have enjoyed many times. Have had many cups of tea from other Persian Samavars & a few puffs on other hubble bubbles.
> I'm writing this in a rush to take it to customs.
> Bye for now
> Love Anne.
>
> PS Just thought I'd fill you in on exactly what this box of junk contains.
> PS Also 3 pairs of slippers, one for Mum (from Bear) also a hand printed cloth of polo design from Esfahan.

Mustafa seemed genuinely pleased with the deal and excited to have Ernie for his carpet buying expeditions to the nomads' camps. We left with the knowledge that Ernie was in loving, and hopefully capable, hands.

Des and I stayed in Esfahan for eight more days. Lynn and Ric bought another rug from a carpet merchant called Karim, and we all sent parcels off home. Included in my box to Australia were a beaten brass hookah, brass samovar set, a Baluchi prayer rug, and a few goodies for the family at home: pistachios, halva, and their Christmas gifts from Turkey. Six months later, Des shared that when his parents received their parcel, noting that the never-seen-before pistachios had all split open exposing a greenish-tinged inner nut, they threw them out. In their minds, they were mouldy. Such a waste! With the revelations about popcorn and pizza, and now pistachios, I was wondering what kind of colonial outpost New Zealand had been in the 1960s and early 1970s.

Ric, Lynn, Des, and I again visited the Shahrazad Restaurant we'd become acquainted with the previous time we were in Esfahan, and sampled some different Persian dishes on the menu. This motivated Lynn and me to move into the camp kitchen one night to prepare a Persian dish from Lynn's Persian Cookery Book. With chelo, we enjoyed *Khoresch Holu* consisting of cubes of lamb with peach sauce. It was quite a hit. We also tried pomegranate soup, but it was an absolute disaster that met its fate by being flushed away.

Fred and Anna breezed into the campsite after a few days. They were heading west on their way home to South Carolina in the USA after spending two years in New Zealand. In their late twenties, their gregarious nature made them a perfect addition to our convivial little group. Our warm abode became the gathering spot for the six of us. Lynn, Ric, Anna, and Fred moved all their cooking gear into our room, and their Land Rovers were used for sleeping. Nights lengthened, as we all gathered around the heater chatting and arguing and engaging in good-natured banter. Fred and Anna entertained us with stories about their attempts to assimilate into New Zealand life, including one about their many failed attempts to get a handle on the nomenclature of the daily meals typically enjoyed around the world. Their experience went something like this:

Invited for 'tea' in New Zealand, they arrived at their hosts' place for the expected cup of tea, so they ate their evening meal before leaving home. On arrival, they were presented with an enormous spread, but not wanting to offend their new friends, they struggled through what was a second substantial meal within a couple of hours.

When invited for 'supper,' they didn't want to make the same mistake by eating in advance, so they arrived hungry. As the night wore on and no food appeared, by the time supper was served around midnight, they were ravenous.

When invited for 'dinner' ... unfortunately, I didn't record the tale in my journal and I don't remember this part except they had us in stitches. I recall that it was another botched attempt with the outcome that they were uncomfortably hungry or full as a goog.

We took Fred and Anna to Karim's warehouse, where they bought two rugs: an Esfahan wall rug and a nomad prayer rug. Karim took us all to a sports night where the age-old tradition of *Zurkhaneh* was practised. Men exercised in a pit-like area to singing accompanied by the rhythm of a drum, or *zarb*. One of the activities involved two large wooden clubs swung rhythmically around the shoulders. The clubs were of various weights, the largest being 40 kilograms. After sets of exercises with and without the clubs, everyone moved to the perimeter of the exercise area and one at a time each man spun on one foot in the centre, completing as many turns as possible. The whole routine was conducted according to tradition spanning hundreds of years. Being afforded a glimpse into this ancient art was a privilege.

Having left Ernie with Mustafa, Des and I were now without wheels, so Ric and Lynn invited us to ride with them to Tehran.

Our distinctly different vehicles had led to an unequal relationship with Ric and Lynn, with Des and me grateful beneficiaries. We'd relied on them to collect our strewn possessions on inhospitable roads, to provide shelter during cyclonic conditions, and now transportation from Esfahan to Tehran. Despite our obvious disparity in choice of vehicles and nationalities, we shared a love of being on the road, hanging out with other travellers, interacting with residents, and basking in the benefits of travel. At the heart of the relationship was a friendship that Des and I appreciated, and we felt it was reciprocated. It would be 45 years later that I'd join Ric in a San Francisco bar and reminisce about our earlier adventures over a few beers.

It was now January 15, 1974. It had snowed three times while we were in Esfahan, and patches of snow remained. As we left the warmth of the people and the heat from the buildings, the snow on the ground became thicker and more uniformly settled as we ventured north. The road remained clear of snow and ice for 200 kilometres. Halfway through our journey, it began to snow, and as the wind moaned, skeins of snow drifted across the road. For the last 150 kilometres, the snow collected on the pavement and Ric changed to four-wheel drive. The few cars we saw had snow chains. The many trucks with their heavy wheels and hot exhausts made the going a little easier, keeping the road relatively clear. On one occasion, we stopped to clean the windscreen, and as Ric braked, the Land Rover slid across to the other side of the road, turning a complete circle as we did so. It was a long and slow ride back to all the comforts of Gol-e-Sahra.

Before turning into the campsite, we stopped for a well-earned feed of chelo kabab, inhaled with appreciative sighs.

Gol-e-Sahra had changed during our absence. The snow on the ground was thick and fluffy, and the trees and shrubs sagged under the added weight. Ric circled the campsite to find a few crazy campers, their vans camouflaged by the snow. The ground was clothed in thousands of illuminated particles, brightened by the artificial lights of the campsite. The pool we'd slept beside five weeks earlier was covered in a sheet of ice, and the snow surrounding it was two feet thick. It was even too cold to camp in the recreation room, so

Des and I obtained a heated room for our two-night stay.

The following day was dizzy with errands in Tehran in preparation for departure the next morning.

By this time, I had decided against accepting Ric and Lynn's offer of a ride to India. When it was extended, it felt too generous and too convenient to pass up. They were heading to Bombay (renamed Mumbai in 1995) where they planned to take a ferry or freighter to Kenya in Africa. Bombay felt geographically closer to Australia than I'd been for some time, and I figured it was 'just a hop, step, and a jump' to head home from there. I'd been away for two years, and on some days I felt a gravitational pull to return.

While the prospect of returning home to family and friends was tempting, and at first blush felt like an appropriate choice, I wasn't ready to be imprisoned by more responsible choices than the ones of the last two years. I pictured slipping back into a beat of daily life as predictable as a concentrically swinging metronome. A return home would seriously clip my travel wings and put an end to my peripatetic wandering. Travel had forged a path of awakening that hinted at something greater than mere day-to-day existence, and the thought of being whiplashed back into the routine of my former life felt much less appealing.

In the mix were two countries, in particular, I was yearning to visit — Israel and Canada — and the lure of Israel, as close as it was, helped determine the outcome of the back-and-forth tug.

So, Des and I bought tickets for the train to Istanbul and stocked up on snacks and novels for the three-day trip. We collected mail, changed money, and generally got ourselves organized. Back at Gol-e-Sahra, as Ric and Lynn were leaving early the next day, we toasted them over a few beers and wished them the safest of journeys.

We had met many interesting people during our travels, and Ric and Lynn were no exception. They resembled the free-spirited and adventurous characters in 'Me and Bobby McGee' who loved the freedom of travel and the liberating feeling of being on the road. It wasn't surprising Lynn and Ric were inspired by the words of Kris Kristofferson posted on a small patch of metal in their Land Rover:

> Freedom's just another word for nothin' left to lose
> Nothin' ain't worth nothin' but it's free

We were fortunate to have been wide-eyed twenty-somethings at a time when Iran was a welcome stop on the well-trodden overland route to India. The Islamic Revolution of 1979 changed all that when Iran became off-limits and isolated from much of the international community.

Freedom's just another word for nothing left to lose And nothing aint worth nothing but it's free...

It would be four decades later that I would sit opposite a much younger traveller in an Istanbul hostel common room.

Dara was working on his laptop, but I waded in, hoping to distract him long enough to enjoy a brief conversation. My initial greeting attracted a familiar reaction, signalling a preference that he'd rather not be disturbed. I got it; I've often felt that way myself, but usually not in a travel context. I pressed on with the commonly utilized banality, "Where are you from?" When he responded, "Iran," I gushed, "I L-O-V-E Iran!"

With that, the laptop lid came down, simultaneously accompanied by "You've been to Iran???"

Given the hint of incredulity embodied in his response, I likely appeared as an anomaly — a Westerner who had not only visited his homeland but was clearly enamoured by it. It was obvious to me that Dara had been born after the Islamic Revolution of 1979 and the establishment of the Islamic Republic. He was too young to have experienced the days when a plethora of Westerners drifted across the country. In his relatively short life, he'd likely encountered few Westerners within Iran's borders or any outside of Iran who held a positive image in contrast to that portrayed by the Western media. I was a rarity.

"Yes, back in the 1970s, exactly 40 years ago. Would you like to see some photos from the trip?"

The laptop lid remained firmly closed as he eagerly expressed interest in this sudden turn of events.

Dara was studying in Istanbul, and he appeared to welcome my intrusion into his study time. Despite the generational differences, we bonded over a shared fascination with his homeland. Our interaction took me back to the '70s when conversations with other travellers were expected and welcomed. The key difference in my 2014 conversation with Dara was that my iPad and his laptop held rich repositories of photographs to enhance the dialogue.

His mother was also a traveller, and Dara proudly shared photographs of her recent visits to Esfahan and Tehran. I was intrigued.

So was Dara. He skimmed over my digitalized journal entries interspersed with 40-year-old photographs. He asked for copies and permission to share them with family and friends, to which I happily obliged.

Our connection resulted in an invitation to visit Iran as a guest of his family. Our somewhat brief exchange and resultant invitation embodied what for me was one of the alluring characteristics of Iran. Despite the tense relations between the Islamic Republic and Western governments since 1979, my interaction with Dara confirmed what I'd concluded 40 years earlier — Iranians are friendly, quick to interact positively with strangers, and the tradition of hospitality continues to run deep as it has for centuries. It reinforced, yet again, why ordinary people shouldn't be confused with the dogma, rhetoric, posturing, personalities, and political ideologies of their respective governments.

Persian Gulf to Terhran, Iran

Chapter 16:
The Home Straight

Des Molloy

"Travel isn't always pretty. It isn't always comfortable. Sometimes it hurts, it even breaks your heart. But that's okay. The journey changes you; it should change you. It leaves marks on your memory, on your consciousness, on your heart, and on your body. You take something with you. Hopefully, you leave something good behind."
Anthony Bourdain

As Anne has already mentioned, in the five weeks that we had been away, Tehran had changed. Winter had well and truly arrived. While our failure to get work permits had left us disappointed, maybe it was just as well that our quest for employment hadn't materialised. It had seemed an exciting and exotic prospect, an experience we would have treasured for the rest of our lives.

Now, the overarching impression of Tehran was one of bitter cold and an all-encompassing white blanket of snow.

We'd noted with a wry smile that the abandoned tent down the back of the camp was now just a white mound. The mystery of the tent was never solved. It was there when we arrived in early November, and it remained so: aloof and deserted. We eyed it with envy. While faded, it was a superior version to our hand-me-down pup tent, and the thought had crossed our minds of executing a switch. We speculated that the owner had lightened his or her luggage and moved on, or struck a deal with Gol-e-Sahra management to gain several nights' lodging free of charge in exchange for the tent.

I still chuckle at the memory of waiting outside the camp gates for a minibus on our last day, and my eyes attracted to a distant car heading our way. It seemed to glow from the inside. Then, as it came closer, it looked like it was on fire. It was a VW Beetle, and as it passed by, finally we could see the source of the glow. Sitting in the back seat, diagonally opposite the driver, was a man operating a butane or propane burner, presumably to heat the interior and keep the windscreen de-iced.

We had wavered from time to time in our plans when something possibly more exciting presented itself. Now, for me, there was an additional influence. I was running on empty; the coffers were almost bare. Yes, I was wrapped up in our adventure, but there weren't the funds to continue. I was also missing the frisson of London, the rugby club, and our mates. I was looking forward to lacing up my boots and chasing a leather ball around a rugby field, and I was interested in finding out what everyone had been up to. Plus, I was keen to share highlights of the adventures that Anne and I had enjoyed and endured.

Anne's coffers weren't in a similarly dismal state, and she was refocussed on getting to Israel and Palestine.

It is interesting to reflect on the pro-Israel sentiments of our generation. Anne and I had discovered the historical fiction of Leon Uris, including his novel *Exodus* that highlighted the tragic treatment of Jews during the Holocaust, the post-war detention of survivors in Cyprus, and the establishment of the state of Israel in Palestine. Just like our interest in the Nazi era, this period of history intrigued us. Our pro-Israel leanings had been influenced by the horrors of the Holocaust and the rhetoric of pro-Israel Western governments.

A couple of decades later, I had a discourse with a young English woman who had recently travelled in the Middle East and North Africa. Clearly, she was pro-Palestine, something I couldn't envisage. From our ill-informed youthful perspective, Palestine was a biblical country that no longer existed, and a breeding ground for terrorists. There was total clarity, but very little knowledge. So many of us dreamed of the kibbutz life as something we needed to do whilst on our big OE. I was a little envious that Anne would soon experience that and likely return to London with a more in-depth critical analysis of the Israeli-Palestinian conflict.

The prospect of leaving Iran was bittersweet. I think that ultimately the Persians had topped our list of favourite people. It was a toss-up between Iranians and Turks, with Turks a close second. We'd uncovered much more that connected us than separated us.

We had only one slightly unsavoury experience in Iran, and that had been in broad daylight in a Tehran city-centre street. A short, youngish, besuited man carrying a briefcase was walking the opposite way, looking very much like a fine example of modern westernized Iran that the shah tried to portray and encourage. As he passed us, he reached out and stuck his free hand right into Anne's crotch area. What he was trying to do, or what reaction he was expecting, baffled me. It was unexpected and totally out of character for an Iranian based on our experience to date. I instinctively chased him down the footpath a short distance but gave up as he scurried off as fast as his stumpy legs could carry him. Anne's time in Eastern Turkey had been fairly torrid, but Iran had otherwise been mellow and enjoyable.

Our brief stay in Iran was also quite reflective. In terms of travel styles, guided tours were a perfect choice for some people and some situations, but our preference for independent travel was based on the belief that we'd meet a wider variety of travellers and enjoy more meaningful encounters with local merchants, workers, and residents. It also meant that our travel dollars, while not substantial, would flow directly into the pockets of independent merchants and their communities, and not leak out of local economies into the hands of offshore businesses.

For the most part, this was indeed the case. We interacted with many interesting travellers of different nationalities. Most were ships that passed in the night; there was usually not enough time to bond. The exceptions were Ken and Jill, and Ric and Lynn. With them, there had been quality time — time to become friends. Both couples had helped us in times of need, and we hoped that they saw us as more than just an obligation. We'd enjoyed our times with them, and in the optimistic way of the young, we presumed our paths would again intersect at some point in the future.

Our chance encounters with locals fuelled our memories of the trip well into the future. The goodness and kindness of people willing to offer assistance or extend hospitality enriched our journey, and fortified our faith in humanity. The people we met helped expand our worldviews and contributed to our unwavering belief in positive outcomes where events would inevitably unfold in our favour.

Evil evaded us. Horror stories of theft and assault (or worse) were absent from our journey. Besides the blue stretchy cord in Yugoslavia, and Anne's orange helmet in Eastern Turkey, other losses of possessions were due to our own negligence. Except for the sexist galahs in Van and the small-minded besuited drongo in Tehran, we were overwhelmed by how well we were treated, and the generosity of the human spirit.

Already our team was one down. I was reasonably happy with Mustafa's having Ernie. Initially, I felt a little mercenary. I didn't think Mustafa had the skills to keep our old friend going, but I was happy to get two of the three prayer rugs that were part of our deal. I felt a lot better when a day or two after Ernie was in Mustafa's care, we went to a motorbike workshop with him. To my delight, I saw the mechanic was tuning a late 1950s BSA Goldstar, the crème de la crème of British sporting single-cylinder motorcycles. It was the pinnacle of the genre. With the universal language of gestures and with our few words of German, I learned that the bike had been sourced from Dubai across the Persian Gulf. It was indeed fast, and to prove it, the mechanic proudly pointed to the 120-mph mark on the speedo. Of course, there were no manuals written in Farsi, and the mechanic had to face doing everything from first principles or iteratively. I noted that the engine had a distinct whine when he fired it up for me. I tore a piece of cardboard from a box and sketched the problem for him. The magneto pinion was meshing too deeply with the intermediate timing pinion. The remedy is to place a thin shim under the magneto, thus spacing the pinions further apart, so the teeth don't bottom in the adjacent groove. Lucas produced a range of suitable shims to enable this. I drew him a shim and pointed at a tin can. He caught on instantly, giving me confidence that he'd be able to fettle Ernie when needed. I wrote in Farsi numerals the tappet clearances and the timing distance 'before top-dead-centre' on full advance. Everything else I reckoned he could guess.

Thirty-one years later, I rode across Asia and Europe from Beijing to Arnhem on another old British single-cylinder motorcycle. One goal of the ride was to locate Ernie and 'Shaking-Minarets' Mustafa. Sadly, because of unavoidable delays earlier in the ride, and the immoveable itinerary of pre-booked air tickets and work commitments, we had to put my similarly aged Yorkshire-made Panther motorcycle 'Penelope' on a train in Kerman, Iran and we whistled past Esfahan without stopping.

On our adventure with Ernie, we'd not seen another Norton (or many of the more-fancied marques or models). Ernie was the first and only Norton I've owned. I often think of him, and as a vicarious link, I have a now-tattered T-shirt proclaiming Norton's slogan of being 'Unapproachable.' He'd done well for an obsolete old boy. Ernie had been true to the ethos of the ride. Or did he create the ethos of the ride? Of one thing I'm certain: he significantly influenced it.

On the Isle of Man in 2006, I was to meet the person who, at the time of our ride, I had thought of as my nemesis. Before we set off in 1973, with youthful naivety, I had written to my favourite motorcycle publication with a proposal that I write for them. I was going off to Europe on an old Norton, and I could send in regular reports. Of course, I thought this might also enable some sponsorship. The magazine, a prestigious monthly, responded in what I thought was a high-handed, almost derogatory fashion, telling me they already had lined up someone who was going to tour Europe on a new Norton — the big-tanked 850cc Interstate.

There is a delightful twist to this tale because Norton had rushed the release of the new 850 and hadn't tested it fully. They soon found the engine's main bearings were prematurely failing. A quick-and-dirty solution was found by changing the roller bearings to ones with the very slightest of barrel-shape to them. These bearings were called 'Superblends,' and when my nemesis went to pick up his brand-new Norton from the factory in early 1973, he was given a secret package of bearings for 'just in case.' Over a convivial beer, I learned that his mighty Norton had shat itself in Norway. In his case, he did a full engine strip and bearing replacement at the Swedish border. No magazine articles ever eventuated, and I concluded that Ernie had well and truly outdone his shiny descendant.

Pillioning is quite an intimate pairing. There is no avoiding close physical contact, and you both have to work together to make it work well. Anne was a champion at ensuring the three of us were always 'as one' on the road, no matter how bad the conditions.

On a related note, how was the hoped-for romance with Anne unfolding? Well, it had got no worse. I was so discreet and secretive about my feelings towards her that the embryo was never fertilized. We may have shared a tiny pup tent and a few double beds, but we were never 'a couple.' She never fell for my latent, and possibly well-hidden, charms. I like to think it was a struggle for her. Certainly, her resolve never wavered. This disappointment could have affected our times together but didn't, because we had quickly transitioned into a tight and effective pairing. There were so many good times that more than made up for the lack of obvious physical release.

Now might be a good time to hand the pen to Anne for her related comments:

> I treasure my close relationship with Des, developed over the five months we spent in close quarters with our buddy Ernie. During the early iterations of the book, I was surprised to learn of Des's romantic aspirations. I was oblivious to his feelings. When I received his earlier drafts, I felt a need to express how much I valued our friendship and sent him the following recollection of a moment together, 44 years after our travels with Ernie:
>
> Sometimes, friendship trumps romance.
>
> It was in a campground hut in Naseby, New Zealand that a friend inserted a by-the-by comment along the lines of "I have you all to myself" as we were enjoying conversation over morning coffee. What I took from it was that my friend was basking in my company and there was no other place he would prefer to be at that moment.
>
> It's one of the nicest compliments I've ever received.
>
> Forty-four years after Des and I travelled with Ernie, we passed through Naseby on another motorcycling adventure in the South Island of New Zealand. The trip had been prompted by my email to Des titled "Fancy a moto adventure?" that garnered the expected response, received within minutes. In my email, I'd explained that I was keen to see Des before meeting up with cycling buddies in Arrowtown, 800 kilometres from where Des lived in Pohara. As a result, Des planned a phenomenal four-day journey. I couldn't wait to rekindle our friendship and perhaps relive and reminisce about some of the highlights of our youthful adventures with Ernie.
>
> As an aside, what I found interesting were the responses of our respective spouses. When I excitedly shared Des's plan with my partner, he nodded approvingly. When I shared Aldric's reaction with

Des, he indicated that Steph's response was just as positive. She was relieved that she wasn't being dragged along on yet another motorcycle jaunt. These reactions reassured me we'd each chosen our life partners well.

The Naseby hut was as basic as the single-skin nylon tent Des and I had shared more than four decades earlier. It had one electrical outlet, a small table, a double bed, an upper-and-lower bunk, and not much else. Des insisted I take the bed, and he took the lower bunk. With a steady overnight rain continuing into the morning, we lingered over conversation and several cups of coffee made with Des's Aeropress. If the truth be known, the "I have you all to myself" comment was at the heart of my request for a third cup.

Being in the company of a good friend is a powerful gift.

There was now an unusual feel to the immediate future. Anne wouldn't be there to talk to, reflect on what we were experiencing, or share dreams, fantasies, and aspirations. Without ever articulating it, I think we both knew we'd been part of something special and that we'd always enjoy a close relationship.

Being as we expected to be on the train for three days, possibly longer going by our eastbound experience, we stocked up on books and as many edible goodies as we could manage. Extended train rides were still a novelty to us, and the journey from Kayseri to Tehran had been our first to include overnighters. When it wasn't too full, too hot, or too cold, we had enjoyed the kilometre-eating comfort surrounding us, even when we were asleep. If only we'd been able to train Ernie to facilitate something similar.

On our westwards train ride from Tehran to Istanbul, we were allocated a six-berth compartment with three others, the journal recording them as "Patti from the USA, Claude from France, and a guy from Finland." I hope they enjoyed our company and apologise for having no memory of them. The vagaries of the senior citizen recall have purged them. They may be in the filing cabinet somewhere, but I cannot find the folder.

It wasn't long before we were out of Tehran and happily clickety-clacking through a Santa Claus landscape. The scheduled three-day journey stretched to five days, a long time to be on a train. There are only a few memories that stand out after 45 years. Unfortunately, Anne's journal isn't helpful as she had slipped into home-stretch relaxation, and the scribbles of her pen were limited to a concise summary of the journey.

I recall that once more, Anne had to endure a difficult time in the Lake Van area. On the ferry across the lake, we needed to ascend from one deck to another. Anne was ahead of me, and a swarthy young Turk was on the upper level. He waited until Anne had started to climb the narrow stairs when he scampered down about four or five steps, ensuring they would have to pass mid-flight. He then turned sideways and flattened his back against the wall. Just as Anne went by, he gently thrust his pelvic area forward so she would have to brush by him.

We'd enjoyed so much about Turkey and their people, but this region gave us nothing but grief. We'd noticed during our time in Van on the way east that the movie theatres were occasionally screening low-budget, semi-pornographic Scandinavian movies starring vacuous blonde bombshells who appeared willing and eager to please men in all sorts of base ways. Obviously, these movies were for the town's version of the 'dirty old men in trench coats' seen in London's Soho and Hamburg's Reeperbahn. Possibly these sleazos, upon seeing a blonde in tightish jeans, thought that all their dreams had come true as a 'hottie' from the silver screen had appeared in their lives, just waiting to be hit on in a crude way.

Fortunately, our good experiences outweighed the bad by more than a hundredfold. Still, I felt for Anne on each of these occasions when my gender did not treat her respectfully.

One of the unexplained delays along the way also sticks with me as an example of the mischievous and amusing nature of the Turk. The train was stationary out in the wops somewhere and hadn't moved for a couple of hours. Finally, passengers started getting off to stretch their legs and have a change of scenery. At some stage, we joined in, dropping from the train into soft snow that, as my mum would say, was up to our hocks. It translated into a novel experience of wading through this cold, white medium. When there were enough people off the train and semi-snowbound, the engineer started to move the train along. Of course, this brought panic to those not on board, and amusement to those who were. Once all the panicked folk were back on board, we remained stationary for several more hours. It had just been a bit of fun.

We had been on the road for over five months, usually sleeping rough and mostly living outdoors. During that time, we had been rudely healthy, with just a couple of minor exceptions. Our first train ride had put us in close quarters with a lot of people, and within 24 hours, we both had colds that took a while to shake off once we got to Tehran. History repeated itself on our westward train ride. Within the first day, we once more succumbed to colds. Nothing particularly bad, but enough to remind us it is not the amount of precipitation you are subjected to, nor the temperatures you endure — it is the germs from others that will lay you low.

Snow was with us for almost the entire 3,000 kilometres to Istanbul. This made for stunning vistas, but ultimately it became a little overwhelming in its sameness, showing that you can suffer from a surfeit of beauty. Finally, we were back in our favourite city, even though we knew it was only for a couple of days. Our not-very express had dropped us on the Asian side of the Bosphorus, and it was quite a struggle to get us and our gear across to the European side that we ordained as being closer to the action and easier from which to exit. Anne lamented the fact that her rucksack she'd lent Steve for his trip to the USA was sitting idle in London when it could have been invaluable for the next stage of her journey.

We found cheap lodging at the Stop Hotel in the Sultanahmet area, sharing a four-bed room with David, a guy from Yorkshire.

The next day brought an encounter that falsely went into my family folklore. We'd decided on a Turkish bath, and when we got there, an excited attendant told us that the 'feelm star Rex Harrison' was there. Well, Anne went her way, and I ambled into the men's area to find no sign of the effete English star of *My Fair Lady and Dr Doolittle*. There was, however, a big hunk of an American who seemed to have an English manager. We spent an enjoyable enough time together, sharing the good, the bad, and the ugly that is a civic Turkish bath. Later, Anne was encouraged to have her photo taken with 'the hunk,' and we saw a magazine or newspaper board with the name 'Harrison' on it. Subsequently, this brief couple of hours morphed into 'the time me and Harrison Ford nakedly shared a hot tub before either of us were famous!' It took until 2009 and the first iteration of The Ernie Diaries for the truth to out. Anne had recorded the day in her journal, including the proper name of the actor. He was Richard Harrison, who Google tells me is/was a briefly popular American actor who starred in B-grade European movies during the period.

Our farewells at the airport were suitably low key. I was envious of Anne's being able to continue to Israel and more adventures, but I presumed she'd turn up in London in a few months and that I'd still be there.

And so it was that at 3.30 p.m. on Wednesday, January 23, 1974, I flew off to Heathrow and back to the 603 girls, with less than £20 in my pocket. I would subsequently break my last £1 whilst waiting for my first pay from my new job. Anne's El Al flight left for Tel Aviv at 10.30 p.m. amidst security so stringent and so alien that it warranted five full pages in her journal.

For nearly half a year, we'd experienced many escapades and enjoyed many adventures. We'd honed our love of travel, elevating the highlights to lofty prominence and relegating the low points to quickly forgotten status. Faithful old Ernie had taken us from near the Arctic Circle to the Persian Gulf. We were pretty proud of our threesome, and we had memories to last a lifetime.

Chapter 17:
The Cast

Ernie

Ernie was a 1957 500cc Norton ES2. We'd assembled him from a barn-find status. Whilst he was part of a lineage of 79mm x 100mm long-stroke single-cylinder models dating from 1928, by 1957 the ES2 was already seen as a throwback to earlier times. The post-war years had also seen a move to cheapen each succeeding model rather than improve it. There were design flaws like having insufficient fixing restraints to the exhaust system that regularly drove us to the brink of despair. The poor design of the supposedly oil-filled primary chaincase was also a nightmare. The clutch and chain needed oil, yet the design seemed to preclude the pressed-steel chaincase from keeping it in. After conventional gaskets and unguents failed, we tried molten candle wax and high-temperature grease, with only a modicum of temporary success.

Ernie's single downtube swinging arm frame was also only a transitional iteration. By the time the ES2 had the legendary featherbed frame in 1959, it was too heavy for the limited power delivery of what was a pre-war engine. Loved as the model was, it was discontinued after 1964. The day of the long-stroke single-cylinder lugger was done. Already the reliable and sportier Japanese marques were flooding the marketplace with much more desirable fare.

Norton would last as a mainstream motorcycle manufacturer only until 1976. They'd been part of the glory years, their competition models winning many championships, justifying their catchword of 'Unapproachable.'

Thus, Ernie was not an example of Britain's finest. He was like the elite athlete's stumblebum plodding brother; his glory was only reflected. However, that didn't stop us loving him and his contrary ways. Whilst Ernie had no sporting pedigree, and no valid claims to quality or reliability, he was earnest. When the chips were down, he always came through with the goods. Purely on the evidence of successfully thudding along for nearly 10,000 kilometres with a glued-up piston, he deserves the mantle of a deity.

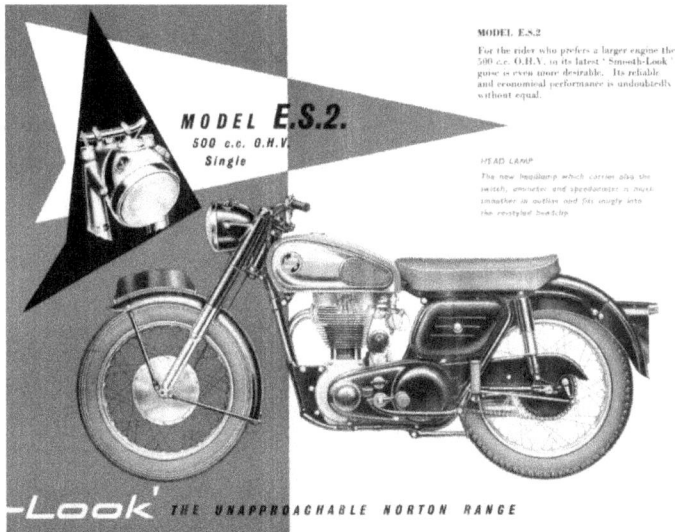

The Cast

Des Molloy

I remained based in the UK for another three years after the Ernie adventure, working in construction, playing rugby during the winters, and travelling in the summers. The wholesome enjoyment, sense of being in the ride, and interacting so closely with the environment and the people inspired other 'Ernie-esque' adventures. A Russian Ural and sidecar outfit took me off to run with the bulls at the Festival of San Fermín in Pamplona, Spain, and to the Isle of Man for the TT (Tourist Trophy) races.

Another Ernie-inspired ride on old British single-cylinder bangers took place in 1976 and 1977, spawning my book *No One Said It Would Be Easy*. It chronicled an incident-filled ride from New Orleans to Buenos Aires.

By that time, I had met my life partner Steph, and a period of domesticity followed back in New Zealand. Three decades produced four children and a lot of love and laughter before I embarked upon another international adventure. As a result of a small inheritance from my mother, I set off on 'Penelope,' (the bike Steph and I had ridden on the America's epic) taking me back across Asia and Europe in 2005 from Beijing to Arnhem. The ride also inspired a book and a movie: *The Last Hurrah*.

Adventuring is addictive. Recreating Robert Pirsig's ride immortalized in his cult book *Zen and the Art of Motorcycle Maintenance* followed in 2006 — on the correct period bikes. Unimaginatively, my book from this adventure is titled *Zen and The Last Hurrah*.

Nearing the end of my waged career in construction, I dragged Penelope once more from the shed and progressively rode around the big red continent that is Australia. My manuscript from that four-year part-time saga is tentatively called *The Big Sit*.

In semi-retirement, I read, I write, I dream, and I love. My remaining goal is to treat our grandchildren to some memorable two-wheeled adventures.

The Cast

Anne Betts

As Des predicted, after another five months shared between Israel, Palestine, Jordan, and Cyprus, I returned to London. During my absence, many of our mates had returned to either Australia or New Zealand. I found Des happily ensconced in familiar surroundings with the 603 girls. Since returning to London, he'd established a construction company side hustle and offered me a job driving the company's old London taxicab to pick up supplies. Des had an uncanny ability to make something appear more alluring or exciting than it was. I pictured driving around in a London icon, soaking up every moment while cruising the streets of a city I loved. However, I've no recollection of collecting supplies, or driving the taxi. I remember working as a chippy's mate and general labourer on various construction jobs. One involved retiling a very steep roof of a three-storey building with no safety gear and living to tell the tale. Our crew of young colonials was the talk of the regulars of the pub across the street where we enjoyed a daily lunch of a ploughman's and a pint.

In November 1974, I realised a dream spawned as an 11-year-old when Canada appeared in the Grade 6 social studies curriculum. It had remained towards the top of my to-visit list ever since. I found work in an isolated fly-in community in the Canadian North where I spent eight years teaching *Dené students in First Nations' communities. Involvement in the union eventually morphed into a 25-year career as a union representative until retirement in 2008.*

A year after arriving in Canada, I made my way back to the UK during the school holidays of Christmas 1975 to spend it with my sister, who was living in South East England. Taking advantage of the fact I was in London, I headed out to 603, curious to find out if any of our mates were still in the UK. The first person I encountered was Des, then Pommie Jim, then Michele, who was flying home to New Zealand the following day. With a farewell party in the works at the Three Blackbirds pub across the road, what was a gal to do? Join the celebration, of course, and crash overnight at 603. It was reminiscent of the pre-Ernie days when Des and I had been welcomed into the flat to camp on the floor of the spacious living room.

Over the next 24 hours, Des and I made plans to meet one year later for a South American adventure on old motorcycles. We found a map and decided that the Poste Restante in Mexicali at noon on December 1, 1976, would work as a convenient meeting place and time. Those plans were eventually derailed by the lure of an extended stay in Canada, fuelled by a job offer with the prospect of working with former colleagues who'd become good friends. With the hint of a romance in the air, Canada won. After reading Des's account of the trip in *No One Said It Would Be Easy*, I thank my lucky stars and Canada that I'd never made it to Mexicali. Our adventure with Ernie had been a walk in the park compared to that ride. The Canadian romance has lasted until this day. Along the way, I became a Canadian citizen and revel in the fact that my Australian and Canadian passports accompany me on all international travels.

Our Mates

The five-week voyage on the SS *Australis* in 1972 set the stage for some lasting friendships. By the time the ship berthed in Southampton, relationships forged through romance, friendship, and likely compatibility as flatmates led to clusters of folks who were willing to share the costs of accommodation. It also resulted in many shared travel adventures.

Over a six-year period from late 1972 to 1977, our mates gradually drifted back to either Australia or New Zealand. Smaller groups of friends stayed in touch, but it wasn't until 2012 that a concerted effort was made to reassemble the entire gang and organize a reunion to mark the 40th anniversary of our voyage on the SS *Australis*. After the initial gathering at Des and Steph's two-acre property in Golden Bay, New Zealand, these get-togethers, alternating between Australia and New Zealand, attract at least two-dozen of our friends and their partners every couple of years. Hugs, conversation, laughter, and camaraderie dominate each gathering, and the years melt away as we piece together the rich memories of our youth.

Ric and Lynn

After receiving *The Ernie Diaries* from Anne in 2009, I sent a Facebook friend request to a Ric Fink, hoping it was our Ric Fink from the '70s. Ric's enthusiastic response shared a few fond memories of our time together. After leaving us in Tehran, Lynn and Ric continued travelling east to India, where their Land Rover was shipped across the Indian Ocean to Mombasa, Kenya. In Kenya, they broke up after nine years of marriage; Lynn stayed in Kenya for five years, and Ric for nine years. They remain friends. Ric lives in San Francisco, California and Lynn lives in Dawsonville, about an hour north of Atlanta, Georgia. Anne communicates with them both through Facebook and had the opportunity to connect face to face with Ric on a visit to San Francisco in 2016.

Ken and Jill

In 2016, Google helped find a Jill Duncalfe residing in Auckland, New Zealand that turned out to be the 'right Jill.' We exchanged emails containing a few photographs and references to each other from our respective journals, reconnecting again in 2020. After leaving Tehran, Ken and Jill continued east to Calcutta, where they flew home to New Zealand after leaving their Kombi with a shipping agent. The van arrived in New Zealand three months later. They raised three children in Hamilton and moved to Auckland in 1997, where Jill worked as a Therapeutic Counsellor and Ken as a Research and Development Manager. They have since returned to Africa to trek with gorillas in Uganda, and are now retired, spending time travelling around NZ in a converted bus to the remotest places they can find.

Monica

After our rendezvous in Stockholm, Monica returned to England, where she met her life partner Sandy and set down roots within commuting distance of London. Anne and Monica have remained friends and enjoyed several face-to-face visits in the UK and Canada.

SS Australis

With the Greek flag flying from her stern, the legendary ship transported thousands of young Australians and New Zealanders to the UK, and just as many ten-pound poms and other immigrants to the antipodes. By the time she was purchased by the Chandris Group in 1964 to ply the route between the UK and Australia and New Zealand, the soon-to-be named *Australis* was already 24 years old. Facing competition from newer ocean liners and long-range aircraft, the *Australis* filled a perfect niche in the post-war immigration market and offered a tempting option by sea for young adventurous travellers with Europe in their sights.

On her final voyage in 1994, tragedy struck during a severe storm and the ship ran aground off Fuerteventura in the Canary Islands. Over time, the vessel slowly succumbed to the forces of nature and today, she has all but disappeared except for small pieces of steel that may be visible at low tide.

The much-loved ship figures prominently in the memories of many passengers and crew, so much so that websites and Facebook groups have been established for the sharing of photographs and cherished memories.

The Cast

Acknowledgements

Anne Betts

Writing a book was as hard as I thought it would be, but more enjoyable than I'd imagined. Unlike Des, who has three published memoirs of motorcycle travels to his credit, for me this was venturing into uncharted territory. I'll start by thanking Des for his persistence in convincing me to embark on this project, agreement to share the writing, and encouragement and support along the way.

Earlier drafts bear little resemblance to the finished product. This was before we enlisted the help of friends who brought different gifts to the quality of their feedback. Some challenged us to overcome the deficiencies of my 1973 journal and reach into the depths of our memories to make a greater effort to be more descriptive of people and places. Others whose first language isn't English encouraged us to bring greater clarity to our writing by elaborating on certain vocabulary and expressions. And others demonstrated that our grasp of grammar and punctuation, and appreciation of the differences between British and American English, left a lot to be desired. Their feedback prompted a concerted effort to improve in this area of our writing. Everyone inspired us with words of encouragement, praise, and challenges to do better.

Our heartfelt thanks are extended to George, Janet, Kris, Nod, Normand, and Terri-Lee. Thank you, friends.

Des Molloy

Top of my list has to be Steph Molloy who has been a constant in my life since 1976, contributing to and always supporting and encouraging my dreams.

Publishing books about oneself can be seen as vanity projects ... I see them as records of the humdrum adventures of the ordinary folk, something for future generations to pore over. It takes a certain resolve to formalise your fireside yarns into something for your offspring's offspring to be able to hold in their hands and share the banal and not-so-banal snippets from your life. I am not a diarist and always thought the best memories didn't fade so could be recalled and recounted on demand. Age and Anne's journal have proven this to be a fallacy. Inaccuracies in my 'tall tales and true' exploits have been corrected in this book.

Without Anne's journal and her single-mindedness in getting this adventure to you all, Ernie's tale would probably have just remained a fable, parts of which we might or might not recount after a beer or two.

I would be remiss if I didn't also acknowledge The Design Dept's Jess Kelly and her skill in getting this book to publication. She is more than a graphic artist and book designer to me, she is an important muse and advisor willing to help an old duffer through the intricacies and foibles of Mailchimp, Webflow, InCopy and Dropbox. Patient, confident and competent.

So it has been a triumvirate of strong, capable women who have enabled this publication and I thank them all for their forbearance and input.

Available Online Now
www.kahukupublishing.com

An outrageous sortie on a pre-war BSA and two obscure, obsolete Yorkshire-made, single-cylinder Panther motorbikes. Poorly funded, with little planning, the ride depends on good luck, blind loyalty and terminal optimism. The struggle is managed with a youthful naivety.

This is a recollection of a youth well-spent. Love and adventure are in the air with every chapter a precarious adventure.

Des Molloy and Dick Huurdeman look like the sort of guys who should be sedately steering a sleigh in a Santa parade, not riding old single-banger British bikes halfway across the world through some of the most difficult and remote terrain imaginable. Des's son Steve joined this intrepid pair as a cameraman and general factotum for the highs and lows of an incident-packed three-month trek from Beijing to Arnhem on 'Penelope', a 1965 Yorkshire-made 650cc Panther, and 'Dutch Courage', a 1954 Norton 600.

In July 1968 a mentally insecure philosophy teacher began a motorcycle ride across the US with his not-yet 12-year-old son. Robert Pirsig's journey was immortalized in his best-selling book *Zen and the Art of Motorcycle Maintenance*.
Des Molloy and team, on the correct-period 1965 bikes follow the wheel-tracks of their antecedents, recording their thoughts and comparing with the best-selling philosopher.

Everyday People.
Amazing Adventures.

The Ernie Diaries

www.ingramcontent.com/pod-product-compliance
Lightning Source LLC
Chambersburg PA
CBHW071954290426
44109CB00018B/2019